DICTIONARY
THEME–BASED

British English Collection

ENGLISH-
HEBREW

The most useful words
To expand your lexicon and sharpen
your language skills

7000 words

Theme-based dictionary British English-Hebrew - 7000 words
By Andrey Taranov

T&P Books vocabularies are intended for helping you learn, memorize and review foreign words. The dictionary is divided into themes, covering all major spheres of everyday activities, business, science, culture, etc.

The process of learning words using T&P Books' theme-based dictionaries gives you the following advantages:

- Correctly grouped source information predetermines success at subsequent stages of word memorization
- Availability of words derived from the same root allowing memorization of word units (rather than separate words)
- Small units of words facilitate the process of establishing associative links needed for consolidation of vocabulary
- Level of language knowledge can be estimated by the number of learned words

T&P Books Publishing
www.tpbooks.com

This book is also available in E-book formats.
Please visit www.tpbooks.com or the major online bookstores.

HEBREW THEME-BASED DICTIONARY
British English collection

T&P Books vocabularies are intended to help you learn, memorize, and review foreign words. The vocabulary contains over 7000 commonly used words arranged thematically.

- Vocabulary contains the most commonly used words
- Recommended as an addition to any language course
- Meets the needs of beginners and advanced learners of foreign languages
- Convenient for daily use, revision sessions, and self-testing activities
- Allows you to assess your vocabulary

Special features of the vocabulary

- Words are organized according to their meaning, not alphabetically
- Words are presented in three columns to facilitate the reviewing and self-testing processes
- Words in groups are divided into small blocks to facilitate the learning process
- The vocabulary offers a convenient and simple transcription of each foreign word

The vocabulary has 198 topics including:

Basic Concepts, Numbers, Colors, Months, Seasons, Units of Measurement, Clothing & Accessories, Food & Nutrition, Restaurant, Family Members, Relatives, Character, Feelings, Emotions, Diseases, City, Town, Sightseeing, Shopping, Money, House, Home, Office, Working in the Office, Import & Export, Marketing, Job Search, Sports, Education, Computer, Internet, Tools, Nature, Countries, Nationalities and more …

TABLE OF CONTENTS

PRONUNCIATION GUIDE

Letter's name	Letter	Hebrew example	T&P phonetic alphabet	English example
Alef	א	אריה	[ɑ], [ɑ:]	bath, to pass
	א	אחד	[ɛ], [ɛ:]	habit, bad
	א	מָאָה	['] (hamza)	glottal stop
Bet	ב	בית	[b]	baby, book
Gimel	ג	גמל	[g]	game, gold
Gimel+geresh	ג'	ג'ונגל	[ʤ]	joke, general
Dalet	ד	דג	[d]	day, doctor
Hei	ה	הר	[h]	home, have
Vav	ו	וסת	[v]	very, river
Zayin	ז	זאב	[z]	zebra, please
Zayin+geresh	ז'	ז'ורנל	[ʒ]	forge, pleasure
Chet	ח	חוט	[x]	as in Scots 'loch'
Tet	ט	טוב	[t]	tourist, trip
Yud	י	יום	[j]	yes, New York
Kaph	ך כ	בריש	[k]	clock, kiss
Lamed	ל	לחם	[l]	lace, people
Mem	ם מ	מלך	[m]	magic, milk
Nun	ן ג	גר	[n]	name, normal
Samech	ס	סוס	[s]	city, boss
Ayin	ע	עין	[ɑ], [ɑ:]	bath, to pass
	ע	תָשעִים	['] (ayn)	voiced pharyngeal fricative
Pei	ף פ	פיל	[p]	pencil, private
Tsadi	ץ צ	צעצוע	[ts]	cats, tsetse fly
Tsadi+geresh	צ'ץ'	צ'ק	[tʃ]	church, French
Qoph	ק	קוף	[k]	clock, kiss
Resh	ר	רכבת	[r]	French (guttural) R
Shin	ש	שלחן, עָשׂרִים	[s], [ʃ]	city, machine
Tav	ת	תפוז	[t]	tourist, trip

ABBREVIATIONS
used in the dictionary

English abbreviations

ab.	-	about
adj	-	adjective
adv	-	adverb
anim.	-	animate
as adj	-	attributive noun used as adjective
e.g.	-	for example
etc.	-	et cetera
fam.	-	familiar
fem.	-	feminine
form.	-	formal
inanim.	-	inanimate
masc.	-	masculine
math	-	mathematics
mil.	-	military
n	-	noun
pl	-	plural
pron.	-	pronoun
sb	-	somebody
sing.	-	singular
sth	-	something
v aux	-	auxiliary verb
vi	-	intransitive verb
vi, vt	-	intransitive, transitive verb
vt	-	transitive verb

Hebrew abbreviations

ז	-	masculine
ז"ר	-	masculine plural
ז , נ	-	masculine, feminine
נ	-	feminine
נ"ר	-	feminine plural

BASIC CONCEPTS

Basic concepts. Part 1

1. Pronouns

I, me	ani	אֲנִי (ז, נ)
you (masc.)	ata	אַתָּה (ז)
you (fem.)	at	אַתְּ (נ)
he	hu	הוּא (ז)
she	hi	הִיא (נ)
we	a'naxnu	אֲנַחְנוּ (ז, נ)
you (masc.)	atem	אַתֶּם (ז"ר)
you (fem.)	aten	אַתֶּן (נ"ר)
you (polite, sing.)	ata, at	אַתָּה (ז), אַתְּ (נ)
you (polite, pl)	atem, aten	אַתֶּם (ז"ר), אַתֶּן (נ"ר)
they (masc.)	hem	הֵם (ז"ר)
they (fem.)	hen	הֵן (נ"ר)

2. Greetings. Salutations. Farewells

Hello! (fam.)	ʃalom!	שָׁלוֹם!
Hello! (form.)	ʃalom!	שָׁלוֹם!
Good morning!	'boker tov!	בּוֹקֶר טוֹב!
Good afternoon!	tsaha'rayim tovim!	צָהֳרַיִם טוֹבִים!
Good evening!	'erev tov!	עֶרֶב טוֹב!
to say hello	lomar ʃalom	לוֹמַר שָׁלוֹם
Hi! (hello)	hai!	הַיי!
greeting (n)	ahlan	אַהְלַן
to greet (vt)	lomar ʃalom	לוֹמַר שָׁלוֹם
How are you? (form.)	ma ʃlomex?, ma ʃlomxa?	מַה שְׁלוֹמֵךְ? (נ), מַה שְׁלוֹמְךָ? (ז)
How are you? (fam.)	ma niʃma?	מַה נִשְׁמָע?
What's new?	ma xadaʃ?	מַה חָדָשׁ?
Bye-Bye! Goodbye!	lehitra'ot!	לְהִתְרָאוֹת!
Bye!	bai!	בַּיי!
See you soon!	lehitra'ot bekarov!	לְהִתְרָאוֹת בְּקָרוֹב!
Farewell!	heye ʃalom!	הֱיֵה שָׁלוֹם!
Farewell! (form.)	lehitra'ot!	לְהִתְרָאוֹת!
to say goodbye	lomar lehitra'ot	לוֹמַר לְהִתְרָאוֹת
Cheers!	bai!	בַּיי!
Thank you! Cheers!	toda!	תּוֹדָה!
Thank you very much!	toda raba!	תּוֹדָה רַבָּה!

My pleasure!	bevakaʃa	בְּבַקָשָׁה
Don't mention it!	al lo davar	עַל לֹא דָבָר
It was nothing	ein be'ad ma	אֵין בְּעַד מָה

| Excuse me! | sliχa! | סְלִיחָה! |
| to excuse (forgive) | lis'loaχ | לִסְלוֹחַ |

to apologize (vi)	lehitnatsel	לְהִתְנַצֵל
My apologies	ani mitnatsel, ani mitna'tselet	אֲנִי מִתְנַצֵל (ז), אֲנִי מִתְנַצֶלֶת (נ)
I'm sorry!	ani mitsta'er, ani mitsta''eret	אֲנִי מִצְטַעֵר (ז), אֲנִי מִצְטַעֶרֶת (נ)
to forgive (vt)	lis'loaχ	לִסְלוֹחַ
It's okay! (that's all right)	lo nora	לֹא נוֹרָא
please (adv)	bevakaʃa	בְּבַקָשָׁה

Don't forget!	al tiʃkaχ!	אַל תִשְׁכַּח! (ז)
Certainly!	'betaχ!	בֶּטַח!
Of course not!	'betaχ ʃelo!	בֶּטַח שֶׁלֹא!
Okay! (I agree)	okei!	אוֹקֵיי!
That's enough!	maspik!	מַסְפִּיק!

3. Cardinal numbers. Part 1

0 zero	'efes	אֶפֶס (ז)
1 one	eχad	אֶחָד (ז)
1 one (fem.)	aχat	אַחַת (נ)
2 two	'ʃtayim	שְׁתַיִם (נ)
3 three	ʃaloʃ	שָׁלוֹש (נ)
4 four	arba	אַרְבַּע (נ)

5 five	χameʃ	חָמֵש (נ)
6 six	ʃeʃ	שֵׁש (נ)
7 seven	'ʃeva	שֶׁבַע (נ)
8 eight	'ʃmone	שְׁמוֹנֶה (נ)
9 nine	'teʃa	תֵשַׁע (נ)

10 ten	'eser	עֶשֶׂר (נ)
11 eleven	aχat esre	אַחַת־עֶשְׂרֵה (נ)
12 twelve	ʃteim esre	שְׁתֵים־עֶשְׂרֵה (נ)
13 thirteen	ʃloʃ esre	שְׁלוֹש־עֶשְׂרֵה (נ)
14 fourteen	arba esre	אַרְבַּע־עֶשְׂרֵה (נ)

15 fifteen	χameʃ esre	חָמֵש־עֶשְׂרֵה (נ)
16 sixteen	ʃeʃ esre	שֵׁש־עֶשְׂרֵה (נ)
17 seventeen	ʃva esre	שְׁבַע־עֶשְׂרֵה (נ)
18 eighteen	ʃmone esre	שְׁמוֹנֶה־עֶשְׂרֵה (נ)
19 nineteen	tʃa esre	תֵשַׁע־עֶשְׂרֵה (נ)

20 twenty	esrim	עֶשְׂרִים
21 twenty-one	esrim ve'eχad	עֶשְׂרִים וְאֶחָד
22 twenty-two	esrim u'ʃnayim	עֶשְׂרִים וּשְׁנַיִם
23 twenty-three	esrim uʃloʃa	עֶשְׂרִים וּשְׁלוֹשָׁה

| 30 thirty | ʃloʃim | שְׁלוֹשִׁים |
| 31 thirty-one | ʃloʃim ve'eχad | שְׁלוֹשִׁים וְאֶחָד |

32 thirty-two	ʃloʃim u'ʃnayim	שְׁלוֹשִׁים וּשְׁנַיִים
33 thirty-three	ʃloʃim uʃloʃa	שְׁלוֹשִׁים וּשְׁלוֹשָׁה
40 forty	arba'im	אַרְבָּעִים
41 forty-one	arba'im ve'eχad	אַרְבָּעִים וְאָחָד
42 forty-two	arba'im u'ʃnayim	אַרְבָּעִים וּשְׁנַיִים
43 forty-three	arba'im uʃloʃa	אַרְבָּעִים וּשְׁלוֹשָׁה
50 fifty	χamiʃim	חֲמִישִׁים
51 fifty-one	χamiʃim ve'eχad	חֲמִישִׁים וְאָחָד
52 fifty-two	χamiʃim u'ʃnayim	חֲמִישִׁים וּשְׁנַיִים
53 fifty-three	χamiʃim uʃloʃa	חֲמִישִׁים וּשְׁלוֹשָׁה
60 sixty	ʃiʃim	שִׁישִׁים
61 sixty-one	ʃiʃim ve'eχad	שִׁישִׁים וְאָחָד
62 sixty-two	ʃiʃim u'ʃnayim	שִׁישִׁים וּשְׁנַיִים
63 sixty-three	ʃiʃim uʃloʃa	שִׁישִׁים וּשְׁלוֹשָׁה
70 seventy	ʃiv'im	שִׁבְעִים
71 seventy-one	ʃiv'im ve'eχad	שִׁבְעִים וְאָחָד
72 seventy-two	ʃiv'im u'ʃnayim	שִׁבְעִים וּשְׁנַיִים
73 seventy-three	ʃiv'im uʃloʃa	שִׁבְעִים וּשְׁלוֹשָׁה
80 eighty	ʃmonim	שְׁמוֹנִים
81 eighty-one	ʃmonim ve'eχad	שְׁמוֹנִים וְאָחָד
82 eighty-two	ʃmonim u'ʃnayim	שְׁמוֹנִים וּשְׁנַיִים
83 eighty-three	ʃmonim uʃloʃa	שְׁמוֹנִים וּשְׁלוֹשָׁה
90 ninety	tiʃim	תִּשְׁעִים
91 ninety-one	tiʃim ve'eχad	תִּשְׁעִים וְאָחָד
92 ninety-two	tiʃim u'ʃayim	תִּשְׁעִים וּשְׁנַיִים
93 ninety-three	tiʃim uʃloʃa	תִּשְׁעִים וּשְׁלוֹשָׁה

4. Cardinal numbers. Part 2

100 one hundred	'me'a	מֵאָה (נ)
200 two hundred	ma'tayim	מָאתַיִים
300 three hundred	ʃloʃ me'ot	שְׁלוֹשׁ מֵאוֹת (נ)
400 four hundred	arba me'ot	אַרְבַּע מֵאוֹת (נ)
500 five hundred	χameʃ me'ot	חָמֵשׁ מֵאוֹת (נ)
600 six hundred	ʃeʃ me'ot	שֵׁשׁ מֵאוֹת (נ)
700 seven hundred	ʃva me'ot	שְׁבַע מֵאוֹת (נ)
800 eight hundred	ʃmone me'ot	שְׁמוֹנֶה מֵאוֹת (נ)
900 nine hundred	tʃa me'ot	תֵּשַׁע מֵאוֹת (נ)
1000 one thousand	'elef	אָלֶף (ז)
2000 two thousand	al'payim	אַלְפַּיִים (ז)
3000 three thousand	'ʃloʃet alafim	שְׁלוֹשֶׁת אֲלָפִים (ז)
10000 ten thousand	a'seret alafim	עֲשֶׂרֶת אֲלָפִים (ז)
one hundred thousand	'me'a 'elef	מֵאָה אָלֶף (ז)
million	milyon	מִילְיוֹן (ז)
billion	milyard	מִילְיַארְד (ז)

5. Numbers. Fractions

fraction	'ʃever	שֶׁבֶר (ז)
one half	'χetsi	חֲצִי (ז)
one third	ʃliʃ	שְׁלִישׁ (ז)
one quarter	'reva	רֶבַע (ז)
one eighth	ʃminit	שְׁמִינִית (נ)
one tenth	asirit	עֲשִׂירִית (נ)
two thirds	ʃnei ʃliʃim	שְׁנֵי שְׁלִישִׁים (ז)
three quarters	'ʃloʃet riv'ei	שְׁלוֹשֶׁת רְבָעֵי

6. Numbers. Basic operations

subtraction	χisur	חִיסוּר (ז)
to subtract (vi, vt)	leχaser	לְחַסֵר
division	χiluk	חִילוּק (ז)
to divide (vt)	leχalek	לְחַלֵק
addition	χibur	חִיבּוּר (ז)
to add up (vt)	leχaber	לְחַבֵּר
to add (vi)	leχaber	לְחַבֵּר
multiplication	'kefel	כֶּפֶל (ז)
to multiply (vt)	lehaχpil	לְהַכְפִּיל

7. Numbers. Miscellaneous

digit, figure	sifra	סִפְרָה (נ)
number	mispar	מִסְפָּר (ז)
numeral	ʃem mispar	שֵׁם מִסְפָּר (ז)
minus sign	'minus	מִינוּס (ז)
plus sign	plus	פְּלוּס (ז)
formula	nusχa	נוּסְחָה (נ)
calculation	χiʃuv	חִישׁוּב (ז)
to count (vi, vt)	lispor	לִסְפּוֹר
to count up	leχaʃev	לְחַשֵׁב
to compare (vt)	lehaʃvot	לְהַשְׁווֹת
How much?	'kama?	כַּמָה?
How many?	'kama?	כַּמָה?
sum, total	sχum	סְכוּם (ז)
result	totsa'a	תוֹצָאָה (נ)
remainder	ʃe'erit	שְׁאֵרִית (נ)
a few (e.g., ~ years ago)	'kama	כַּמָה
little (I had ~ time)	ktsat	קְצָת
few (I have ~ friends)	me'at	מְעַט
a little (~ water)	me'at	מְעַט
the rest	ʃe'ar	שְׁאָר (ז)
one and a half	eχad va'χetsi	אֶחָד וָחֲצִי (ז)

dozen	tresar	תְרֵיסָר (ז)
in half (adv)	'χetsi 'χetsi	חֲצִי חֲצִי
equally (evenly)	ʃave beʃave	שָׁוֶה בְּשָׁוֶה
half	'χetsi	חֲצִי (ז)
time (three ~s)	'pa'am	פַּעַם (נ)

8. The most important verbs. Part 1

to advise (vt)	leya'ets	לְיָיעֵץ
to agree (say yes)	lehaskim	לְהַסכִּים
to answer (vi, vt)	la'anot	לַעֲנוֹת
to apologize (vi)	lehitnatsel	לְהִתנַצֵל
to arrive (vi)	leha'gi'a	לְהַגִּיעַ

to ask (~ oneself)	liʃol	לִשׁאוֹל
to ask (~ sb to do sth)	levakeʃ	לְבַקֵשׁ
to be (vi)	lihyot	לִהיוֹת

to be afraid	lefaχed	לְפַחֵד
to be hungry	lihyot ra'ev	לִהיוֹת רָעֵב
to be interested in …	lehit'anyen be…	…לְהִתעַנייֵן בְּ
to be needed	lehidareʃ	לְהִידָרֵשׁ
to be surprised	lehitpale	לְהִתפַּלֵא
to be thirsty	lihyot tsame	לִהיוֹת צָמֵא
to begin (vt)	lehatχil	לְהַתחִיל
to belong to …	lehiʃtayeχ	לְהִשׁתַייֵך
to boast (vi)	lehitravrev	לְהִתרַברֵב
to break (split into pieces)	liʃbor	לְשׁבּוֹר
to call (~ for help)	likro	לִקרוֹא

can (v aux)	yaχol	יָכוֹל
to catch (vt)	litfos	לִתפּוֹס
to change (vt)	leʃanot	לְשַׁנוֹת
to choose (select)	livχor	לִבחוֹר
to come down (the stairs)	la'redet	לָרֶדֶת
to compare (vt)	lehaʃvot	לְהַשׁווֹת
to complain (vi, vt)	lehitlonen	לְהִתלוֹנֵן
to confuse (mix up)	lehitbalbel	לְהִתבַּלבֵּל
to continue (vt)	lehamʃiχ	לְהַמשִׁיך
to control (vt)	liʃlot	לִשׁלוֹט
to cook (dinner)	levaʃel	לְבַשֵׁל

to cost (vt)	la'alot	לַעֲלוֹת
to count (add up)	lispor	לִספּוֹר
to count on …	lismoχ al	לִסמוֹך עַל
to create (vt)	litsor	לִיצוֹר
to cry (weep)	livkot	לִבכּוֹת

9. The most important verbs. Part 2

| to deceive (vi, vt) | leramot | לְרַמוֹת |
| to decorate (tree, street) | lekaʃet | לְקַשֵׁט |

to defend (a country, etc.)	lehagen	לְהָגֵן
to demand (request firmly)	lidroʃ	לִדרוֹשׁ
to dig (vt)	laxpor	לַחפּוֹר

to discuss (vt)	ladun	לָדוּן
to do (vt)	la'asot	לַעֲשׂוֹת
to doubt (have doubts)	lefakpek	לְפַקפֵּק
to drop (let fall)	lehapil	לְהַפִּיל
to enter (room, house, etc.)	lehikanes	לְהִיכָּנֵס

to excuse (forgive)	lis'loax	לִסלוֹחַ
to exist (vi)	lehitkayem	לְהִתקַייֵם
to expect (foresee)	laxazot	לַחֲזוֹת
to explain (vt)	lehasbir	לְהַסבִּיר
to fall (vi)	lipol	לִיפּוֹל

to fancy (vt)	limtso xen be'ei'nayim	לִמצוֹא חֵן בְּעֵינַיִים
to find (vt)	limtso	לִמצוֹא
to finish (vt)	lesayem	לְסַייֵם
to fly (vi)	la'uf	לָעוּף
to follow … (come after)	la'akov axarei	לַעֲקוֹב אַחֲרֵי

to forget (vi, vt)	liʃkoax	לִשכּוֹחַ
to forgive (vt)	lis'loax	לִסלוֹחַ
to give (vt)	latet	לָתֵת
to give a hint	lirmoz	לִרמוֹז
to go (on foot)	la'lexet	לָלֶכֶת

to go for a swim	lehitraxets	לְהִתרַחֵץ
to go out (for dinner, etc.)	latset	לָצֵאת
to guess (the answer)	lenaxeʃ	לְנַחֵשׁ

to have (vt)	lehaxzik	לְהַחזִיק
to have breakfast	le'exol aruxat 'boker	לֶאֱכוֹל אֲרוּחַת בּוֹקֶר
to have dinner	le'exol aruxat 'erev	לֶאֱכוֹל אֲרוּחַת עֶרֶב
to have lunch	le'exol aruxat tsaha'rayim	לֶאֱכוֹל אֲרוּחַת צָהֳרַיים
to hear (vt)	liʃmo'a	לִשמוֹעַ

to help (vt)	la'azor	לַעֲזוֹר
to hide (vt)	lehastir	לְהַסתִּיר
to hope (vi, vt)	lekavot	לְקַווֹת
to hunt (vi, vt)	latsud	לָצוּד
to hurry (vi)	lemaher	לְמַהֵר

10. The most important verbs. Part 3

to inform (vt)	leho'dia	לְהוֹדִיעַ
to insist (vi, vt)	lehit'akeʃ	לְהִתעַקֵשׁ
to insult (vt)	leha'aliv	לְהַעֲלִיב
to invite (vt)	lehazmin	לְהַזמִין
to joke (vi)	lehitba'deax	לְהִתבַּדֵחַ

to keep (vt)	liʃmor	לִשמוֹר
to keep silent, to hush	liʃtok	לִשתוֹק

to kill (vt)	laharog	לַהֲרוֹג
to know (sb)	lehakir et	לְהַכִּיר אֶת
to know (sth)	la'da'at	לָדַעַת
to laugh (vi)	litsχok	לִצְחוֹק

to liberate (city, etc.)	leʃaχrer	לְשַׁחְרֵר
to look for ... (search)	leχapes	לְחַפֵּשׂ
to love (sb)	le'ehov	לֶאֱהוֹב
to make a mistake	lit'ot	לִטְעוֹת
to manage, to run	lenahel	לְנַהֵל

to mean (signify)	lomar	לוֹמַר
to mention (talk about)	lehazkir	לְהַזְכִּיר
to miss (school, etc.)	lehaχsir	לְהַחְסִיר
to notice (see)	lasim lev	לָשִׂים לֵב
to object (vi, vt)	lehitnaged	לְהִתְנַגֵּד

to observe (see)	litspot, lehaʃkif	לִצְפּוֹת, לְהַשְׁקִיף
to open (vt)	lif'toaχ	לִפְתוֹחַ
to order (meal, etc.)	lehazmin	לְהַזְמִין
to order (mil.)	lifkod	לִפְקוֹד
to own (possess)	lihyot 'ba'al ʃel	לִהְיוֹת בַּעַל שֶׁל

to participate (vi)	lehiʃtatef	לְהִשְׁתַּתֵּף
to pay (vi, vt)	leʃalem	לְשַׁלֵּם
to permit (vt)	leharʃot	לְהַרְשׁוֹת
to plan (vt)	letaχnen	לְתַכְנֵן
to play (children)	lesaχek	לְשַׂחֵק

to pray (vi, vt)	lehitpalel	לְהִתְפַּלֵּל
to prefer (vt)	leha'adif	לְהַעֲדִיף
to promise (vt)	lehav'tiaχ	לְהַבְטִיחַ
to pronounce (vt)	levate	לְבַטֵּא
to propose (vt)	leha'tsi'a	לְהַצִּיעַ
to punish (vt)	leha'aniʃ	לְהַעֲנִישׁ

11. The most important verbs. Part 4

to read (vi, vt)	likro	לִקְרוֹא
to recommend (vt)	lehamlits	לְהַמְלִיץ
to refuse (vi, vt)	lesarev	לְסָרֵב
to regret (be sorry)	lehitsta'er	לְהִצְטַעֵר
to rent (sth from sb)	liskor	לִשְׂכּוֹר

to repeat (say again)	laχazor al	לַחֲזוֹר עַל
to reserve, to book	lehazmin meroʃ	לְהַזְמִין מֵרֹאשׁ
to run (vi)	laruts	לָרוּץ
to save (rescue)	lehatsil	לְהַצִּיל

to say (~ thank you)	lomar	לוֹמַר
to scold (vt)	linzof	לִנְזוֹף
to see (vt)	lir'ot	לִרְאוֹת
to sell (vt)	limkor	לִמְכּוֹר
to send (vt)	liʃ'loaχ	לִשְׁלוֹחַ

to shoot (vi)	lirot	לִירוֹת
to shout (vi)	lits'ok	לִצְעוֹק
to show (vt)	lehar'ot	לְהַרְאוֹת
to sign (document)	laxtom	לַחְתוֹם

to sit down (vi)	lehityaʃev	לְהִתְיַישֵׁב
to smile (vi)	lexayex	לְחַייֵך
to speak (vi, vt)	ledaber	לְדַבֵּר
to steal (money, etc.)	lignov	לִגְנוֹב
to stop (for pause, etc.)	la'atsor	לַעֲצוֹר

to stop (please ~ calling me)	lehafsik	לְהַפְסִיק
to study (vt)	lilmod	לִלְמוֹד
to swim (vi)	lisxot	לִשְׂחוֹת
to take (vt)	la'kaxat	לָקַחַת
to think (vi, vt)	laxʃov	לַחְשוֹב

to threaten (vt)	le'ayem	לְאַייֵם
to touch (with hands)	la'ga'at	לָגַעַת
to translate (vt)	letargem	לְתַרְגֵּם
to trust (vt)	liv'toax	לִבְטוֹחַ
to try (attempt)	lenasot	לְנַסוֹת

to turn (e.g., ~ left)	lifnot	לִפְנוֹת
to underestimate (vt)	leham'it be''erex	לְהַמְעִיט בְּעֶרֶך
to understand (vt)	lehavin	לְהָבִין
to unite (vt)	le'axed	לְאַחֵד
to wait (vt)	lehamtin	לְהַמְתִּין

to want (wish, desire)	lirtsot	לִרְצוֹת
to warn (vt)	lehazhir	לְהַזְהִיר
to work (vi)	la'avod	לַעֲבוֹד
to write (vt)	lixtov	לִכְתוֹב
to write down	lirʃom	לִרְשוֹם

12. Colours

colour	'tseva	צֶבַע (ז)
shade (tint)	gavan	גָוֶון (ז)
hue	gavan	גָוֶון (ז)
rainbow	'keʃet	קֶשֶׁת (נ)

white (adj)	lavan	לָבָן
black (adj)	ʃaxor	שָׁחוֹר
grey (adj)	afor	אָפוֹר

green (adj)	yarok	יָרוֹק
yellow (adj)	tsahov	צָהוֹב
red (adj)	adom	אָדוֹם

blue (adj)	kaxol	כָּחוֹל
light blue (adj)	taxol	תָכוֹל
pink (adj)	varod	וָרוֹד
orange (adj)	katom	כָּתוֹם

19

| violet (adj) | segol | סָגוֹל |
| brown (adj) | χum | חוּם |

| golden (adj) | zahov | זָהוֹב |
| silvery (adj) | kasuf | כָּסוּף |

beige (adj)	beʒ	בֶּז'
cream (adj)	be'tseva krem	בְּצֶבַע קרֶם
turquoise (adj)	turkiz	טוּרקִיז
cherry red (adj)	bordo	בּוֹרדוֹ
lilac (adj)	segol	סָגוֹל
crimson (adj)	patol	פָּטוֹל

light (adj)	bahir	בָּהִיר
dark (adj)	kehe	כֵּהֶה
bright, vivid (adj)	bohek	בּוֹהֵק

coloured (pencils)	tsiv'oni	צִבעוֹנִי
colour (e.g. ~ film)	tsiv'oni	צִבעוֹנִי
black-and-white (adj)	ʃaχor lavan	שָׁחוֹר־לָבָן
plain (one-coloured)	χad tsiv'i	חַד־צִבעִי
multicoloured (adj)	sasgoni	סַסגוֹנִי

13. Questions

Who?	mi?	מִי?
What?	ma?	מָה?
Where? (at, in)	'eifo?	אֵיפֹה?
Where (to)?	le'an?	לְאָן?
From where?	me"eifo?	מֵאֵיפֹה?
When?	matai?	מָתַי?
Why? (What for?)	'lama?	לָמָה?
Why? (~ are you crying?)	ma'du'a?	מַדוּעַ?

What for?	biʃvil ma?	בִּשׁבִיל מָה?
How? (in what way)	eiχ, keitsad?	כֵּיצַד? אֵיך?
What? (What kind of ...?)	'eize?	אֵיזֶה?
Which?	'eize?	אֵיזֶה?

To whom?	lemi?	לְמִי?
About whom?	al mi?	עַל מִי?
About what?	al ma?	עַל מָה?
With whom?	im mi?	עִם מִי?

| How many? How much? | 'kama? | כַּמָה? |
| Whose? | ʃel mi? | שֶׁל מִי? |

14. Function words. Adverbs. Part 1

Where? (at, in)	'eifo?	אֵיפֹה?
here (adv)	po, kan	פֹּה, כָּאן
there (adv)	ʃam	שָׁם

somewhere (to be)	'eifo ʃehu	אֵיפֹה שֶׁהוּא
nowhere (not in any place)	beʃum makom	בְּשׁוּם מָקוֹם
by (near, beside)	leyad …	לְיַד ...
by the window	leyad haχalon	לְיַד הַחַלוֹן
Where (to)?	le'an?	לְאָן?
here (e.g. come ~!)	'hena, lekan	הֵנָה; לְכָאן
there (e.g. to go ~)	leʃam	לְשָׁם
from here (adv)	mikan	מִכָּאן
from there (adv)	miʃam	מִשָׁם
close (adv)	karov	קָרוֹב
far (adv)	raχok	רָחוֹק
near (e.g. ~ Paris)	leyad	לְיַד
nearby (adv)	karov	קָרוֹב
not far (adv)	lo raχok	לֹא רָחוֹק
left (adj)	smali	שׂמָאלִי
on the left	mismol	מִשׂמֹאל
to the left	'smola	שׂמֹאלָה
right (adj)	yemani	יְמָנִי
on the right	miyamin	מִיָמִין
to the right	ya'mina	יָמִינָה
in front (adv)	mika'dima	מִקָדִימָה
front (as adj)	kidmi	קָדמִי
ahead (the kids ran ~)	ka'dima	קָדִימָה
behind (adv)	me'aχor	מֵאָחוֹר
from behind	me'aχor	מֵאָחוֹר
back (towards the rear)	a'χora	אָחוֹרָה
middle	'emtsa	אָמצַע (ז)
in the middle	ba''emtsa	בָּאֶמצַע
at the side	mehatsad	מֵהַצָד
everywhere (adv)	beχol makom	בְּכָל מָקוֹם
around (in all directions)	misaviv	מִסָבִיב
from inside	mibifnim	מִבִּפנִים
somewhere (to go)	le'an ʃehu	לְאָן שֶׁהוּא
straight (directly)	yaʃar	יָשָׁר
back (e.g. come ~)	baχazara	בַּחֲזָרָה
from anywhere	me'ei ʃam	מֵאֵי שָׁם
from somewhere	me'ei ʃam	מֵאֵי שָׁם
firstly (adv)	reʃit	רֵאשִׁית
secondly (adv)	ʃenit	שֵׁנִית
thirdly (adv)	ʃliʃit	שׁלִישִׁית
suddenly (adv)	pit'om	פִּתאוֹם
at first (in the beginning)	behatslaχa	בַּהַתחָלָה

for the first time	lariʃona	לָרִאשׁוֹנָה
long before …	zman rav lifnei …	זְמַן רַב לִפְנֵי …
anew (over again)	meχadaʃ	מֵחָדָשׁ
for good (adv)	letamid	לְתָמִיד

never (adv)	af 'pa'am, me'olam	מֵעוֹלָם, אַף פַּעַם
again (adv)	ʃuv	שׁוּב
now (at present)	aχʃav, ka'et	עַכְשָׁיו, כָּעֵת
often (adv)	le'itim krovot	לְעִיתִים קְרוֹבוֹת
then (adv)	az	אָז
urgently (quickly)	bidχifut	בִּדְחִיפוּת
usually (adv)	be'dereχ klal	בְּדֶרֶךְ כְּלָל

by the way, …	'dereχ 'agav	דֶּרֶךְ אַגַּב
possibly	efʃari	אֶפְשָׁרִי
probably (adv)	kanir'e	כַּנִּרְאָה
maybe (adv)	ulai	אוּלַי
besides …	χuts mize …	חוּץ מִזֶּה …
that's why …	laχen	לָכֵן
in spite of …	lamrot …	לַמְרוֹת …
thanks to …	hodot le…	הוֹדוֹת לְ…

what (pron.)	ma	מָה
that (conj.)	ʃe	שׁ
something	'maʃehu	מַשֶׁהוּ
anything (something)	'maʃehu	מַשֶׁהוּ
nothing	klum	כְּלוּם

who (pron.)	mi	מִי
someone	'miʃehu, 'miʃehi	מִישֶׁהוּ (ז), מִישֶׁהִי (נ)
somebody	'miʃehu, 'miʃehi	מִישֶׁהוּ (ז), מִישֶׁהִי (נ)

nobody	af eχad, af aχat	אַף אֶחָד (ז), אַף אַחַת (נ)
nowhere (a voyage to ~)	leʃum makom	לְשׁוּם מָקוֹם
nobody's	lo ʃayaχ le'af eχad	לֹא שַׁיָּךְ לְאַף אֶחָד
somebody's	ʃel 'miʃehu	שֶׁל מִישֶׁהוּ

so (I'm ~ glad)	kol kaχ	כָּל־כָּךְ
also (as well)	gam	גַּם
too (as well)	gam	גַּם

15. Function words. Adverbs. Part 2

Why?	ma'du'a?	מַדּוּעַ?
for some reason	miʃum ma	מִשׁוּם־מָה
because …	miʃum ʃe	מִשׁוּם שׁ
for some purpose	lematara 'kolʃehi	לְמַטָּרָה כָּלְשֶׁהִי

and	ve …	וְ …
or	o	אוֹ
but	aval, ulam	אֲבָל, אוּלָם
for (e.g. ~ me)	biʃvil	בִּשְׁבִיל
too (excessively)	yoter midai	יוֹתֵר מִדַּי
only (exclusively)	rak	רַק

| exactly (adv) | bediyuk | בְּדִיוּק |
| about (more or less) | be''erex | בְּעֵרֶךְ |

approximately (adv)	be''erex	בְּעֵרֶךְ
approximate (adj)	meʃo'ar	מְשׁוֹעָר
almost (adv)	kim'at	כְּמְעַט
the rest	ʃe'ar	שְׁאָר (ז)

the other (second)	axer	אַחֵר
other (different)	axer	אַחֵר
each (adj)	kol	כֹּל
any (no matter which)	kolʃehu	כָּלְשֶׁהוּ
many, much (a lot of)	harbe	הַרְבֵּה
many people	harbe	הַרְבֵּה
all (everyone)	kulam	כֻּלָּם

in return for ...	tmurat ...	תְּמוּרַת ...
in exchange (adv)	bitmura	בִּתְמוּרָה
by hand (made)	bayad	בְּיָד
hardly (negative opinion)	safek im	סָפֵק אִם

probably (adv)	karov levadai	קָרוֹב לְוַדַּאי
on purpose (intentionally)	'davka	דַּוְוקָא
by accident (adv)	bemikre	בְּמִקְרֶה

very (adv)	me'od	מְאֹד
for example (adv)	lemaʃal	לְמָשָׁל
between	bein	בֵּין
among	be'kerev	בְּקֶרֶב
so much (such a lot)	kol kax harbe	כָּל־כָּךְ הַרְבֵּה
especially (adv)	bimyuxad	בְּמִיוּחָד

Basic concepts. Part 2

16. Opposites

rich (adj)	aʃir	עָשִׁיר
poor (adj)	ani	עָנִי
ill, sick (adj)	χole	חוֹלֶה
well (not sick)	bari	בָּרִיא
big (adj)	gadol	גָּדוֹל
small (adj)	katan	קָטָן
quickly (adv)	maher	מַהֵר
slowly (adv)	le'at	לְאַט
fast (adj)	mahir	מָהִיר
slow (adj)	iti	אִיטִי
glad (adj)	sa'meaχ	שָׂמֵחַ
sad (adj)	atsuv	עָצוּב
together (adv)	be'yaχad	בְּיַחַד
separately (adv)	levad	לְבַד
aloud (to read)	bekol ram	בְּקוֹל רָם
silently (to oneself)	belev, be'ʃeket	בְּלֵב, בְּשֶׁקֶט
tall (adj)	ga'voha	גָּבוֹהַ
low (adj)	namuχ	נָמוּךְ
deep (adj)	amok	עָמוֹק
shallow (adj)	radud	רָדוּד
yes	ken	כֵּן
no	lo	לֹא
distant (in space)	raχok	רָחוֹק
nearby (adj)	karov	קָרוֹב
far (adv)	raχok	רָחוֹק
nearby (adv)	samuχ	סָמוּךְ
long (adj)	aroχ	אָרוֹךְ
short (adj)	katsar	קָצָר
good (kindhearted)	tov lev	טוֹב לֵב
evil (adj)	raʃa	רָשָׁע

| married (adj) | nasui | נָשׂוּי |
| single (adj) | ravak | רַוָּק |

| to forbid (vt) | le'esor al | לֶאֱסוֹר עַל |
| to permit (vt) | leharʃot | לְהַרְשׁוֹת |

| end | sof | סוֹף (ז) |
| beginning | hatχala | הַתְחָלָה (נ) |

| left (adj) | smali | שְׂמָאלִי |
| right (adj) | yemani | יְמָנִי |

| first (adj) | riʃon | רִאשׁוֹן |
| last (adj) | aχaron | אַחֲרוֹן |

| crime | 'peʃa | פֶּשַׁע (ז) |
| punishment | 'oneʃ | עוֹנֶשׁ (ז) |

| to order (vt) | letsavot | לְצַווֹת |
| to obey (vi, vt) | letsayet | לְצַיֵּית |

| straight (adj) | yaʃar | יָשָׁר |
| curved (adj) | me'ukal | מְעוּקָל |

| paradise | gan 'eden | גַּן עֵדֶן (ז) |
| hell | gehinom | גֵּיהִינוֹם (ז) |

| to be born | lehivaled | לְהִיווָלֵד |
| to die (vi) | lamut | לָמוּת |

| strong (adj) | χazak | חָזָק |
| weak (adj) | χalaʃ | חַלָּשׁ |

| old (adj) | zaken | זָקֵן |
| young (adj) | tsa'ir | צָעִיר |

| old (adj) | yaʃan | יָשָׁן |
| new (adj) | χadaʃ | חָדָשׁ |

| hard (adj) | kaʃe | קָשֶׁה |
| soft (adj) | raχ | רַךְ |

| warm (tepid) | χamim | חָמִים |
| cold (adj) | kar | קַר |

| fat (adj) | ʃamen | שָׁמֵן |
| thin (adj) | raze | רָזֶה |

| narrow (adj) | tsar | צַר |
| wide (adj) | raχav | רָחָב |

| good (adj) | tov | טוֹב |
| bad (adj) | ra | רַע |

| brave (adj) | amits | אַמִּיץ |
| cowardly (adj) | paχdani | פַחְדָנִי |

17. Weekdays

Monday	yom ʃeni	יוֹם שֵׁנִי (ז)
Tuesday	yom ʃliʃi	יוֹם שלִישִׁי (ז)
Wednesday	yom reviʿi	יוֹם רְבִיעִי (ז)
Thursday	yom χamiʃi	יוֹם חֲמִישִׁי (ז)
Friday	yom ʃiʃi	יוֹם שִׁישִׁי (ז)
Saturday	ʃabat	שַׁבָּת (נ)
Sunday	yom riʃon	יוֹם רִאשׁוֹן (ז)
today (adv)	hayom	הַיוֹם
tomorrow (adv)	maχar	מָחָר
the day after tomorrow	maχara'tayim	מָחֳרָתַיִים
yesterday (adv)	etmol	אֶתמוֹל
the day before yesterday	ʃilʃom	שִׁלשׁוֹם
day	yom	יוֹם (ז)
working day	yom avoda	יוֹם עֲבוֹדָה (ז)
public holiday	yom χag	יוֹם חַג (ז)
day off	yom menuχa	יוֹם מְנוּחָה (ז)
weekend	sof ʃa'vuʿa	סוֹף שָׁבוּעַ
all day long	kol hayom	כָּל הַיוֹם
the next day (adv)	lamaχarat	לַמָחֳרָת
two days ago	lifnei yo'mayim	לִפנֵי יוֹמַיִים
the day before	'erev	עֶרֶב
daily (adj)	yomyomi	יוֹמיוֹמִי
every day (adv)	midei yom	מִדֵי יוֹם
week	ʃa'vua	שָׁבוּעַ (ז)
last week (adv)	baʃa'vuʿa ʃeʿavar	בַּשָׁבוּעַ שֶׁעָבַר
next week (adv)	baʃa'vuʿa haba	בַּשָׁבוּעַ הַבָּא
weekly (adj)	ʃvuʿi	שבוּעִי
every week (adv)	kol ʃa'vuʿa	כָּל שָׁבוּעַ
twice a week	paʿa'mayim beʃa'vuʿa	פַּעֲמַיִים בְּשָׁבוּעַ
every Tuesday	kol yom ʃliʃi	כָּל יוֹם שלִישִׁי

18. Hours. Day and night

morning	'boker	בּוֹקֶר (ז)
in the morning	ba'boker	בַּבּוֹקֶר
noon, midday	tsaha'rayim	צָהֳרַיִים (ז"ר)
in the afternoon	aχar hatsaha'rayim	אַחַר הַצָהֳרַיִים
evening	'erev	עֶרֶב (ז)
in the evening	ba'ʿerev	בָּעֶרֶב
night	'laila	לַילָה (ז)
at night	ba'laila	בַּלַילָה
midnight	χatsot	חֲצוֹת (נ)
second	ʃniya	שנִייָה (נ)
minute	daka	דַקָה (נ)
hour	ʃaʿa	שָׁעָה (נ)

half an hour	χatsi ʃaʿa	חֲצִי שָׁעָה (נ)
a quarter-hour	'reva ʃaʿa	רֶבַע שָׁעָה (ז)
fifteen minutes	χameʃ esre dakot	חָמֵשׁ עֶשְׂרֵה דַקוֹת
24 hours	yemama	יְמָמָה (נ)

sunrise	zriχa	זְרִיחָה (נ)
dawn	ʃaχar	שַׁחַר (ז)
early morning	ʃaχar	שַׁחַר (ז)
sunset	ʃkiʿa	שְׁקִיעָה (נ)

early in the morning	mukdam ba'boker	מוּקְדָם בַּבּוֹקֶר
this morning	ha'boker	הַבּוֹקֶר
tomorrow morning	maχar ba'boker	מָחָר בַּבּוֹקֶר

this afternoon	hayom aχarei hatzaha'rayim	הַיוֹם אַחֲרֵי הַצָהֳרַיִים
in the afternoon	aχar hatsaha'rayim	אַחַר הַצָהֳרַיִים
tomorrow afternoon	maχar aχarei hatsaha'rayim	מָחָר אַחֲרֵי הַצָהֳרַיִים

| tonight (this evening) | ha"erev | הָעֶרֶב |
| tomorrow night | maχar ba"erev | מָחָר בָּעֶרֶב |

at 3 o'clock sharp	baʃaʿa ʃaloʃ bediyuk	בְּשָׁעָה שָׁלוֹשׁ בְּדִיוּק
about 4 o'clock	bisvivot arba	בִּסְבִיבוֹת אַרְבַּע
by 12 o'clock	ad ʃteim esre	עַד שְׁתַּיִם-עֶשְׂרֵה

in 20 minutes	be'od esrim dakot	בְּעוֹד עֶשְׂרִים דַקוֹת
in an hour	be'od ʃaʿa	בְּעוֹד שָׁעָה
on time (adv)	bazman	בַּזְמַן

a quarter to ...	'reva le...	רֶבַע לְ...
within an hour	toχ ʃaʿa	תוֹךְ שָׁעָה
every 15 minutes	kol 'reva ʃaʿa	כָּל רֶבַע שָׁעָה
round the clock	misaviv laʃaʿon	מִסָבִיב לַשָׁעוֹן

19. Months. Seasons

January	'yanuʾar	יָנוּאָר (ז)
February	'februʾar	פֶבְּרוּאָר (ז)
March	merts	מֶרְץ (ז)
April	april	אַפְּרִיל (ז)
May	mai	מַאִי (ז)
June	'yuni	יוּנִי (ז)

July	'yuli	יוּלִי (ז)
August	'ogust	אוֹגוּסְט (ז)
September	sep'tember	סֶפְּטֶמְבָּר (ז)
October	ok'tober	אוֹקְטוֹבָּר (ז)
November	no'vember	נוֹבֶמְבָּר (ז)
December	de'tsember	דֶצֶמְבָּר (ז)

spring	aviv	אָבִיב (ז)
in spring	ba'aviv	בָּאָבִיב
spring (as adj)	avivi	אֲבִיבִי
summer	'kayits	קַיִץ (ז)

| in summer | ba'kayits | בַּקַּיִץ |
| summer (as adj) | ketsi | קַיְצִי |

autumn	stav	סְתָיו (ז)
in autumn	bestav	בִּסְתָיו
autumn (as adj)	stavi	סְתָווִי

winter	'χoref	חוֹרֶף (ז)
in winter	ba'χoref	בַּחוֹרֶף
winter (as adj)	χorpi	חוֹרְפִּי
month	'χodeʃ	חוֹדֶשׁ (ז)
this month	ha'χodeʃ	הַחוֹדֶשׁ
next month	ba'χodeʃ haba	בַּחוֹדֶשׁ הַבָּא
last month	ba'χodeʃ ʃe'avar	בַּחוֹדֶשׁ שֶׁעָבַר

a month ago	lifnei 'χodeʃ	לִפְנֵי חוֹדֶשׁ
in a month (a month later)	be'od 'χodeʃ	בְּעוֹד חוֹדֶשׁ
in 2 months (2 months later)	be'od χod'ʃayim	בְּעוֹד חוֹדְשַׁיִים
the whole month	kol ha'χodeʃ	כָּל הַחוֹדֶשׁ
all month long	kol ha'χodeʃ	כָּל הַחוֹדֶשׁ

monthly (~ magazine)	χodʃi	חוֹדְשִׁי
monthly (adv)	χodʃit	חוֹדְשִׁית
every month	kol 'χodeʃ	כָּל חוֹדֶשׁ
twice a month	pa'a'mayim be'χodeʃ	פַּעֲמַיִים בְּחוֹדֶשׁ

year	ʃana	שָׁנָה (נ)
this year	haʃana	הַשָּׁנָה
next year	baʃana haba'a	בַּשָּׁנָה הַבָּאָה
last year	baʃana ʃe'avra	בַּשָּׁנָה שֶׁעָבְרָה
a year ago	lifnei ʃana	לִפְנֵי שָׁנָה
in a year	be'od ʃana	בְּעוֹד שָׁנָה
in two years	be'od ʃna'tayim	בְּעוֹד שְׁנָתַיִים
the whole year	kol haʃana	כָּל הַשָּׁנָה
all year long	kol haʃana	כָּל הַשָּׁנָה

every year	kol ʃana	כָּל שָׁנָה
annual (adj)	ʃnati	שְׁנָתִי
annually (adv)	midei ʃana	מְדֵי שָׁנָה
4 times a year	arba pa'amim be'χodeʃ	אַרְבַּע פְּעָמִים בְּחוֹדֶשׁ

date (e.g. today's ~)	ta'ariχ	תַּאֲרִיךְ (ז)
date (e.g. ~ of birth)	ta'ariχ	תַּאֲרִיךְ (ז)
calendar	'luaχ ʃana	לוּחַ שָׁנָה (ז)

half a year	χatsi ʃana	חֲצִי שָׁנָה (ז)
six months	ʃiʃa χodaʃim, χatsi ʃana	חֲצִי שָׁנָה, שִׁישָׁה חוֹדָשִׁים
season (summer, etc.)	ona	עוֹנָה (נ)
century	'me'a	מֵאָה (נ)

20. Time. Miscellaneous

| time | zman | זְמַן (ז) |
| moment | 'rega | רֶגַע (ז) |

instant (n)	'rega	רֶגַע (ז)
instant (adj)	miyadi	מְיָדִי
lapse (of time)	tkufa	תְּקוּפָה (נ)
life	χayim	חַיִּים (ז"ר)
eternity	'netsaχ	נֵצַח (ז)
epoch	idan	עִידָן (ז)
era	idan	עִידָן (ז)
cycle	maχzor	מַחְזוֹר (ז)
period	tkufa	תְּקוּפָה (נ)
term (short-~)	tkufa	תְּקוּפָה (נ)
the future	atid	עָתִיד (ז)
future (as adj)	haba	הַבָּא
next time	ba'pa'am haba'a	בַּפַּעַם הַבָּאָה
the past	avar	עָבָר (ז)
past (recent)	ʃe'avar	שֶׁעָבַר
last time	ba'pa'am hako'demet	בַּפַּעַם הַקּוֹדֶמֶת
later (adv)	me'uχar yoter	מְאוּחָר יוֹתֵר
after (prep.)	aχarei	אַחֲרֵי
nowadays (adv)	kayom	כַּיּוֹם
now (at this moment)	aχʃav, ka'et	עַכְשָׁיו, כָּעֵת
immediately (adv)	miyad	מִיָּד
soon (adv)	bekarov	בְּקָרוֹב
in advance (beforehand)	meroʃ	מֵרֹאשׁ
a long time ago	mizman	מִזְּמַן
recently (adv)	lo mizman	לֹא מִזְּמַן
destiny	goral	גּוֹרָל (ז)
recollections	ziχronot	זִיכְרוֹנוֹת (ז"ר)
archives	arχiyon	אַרְכִיּוֹן (ז)
during ...	bezman ʃel ...	בִּזְמַן שֶׁל ...
long, a long time (adv)	zman rav	זְמַן רַב
not long (adv)	lo zman rav	לֹא זְמַן רַב
early (in the morning)	mukdam	מוּקְדָּם
late (not early)	me'uχar	מְאוּחָר
forever (for good)	la'netsaχ	לָנֶצַח
to start (begin)	lehatχil	לְהַתְחִיל
to postpone (vt)	lidχot	לִדְחוֹת
at the same time	bo zmanit	בּוֹ זְמַנִּית
permanently (adv)	bikvi'ut	בִּקְבִיעוּת
constant (noise, pain)	ka'vu'a	קָבוּעַ
temporary (adj)	zmani	זְמַנִּי
sometimes (adv)	lif'amim	לִפְעָמִים
rarely (adv)	le'itim reχokot	לְעִיתִּים רְחוֹקוֹת
often (adv)	le'itim krovot	לְעִיתִּים קְרוֹבוֹת

21. Lines and shapes

square	ri'bu'a	רִיבּוּעַ (ז)
square (as adj)	meruba	מְרוּבָּע

circle	maʿagal, igul	מַעֲגָל, עִיגוּל (ז)
round (adj)	agol	עָגוֹל
triangle	meʃulaʃ	מְשׁוּלָשׁ (ז)
triangular (adj)	meʃulaʃ	מְשׁוּלָשׁ

oval	eʾlipsa	אֱלִיפְּסָה (נ)
oval (as adj)	eʾlipti	אֱלִיפְּטִי
rectangle	malben	מַלְבֵּן (ז)
rectangular (adj)	malbeni	מַלְבֵּנִי

pyramid	piraʾmida	פִּירָמִידָה (נ)
rhombus	meʿuyan	מְעוּיָן (ז)
trapezium	trapez	טְרַפֵּז (ז)
cube	kubiya	קוּבִּיָּה (נ)
prism	minsara	מִנְסָרָה (נ)

circumference	maʿagal	מַעֲגָל (ז)
sphere	sfira	סְפִירָה (נ)
ball (solid sphere)	kadur	כַּדּוּר (ז)
diameter	ʾkoter	קוֹטֶר (ז)
radius	ʾradyus	רַדְיוּס (ז)
perimeter (circle's ~)	hekef	הֶיקֵּף (ז)
centre	merkaz	מֶרְכָּז (ז)

horizontal (adj)	ofki	אוֹפְקִי
vertical (adj)	anaχi	אֲנָכִי
parallel (n)	kav makbil	קַו מַקְבִּיל (ז)
parallel (as adj)	makbil	מַקְבִּיל

line	kav	קַו (ז)
stroke	kav	קַו (ז)
straight line	kav yaʃar	קַו יָשָׁר (ז)
curve (curved line)	akuma	עֲקוּמָה (נ)
thin (line, etc.)	dak	דַּק
contour (outline)	mitʾar	מִתְאָר (ז)

intersection	χituχ	חִיתּוּךְ (ז)
right angle	zavit yaʃara	זָווִית יְשָׁרָה (נ)
segment	mikta	מִקְטָע (ז)
sector (circular ~)	gizra	גִּזְרָה (נ)
side (of a triangle)	ʾtsela	צֶלַע (ז)
angle	zavit	זָווִית (נ)

22. Units of measurement

weight	miʃkal	מִשְׁקָל (ז)
length	ʾoreχ	אוֹרֶךְ (ז)
width	ʾroχav	רוֹחַב (ז)
height	ʾgova	גּוֹבַהּ (ז)
depth	ʾomek	עוֹמֶק (ז)
volume	ʾnefaχ	נֶפַח (ז)
area	ʾʃetaχ	שֶׁטַח (ז)
gram	gram	גְּרָם (ז)
milligram	miligram	מִילִיגְרָם (ז)

kilogram	kilogram	קִילוֹגְרָם (ז)
ton	ton	טוֹן (ז)
pound	'pa'und	פָּאוּנְד (ז)
ounce	'unkiya	אוּנְקְיָה (נ)

metre	'meter	מֶטֶר (ז)
millimetre	mili'meter	מִילִימֶטֶר (ז)
centimetre	senti'meter	סֶנְטִימֶטֶר (ז)
kilometre	kilo'meter	קִילוֹמֶטֶר (ז)
mile	mail	מַייל (ז)

inch	intʃ	אִינְצ' (ז)
foot	'regel	רֶגֶל (נ)
yard	yard	יַרְד (ז)

| square metre | 'meter ra'vuʿa | מֶטֶר רָבוּעַ (ז) |
| hectare | hektar | הֶקְטָר (ז) |

litre	litr	לִיטֶר (ז)
degree	maʿala	מַעֲלָה (נ)
volt	volt	ווֹלְט (ז)
ampere	amper	אַמְפֶּר (ז)
horsepower	'koaχ sus	כּוֹחַ סוּס (ז)

quantity	kamut	כַּמוּת (נ)
a little bit of …	ktsat …	קְצָת …
half	'χetsi	חֲצִי (ז)
dozen	tresar	תְרֵיסָר (ז)
piece (item)	yeχida	יְחִידָה (נ)

| size | 'godel | גּוֹדֶל (ז) |
| scale (map ~) | kne mida | קְנֵה מִידָה (ז) |

minimal (adj)	mini'mali	מִינִימָאלִי
the smallest (adj)	hakatan beyoter	הַקָטָן בְּיוֹתֵר
medium (adj)	memutsa	מְמוּצָע
maximal (adj)	maksi'mali	מַקְסִימָלִי
the largest (adj)	hagadol beyoter	הַגָּדוֹל בְּיוֹתֵר

23. Containers

canning jar (glass ~)	tsin'tsenet	צִנְצֶנֶת (נ)
tin, can	paχit	פַּחִית (נ)
bucket	dli	דְלִי (ז)
barrel	χavit	חָבִית (נ)

wash basin (e.g., plastic ~)	gigit	גִּיגִית (נ)
tank (100L water ~)	meiχal	מֵיכָל (ז)
hip flask	meimiya	מֵימִיָה (נ)
jerrycan	'dʒerikan	גָ'רִיקָן (ז)
tank (e.g., tank car)	meχalit	מֵיכָלִית (נ)

| mug | 'sefel | סֵפֶל (ז) |
| cup (of coffee, etc.) | 'sefel | סֵפֶל (ז) |

saucer	taχtit	תַּחְתִּית (נ)
glass (tumbler)	kos	כּוֹס (נ)
wine glass	ga'vi'a	גָּבִיעַ (ז)
stock pot (soup pot)	sir	סִיר (ז)

bottle (~ of wine)	bakbuk	בַּקְבּוּק (ז)
neck (of the bottle, etc.)	tsavar habakbuk	צַוָּאר הַבַּקְבּוּק (ז)

carafe (decanter)	kad	כַּד (ז)
pitcher	kankan	קַנְקַן (ז)
vessel (container)	kli	כְּלִי (ז)
pot (crock, stoneware ~)	sir 'χeres	סִיר חֶרֶס (ז)
vase	agartal	אֲגַרְטָל (ז)

flacon, bottle (perfume ~)	tsloχit	צְלוֹחִית (נ)
vial, small bottle	bakbukon	בַּקְבּוּקוֹן (ז)
tube (of toothpaste)	ʃfo'feret	שְׁפוֹפֶרֶת (נ)

sack (bag)	sak	שַׂק (ז)
bag (paper ~, plastic ~)	sakit	שַׂקִּית (נ)
packet (of cigarettes, etc.)	χafisa	חֲפִיסָה (נ)

box (e.g. shoebox)	kufsa	קוּפְסָה (נ)
crate	argaz	אַרְגָּז (ז)
basket	sal	סַל (ז)

24. Materials

material	'χomer	חוֹמֶר (ז)
wood (n)	ets	עֵץ (ז)
wood-, wooden (adj)	me'ets	מֵעֵץ

glass (n)	zχuχit	זְכוּכִית (נ)
glass (as adj)	mizχuχit	מִזְכוּכִית

stone (n)	'even	אֶבֶן (נ)
stone (as adj)	me''even	מֵאֶבֶן

plastic (n)	'plastik	פְּלַסְטִיק (ז)
plastic (as adj)	mi'plastik	מִפְּלַסְטִיק

rubber (n)	'gumi	גוּמִי (ז)
rubber (as adj)	mi'gumi	מִגּוּמִי

cloth, fabric (n)	bad	בַּד (ז)
fabric (as adj)	mibad	מִבַּד

paper (n)	neyar	נְיָר (ז)
paper (as adj)	mineyar	מִנְּיָר

cardboard (n)	karton	קַרְטוֹן (ז)
cardboard (as adj)	mikarton	מִקַּרְטוֹן
polyethylene	'nailon	נַיְילוֹן (ז)
cellophane	tselofan	צֶלוֹפָן (ז)

| linoleum | li'nole·um | לִינוֹלֵיאוּם (ז) |
| plywood | dikt | דִּיקְט (ז) |

porcelain (n)	xar'sina	חַרְסִינָה (נ)
porcelain (as adj)	mexar'sina	מְחַרְסִינָה
clay (n)	xarsit	חַרְסִית (נ)
clay (as adj)	me'xeres	מֶחֶרֶס
ceramic (n)	ke'ramika	קֶרָמִיקָה (נ)
ceramic (as adj)	ke'rami	קֶרָמִי

25. Metals

metal (n)	ma'texet	מַתֶּכֶת (נ)
metal (as adj)	mataxti	מַתַּכְתִּי
alloy (n)	sag'soget	סַגְסוֹגֶת (נ)

gold (n)	zahav	זָהָב (ז)
gold, golden (adj)	mizahav, zahov	מִזָּהָב, זָהוֹב
silver (n)	'kesef	כֶּסֶף (ז)
silver (as adj)	kaspi	כַּסְפִּי

iron (n)	barzel	בַּרְזֶל (ז)
iron-, made of iron (adj)	mibarzel	מִבַּרְזֶל
steel (n)	plada	פְּלָדָה (נ)
steel (as adj)	miplada	מִפְּלָדָה
copper (n)	ne'xoſet	נְחוֹשֶׁת (נ)
copper (as adj)	mine'xoſet	מִנְחוֹשֶׁת

aluminium (n)	alu'minyum	אֲלוּמִינְיוּם (ז)
aluminium (as adj)	me'alu'minyum	מְאֲלוּמִינְיוּם
bronze (n)	arad	אָרָד (ז)
bronze (as adj)	me'arad	מְאָרָד

brass	pliz	פְּלִיז (ז)
nickel	'nikel	נִיקֶל (ז)
platinum	'platina	פְּלָטִינָה (נ)
mercury	kaspit	כַּסְפִּית (נ)
tin	bdil	בְּדִיל (ז)
lead	o'feret	עוֹפֶרֶת (נ)
zinc	avats	אָבָץ (ז)

HUMAN BEING

Human being. The body

26. Humans. Basic concepts

human being	ben adam	בֶּן אָדָם (ז)
man (adult male)	'gever	גֶּבֶר (ז)
woman	iʃa	אִשָּׁה (נ)
child	'yeled	יֶלֶד (ז)
girl	yalda	יַלְדָּה (נ)
boy	'yeled	יֶלֶד (ז)
teenager	'na'ar	נַעַר (ז)
old man	zaken	זָקֵן (ז)
old woman	zkena	זְקֵנָה (נ)

27. Human anatomy

organism (body)	guf ha'adam	גּוּף הָאָדָם (ז)
heart	lev	לֵב (ז)
blood	dam	דָּם (ז)
artery	'orek	עוֹרֶק (ז)
vein	vrid	וְרִיד (ז)
brain	'moaχ	מוֹחַ (ז)
nerve	atsav	עָצָב (ז)
nerves	atsabim	עֲצַבִּים (ז"ר)
vertebra	χulya	חוּלְיָה (נ)
spine (backbone)	amud haʃidra	עַמּוּד הַשִּׁדְרָה (ז)
stomach (organ)	keiva	קֵיבָה (נ)
intestines, bowels	me''ayim	מֵעַיִים (ז"ר)
intestine (e.g. large ~)	me'i	מְעִי (ז)
liver	kaved	כָּבֵד (ז)
kidney	kilya	כִּלְיָה (נ)
bone	'etsem	עֶצֶם (נ)
skeleton	'ʃeled	שֶׁלֶד (ז)
rib	'tsela	צֵלָע (נ)
skull	gul'golet	גּוּלְגּוֹלֶת (נ)
muscle	ʃrir	שְׁרִיר (ז)
biceps	ʃrir du raʃi	שְׁרִיר דּוּ-רָאשִׁי (ז)
triceps	ʃrir tlat raʃi	שְׁרִיר תְּלָת-רָאשִׁי (ז)
tendon	gid	גִּיד (ז)
joint	'perek	פֶּרֶק (ז)

lungs	re'ot	רֵיאוֹת (נ"ר)
genitals	evrei min	אֶבְרֵי מִין (ז"ר)
skin	or	עוֹר (ז)

28. Head

head	roʃ	רֹאשׁ (ז)
face	panim	פָּנִים (ז"ר)
nose	af	אַף (ז)
mouth	pe	פֶּה (ז)

eye	'ayin	עַיִן (נ)
eyes	ei'nayim	עֵינַיִים (נ"ר)
pupil	iʃon	אִישׁוֹן (ז)
eyebrow	gaba	גַּבָּה (נ)
eyelash	ris	רִיס (ז)
eyelid	afʿaf	עַפְעַף (ז)

tongue	laʃon	לָשׁוֹן (נ)
tooth	ʃen	שֵׁן (נ)
lips	sfa'tayim	שְׂפָתַיִים (נ"ר)
cheekbones	atsamot leχa'yayim	עַצְמוֹת לְחָיַיִם (נ"ר)
gum	χani'χayim	חֲנִיכַיִים (ז"ר)
palate	χeχ	חֵךְ (ז)

nostrils	neχi'rayim	נְחִירַיִים (ז"ר)
chin	santer	סַנְטֵר (ז)
jaw	'leset	לֶסֶת (נ)
cheek	'leχi	לֶחִי (נ)

forehead	'metsaχ	מֵצַח (ז)
temple	raka	רַקָּה (נ)
ear	'ozen	אֹזֶן (נ)
back of the head	'oref	עוֹרֶף (ז)
neck	tsavar	צַוָּאר (ז)
throat	garon	גָּרוֹן (ז)

hair	se'ar	שֵׂיעָר (ז)
hairstyle	tis'roket	תִּסְרוֹקֶת (נ)
haircut	tis'poret	תִּסְפּוֹרֶת (נ)
wig	pe'a	פֵּאָה (נ)

moustache	safam	שָׂפָם (ז)
beard	zakan	זָקָן (ז)
to have (a beard, etc.)	legadel	לְגַדֵּל
plait	tsama	צַמָּה (נ)
sideboards	pe'ot leχa'yayim	פֵּאוֹת לְחָיַיִם (נ"ר)

red-haired (adj)	'dʒindʒi	גִ'ינְגִ'י
grey (hair)	kasuf	כָּסוּף
bald (adj)	ke'reaχ	קֵירֵחַ
bald patch	ka'raχat	קָרַחַת (נ)
ponytail	'kuku	קוּקוּ (ז)
fringe	'poni	פּוֹנִי (ז)

29. Human body

hand	kaf yad	כַּף יָד (ז)
arm	yad	יָד (נ)

finger	'etsba	אֶצְבַּע (נ)
toe	'bohen	בּוֹהֶן (נ)
thumb	agudal	אֲגוּדָל (ז)
little finger	'zeret	זֶרֶת (נ)
nail	tsi'poren	צִיפּוֹרֶן (נ)

fist	egrof	אֶגְרוֹף (ז)
palm	kaf yad	כַּף יָד (נ)
wrist	'ʃoreʃ kaf hayad	שׁוֹרֶשׁ כַּף הַיָד (ז)
forearm	ama	אַמָה (נ)
elbow	marpek	מַרְפֵּק (ז)
shoulder	katef	כָּתֵף (נ)

leg	'regel	רֶגֶל (נ)
foot	kaf 'regel	כַּף רֶגֶל (נ)
knee	'bereχ	בֶּרֶךְ (נ)
calf	ʃok	שׁוֹק (נ)
hip	yareχ	יָרֵךְ (ז)
heel	akev	עָקֵב (ז)

body	guf	גוּף (ז)
stomach	'beten	בֶּטֶן (נ)
chest	χaze	חָזֶה (ז)
breast	ʃad	שַׁד (ז)
flank	tsad	צַד (ז)
back	gav	גַב (ז)
lower back	mot'nayim	מוֹתְנַיִים (ז"ר)
waist	'talya	טַלְיָה (נ)

navel (belly button)	tabur	טַבּוּר (ז)
buttocks	aχo'rayim	אֲחוֹכַיִים (ז"ר)
bottom	yaʃvan	יַשְׁבָן (ז)

beauty spot	nekudat χen	נְקוּדַת חֵן (נ)
birthmark (café au lait spot)	'ketem leida	כֶּתֶם לֵידָה (ז)
tattoo	ka'a'ku'a	קַעֲקוּעַ (ז)
scar	tsa'leket	צַלֶקֶת (נ)

Clothing & Accessories

30. Outerwear. Coats

clothes	bgadim	בְּגָדִים (ז"ר)
outerwear	levuʃ elyon	לְבוּשׁ עֶלְיוֹן (ז)
winter clothing	bigdei 'χoref	בִּגְדֵי חוֹרֶף (ז"ר)
coat (overcoat)	me'il	מְעִיל (ז)
fur coat	me'il parva	מְעִיל פַּרְוָה (ז)
fur jacket	me'il parva katsar	מְעִיל פַּרְוָה קָצָר (ז)
down coat	me'il puχ	מְעִיל פּוּךְ (ז)
jacket (e.g. leather ~)	me'il katsar	מְעִיל קָצָר (ז)
raincoat (trenchcoat, etc.)	me'il 'geʃem	מְעִיל גֶּשֶׁם (ז)
waterproof (adj)	amid be'mayim	עָמִיד בְּמַיִם

31. Men's & women's clothing

shirt (button shirt)	χultsa	חוּלְצָה (נ)
trousers	miχna'sayim	מִכְנָסַיִם (ז"ר)
jeans	miχnesei 'dʒins	מִכְנְסֵי גִ'ינְס (ז"ר)
suit jacket	ʒaket	זָ'קֶט (ז)
suit	χalifa	חֲלִיפָה (נ)
dress (frock)	simla	שִׂמְלָה (נ)
skirt	χatsa'it	חֲצָאִית (נ)
blouse	χultsa	חוּלְצָה (נ)
knitted jacket (cardigan, etc.)	ʒaket 'tsemer	זָ'קֶט צֶמֶר (ז)
jacket (of a woman's suit)	ʒaket	זָ'קֶט (ז)
T-shirt	ti ʃert	טִי שֶׁרְט (ז)
shorts (short trousers)	miχna'sayim ktsarim	מִכְנָסַיִם קְצָרִים (ז"ר)
tracksuit	'trening	טְרֶנִינג (ז)
bathrobe	χaluk raχatsa	חָלוּק רַחְצָה (ז)
pyjamas	pi'dʒama	פִּיגָ'מָה (נ)
jumper (sweater)	'sveder	סְוֶודֶר (ז)
pullover	afuda	אֲפוּדָה (נ)
waistcoat	vest	וֶסְט (ז)
tailcoat	frak	פְרָאק (ז)
dinner suit	tuk'sido	טוּקְסִידוֹ (ז)
uniform	madim	מַדִּים (ז"ר)
workwear	bigdei avoda	בִּגְדֵי עֲבוֹדָה (ז"ר)
boiler suit	sarbal	סַרְבָּל (ז)
coat (e.g. doctor's smock)	χaluk	חָלוּק (ז)

32. Clothing. Underwear

underwear	levanim	לְבָנִים (ז"ר)
pants	taxtonim	תַחתוֹנִים (ז"ר)
panties	taxtonim	תַחתוֹנִים (ז"ר)
vest (singlet)	gufiya	גוּפִיָה (נ)
socks	gar'bayim	גַרבַּיִים (ז"ר)
nightdress	'ktonet 'laila	כתוֹנֶת לַילָה (נ)
bra	xaziya	חֲזִייָה (נ)
knee highs (knee-high socks)	birkon	בִּרכוֹן (ז)
tights	garbonim	גַרבּוֹנִים (ז"ר)
stockings (hold ups)	garbei 'nailon	גַרבֵּי נַילוֹן (ז"ר)
swimsuit, bikini	'beged yam	בֶּגֶד יָם (ז)

33. Headwear

hat	'kova	כּוֹבַע (ז)
trilby hat	'kova 'leved	כּוֹבַע לֶבֶד (ז)
baseball cap	'kova 'beisbol	כּוֹבַע בֵּייסבּוֹל (ז)
flatcap	'kova mitsxiya	כּוֹבַע מִצחִייָה (ז)
beret	baret	בֶּרֶט (ז)
hood	bardas	בַּרדָס (ז)
panama hat	'kova 'tembel	כּוֹבַע טֶמבֶּל (ז)
knit cap (knitted hat)	'kova 'gerev	כּוֹבַע גֶרֶב (ז)
headscarf	mit'paxat	מִטפַּחַת (נ)
women's hat	'kova	כּוֹבַע (ז)
hard hat	kasda	קַסדָה (נ)
forage cap	kumta	כּוּמתָה (נ)
helmet	kasda	קַסדָה (נ)
bowler	mig'ba'at me'u'gelet	מִגבַּעַת מְעוּגֶלֶת (נ)
top hat	tsi'linder	צִילִינדֶר (ז)

34. Footwear

footwear	han'ala	הַנעָלָה (נ)
shoes (men's shoes)	na'a'layim	נַעֲלַיִים (נ"ר)
shoes (women's shoes)	na'a'layim	נַעֲלַיִים (נ"ר)
boots (e.g., cowboy ~)	maga'fayim	מַגָפַיִים (ז"ר)
carpet slippers	na'alei 'bayit	נַעֲלֵי בַּיִת (נ"ר)
trainers	na'alei sport	נַעֲלֵי ספוֹרט (נ"ר)
trainers	na'alei sport	נַעֲלֵי ספוֹרט (נ"ר)
sandals	sandalim	סַנדָלִים (ז"ר)
cobbler (shoe repairer)	sandlar	סַנדלָר (ז)
heel	akev	עָקֵב (ז)

pair (of shoes)	zug	זוּג (ז)
lace (shoelace)	sroχ	שְׂרוֹךְ (ז)
to lace up (vt)	lisroχ	לִשְׂרוֹךְ
shoehorn	kaf na'a'layim	כַּף נַעֲלַיִם (נ)
shoe polish	miʃχat na'a'layim	מִשְׁחַת נַעֲלַיִם (נ)

35. Textile. Fabrics

cotton (n)	kutna	כּוּתְנָה (נ)
cotton (as adj)	mikutna	מִכּוּתְנָה
flax (n)	piʃtan	פִּשְׁתָּן (ז)
flax (as adj)	mipiʃtan	מִפִּשְׁתָּן
silk (n)	'meʃi	מֶשִׁי (ז)
silk (as adj)	miʃyi	מֶשְׁיִי
wool (n)	'tsemer	צֶמֶר (ז)
wool (as adj)	tsamri	צַמְרִי
velvet	ktifa	קְטִיפָה (נ)
suede	zamʃ	זָמְשׁ (ז)
corduroy	'korderoi	קוֹרְדָרוֹי (ז)
nylon (n)	'nailon	נָיְילוֹן (ז)
nylon (as adj)	mi'nailon	מְנָיְילוֹן
polyester (n)	poli''ester	פּוֹלִיאֶסְטֶר (ז)
polyester (as adj)	mipoli''ester	מִפּוֹלִיאֶסְטֶר
leather (n)	or	עוֹר (ז)
leather (as adj)	me'or	מֵעוֹר
fur (n)	parva	פַּרְוָה (נ)
fur (e.g. ~ coat)	miparva	מִפַּרְוָה

36. Personal accessories

gloves	kfafot	כְּפָפוֹת (נ"ר)
mittens	kfafot	כְּפָפוֹת (נ"ר)
scarf (muffler)	tsa'if	צָעִיף (ז)
glasses	miʃka'fayim	מִשְׁקָפַיִם (ז"ר)
frame (eyeglass ~)	mis'geret	מִסְגֶּרֶת (נ)
umbrella	mitriya	מִטְרִיָּה (נ)
walking stick	makel haliχa	מַקֵּל הֲלִיכָה (ז)
hairbrush	miv'reʃet se'ar	מִבְרֶשֶׁת שֵׂיעָר (נ)
fan	menifa	מְנִיפָה (נ)
tie (necktie)	aniva	עֲנִיבָה (נ)
bow tie	anivat parpar	עֲנִיבַת פַּרְפַּר (נ)
braces	ktefiyot	כְּתֵפִיּוֹת (נ"ר)
handkerchief	mimχata	מִמְחָטָה (נ)
comb	masrek	מַסְרֵק (ז)
hair slide	sikat roʃ	סִיכַת רֹאשׁ (נ)

| hairpin | sikat se'ar | סִיכַּת שֵׂעָר (נ) |
| buckle | avzam | אַבְזָם (ז) |

| belt | χagora | חֲגוֹרָה (נ) |
| shoulder strap | retsu'at katef | רְצוּעַת כָּתֵף (נ) |

bag (handbag)	tik	תִּיק (ז)
handbag	tik	תִּיק (ז)
rucksack	tarmil	תַּרְמִיל (ז)

37. Clothing. Miscellaneous

fashion	ofna	אוֹפְנָה (נ)
in vogue (adj)	ofnati	אוֹפְנָתִי
fashion designer	me'atsev ofna	מְעַצֵּב אוֹפְנָה (ז)

collar	tsavaron	צַוָּוארוֹן (ז)
pocket	kis	כִּיס (ז)
pocket (as adj)	ʃel kis	שֶׁל כִּיס
sleeve	ʃarvul	שַׁרְווּל (ז)
hanging loop	mitle	מִתְלֶה (ז)
flies (on trousers)	χanut	חֲנוּת (נ)

zip (fastener)	roχsan	רוֹכְסָן (ז)
fastener	'keres	קֶרֶס (ז)
button	kaftor	כַּפְתּוֹר (ז)
buttonhole	lula'a	לוּלָאָה (נ)
to come off (ab. button)	lehitaleʃ	לְהִיתָּלֵשׁ

to sew (vi, vt)	litpor	לִתְפּוֹר
to embroider (vi, vt)	lirkom	לִרְקוֹם
embroidery	rikma	רִקְמָה (נ)
sewing needle	'maχat tfira	מַחַט תְּפִירָה (נ)
thread	χut	חוּט (ז)
seam	'tefer	תֶּפֶר (ז)

to get dirty (vi)	lehitlaχleχ	לְהִתְלַכְלֵךְ
stain (mark, spot)	'ketem	כֶּתֶם (ז)
to crease, to crumple	lehitkamet	לְהִתְקַמֵּט
to tear, to rip (vt)	lik'ro'a	לִקְרוֹעַ
clothes moth	aʃ	עָשׁ (ז)

38. Personal care. Cosmetics

toothpaste	miʃχat ʃi'nayim	מִשְׁחַת שִׁינַיִים (נ)
toothbrush	miv'reʃet ʃi'nayim	מִבְרֶשֶׁת שִׁינַיִים (נ)
to clean one's teeth	letsaχ'tseaχ ʃi'nayim	לְצַחְצֵחַ שִׁינַיִים

razor	'ta'ar	תַּעַר (ז)
shaving cream	'ketsef gi'luaχ	קֶצֶף גִּילּוּחַ (ז)
to shave (vi)	lehitga'leaχ	לְהִתְגַּלֵּחַ
soap	sabon	סַבּוֹן (ז)

shampoo	ʃampu	שַׁמְפּוּ (ז)
scissors	mispa'rayim	מִסְפָּרַיִם (ז"ר)
nail file	pʦira	פְּצִירָה (נ)
nail clippers	gozez ʦipor'nayim	גּוֹזֵז צִיפּוֹרְנַיִם (ז)
tweezers	pin'ʦeta	פִּינְצֶטָה (נ)
cosmetics	tamrukim	תַּמְרוּקִים (ז"ר)
face mask	maseχa	מַסֵכָה (נ)
manicure	manikur	מָנִיקוּר (ז)
to have a manicure	laˤasot manikur	לַעֲשׂוֹת מָנִיקוּר
pedicure	pedikur	פֵּדִיקוּר (ז)
make-up bag	tik ipur	תִּיק אִיפּוּר (ז)
face powder	'pudra	פּוּדְרָה (נ)
powder compact	pudriya	פּוּדְרִיָה (נ)
blusher	'somek	סוֹמֵק (ז)
perfume (bottled)	'bosem	בּוֹשֶׂם (ז)
toilet water (lotion)	mei 'bosem	מֵי בּוֹשֶׂם (ז"ר)
lotion	mei panim	מֵי פָּנִים (ז"ר)
cologne	mei 'bosem	מֵי בּוֹשֶׂם (ז"ר)
eyeshadow	ʦlalit	צְלָלִית (נ)
eyeliner	ai 'lainer	אַי לַיינֶר (ז)
mascara	'maskara	מַסְקָרָה (נ)
lipstick	sfaton	שְׂפָתוֹן (ז)
nail polish	'laka leʦipor'nayim	לַכָּה לְצִיפּוֹרְנַיִם (נ)
hair spray	tarsis leseˤar	תַּרְסִיס לְשֵׂיעָר (ז)
deodorant	de'odo'rant	דָאוֹדוֹרַנט (ז)
cream	krem	קְרֶם (ז)
face cream	krem panim	קְרֶם פָּנִים (ז)
hand cream	krem ya'dayim	קְרֶם יָדַיִם (ז)
anti-wrinkle cream	krem 'neged kmatim	קְרֶם נֶגֶד קְמָטִים (ז)
day cream	krem yom	קְרֶם יוֹם (ז)
night cream	krem 'laila	קְרֶם לַיְלָה (ז)
day (as adj)	yomi	יוֹמִי
night (as adj)	leili	לֵילִי
tampon	tampon	טַמְפּוֹן (ז)
toilet paper (toilet roll)	neyar tuʾalet	נְיַיר טוֹאָלֶט (ז)
hair dryer	meyabeʃ seˤar	מְייַבֵּשׁ שֵׂיעָר (ז)

39. Jewellery

jewellery, jewels	taχʃitim	תַּכְשִׁיטִים (ז"ר)
precious (e.g. ~ stone)	yekar 'ereχ	יְקַר עֵרֶךְ
hallmark stamp	tav ʦorfim, bχina	תָּו צוֹרְפִים (ז), בְּחִינָה (נ)
ring	ta'baˤat	טַבַּעַת (נ)
wedding ring	ta'baˤat nisuˤin	טַבַּעַת נִישׂוּאִין (נ)
bracelet	ʦamid	צָמִיד (ז)
earrings	agilim	עֲגִילִים (ז"ר)

necklace (~ of pearls)	maχ'rozet	מַחֲרוֹזֶת (נ)
crown	'keter	כֶּתֶר (ז)
bead necklace	maχ'rozet	מַחֲרוֹזֶת (נ)

diamond	yahalom	יַהֲלוֹם (ז)
emerald	ba'reket	בָּרֶקֶת (נ)
ruby	'odem	אוֹדֶם (ז)
sapphire	sapir	סַפִּיר (ז)
pearl	pnina	פְּנִינָה (נ)
amber	inbar	עִנבָּר (ז)

40. Watches. Clocks

watch (wristwatch)	ʃe'on yad	שְׁעוֹן יָד (ז)
dial	'luaχ ʃa'on	לוּחַ שָׁעוֹן (ז)
hand (clock, watch)	maχog	מָחוֹג (ז)
metal bracelet	tsamid	צָמִיד (ז)
watch strap	retsu'a leʃa'on	רְצוּעָה לְשָׁעוֹן (נ)

battery	solela	סוֹלְלָה (נ)
to be flat (battery)	lehitroken	לְהִתרוֹקֵן
to change a battery	lehaχlif	לְהַחֲלִיף
to run fast	lemaher	לְמַהֵר
to run slow	lefager	לְפַגֵּר

wall clock	ʃe'on kir	שְׁעוֹן קִיר (ז)
hourglass	ʃe'on χol	שְׁעוֹן חוֹל (ז)
sundial	ʃe'on 'ʃemeʃ	שְׁעוֹן שֶׁמֶשׁ (ז)
alarm clock	ʃa'on me'orer	שְׁעוֹן מְעוֹרֵר (ז)
watchmaker	ʃa'an	שָׁעָן (ז)
to repair (vt)	letaken	לְתַקֵּן

Food. Nutricion

41. Food

meat	basar	בָּשָׂר (ז)
chicken	of	עוֹף (ז)
poussin	pargit	פַּרְגִּית (נ)
duck	barvaz	בַּרְוָז (ז)
goose	avaz	אַוָּז (ז)
game	'tsayid	צַיִד (ז)
turkey	'hodu	הוֹדוּ (ז)

pork	basar χazir	בְּשַׂר חֲזִיר (ז)
veal	basar 'egel	בְּשַׂר עֵגֶל (ז)
lamb	basar 'keves	בְּשַׂר כֶּבֶשׂ (ז)
beef	bakar	בָּקָר (ז)
rabbit	arnav	אַרְנָב (ז)

sausage (bologna, etc.)	naknik	נַקְנִיק (ז)
vienna sausage (frankfurter)	naknikiya	נַקְנִיקִיָּה (נ)
bacon	'kotel χazir	קוֹתֶל חֲזִיר (ז)
ham	basar χazir me'uʃan	בְּשַׂר חֲזִיר מְעוּשָׁן (ז)
gammon	'kotel χazir me'uʃan	קוֹתֶל חֲזִיר מְעוּשָׁן (ז)

pâté	pate	פָּטֶה (ז)
liver	kaved	כָּבֵד (ז)
mince (minced meat)	basar taχun	בְּשַׂר טָחוּן (ז)
tongue	laʃon	לָשׁוֹן (נ)

egg	beitsa	בֵּיצָה (נ)
eggs	beitsim	בֵּיצִים (נ"ר)
egg white	χelbon	חֶלְבּוֹן (ז)
egg yolk	χelmon	חֶלְמוֹן (ז)

fish	dag	דָּג (ז)
seafood	perot yam	פֵּירוֹת יָם (ז"ר)
crustaceans	sartana'im	סַרְטָנָאִים (ז"ר)
caviar	kavyar	קָווִיאָר (ז)

crab	sartan yam	סַרְטָן יָם (ז)
prawn	ʃrimps	שְׁרִימְפְּס (ז"ר)
oyster	tsidpat ma'aχal	צִדְפַּת מַאֲכָל (נ)
spiny lobster	'lobster kotsani	לוֹבְּסְטֶר קוֹצָנִי (ז)
octopus	tamnun	תַּמְנוּן (ז)
squid	kala'mari	קָלָמָארִי (ז)

sturgeon	basar haχidkan	בְּשַׂר הַחִדְקָן (ז)
salmon	'salmon	סַלְמוֹן (ז)
halibut	putit	פּוּטִית (נ)
cod	ʃibut	שִׁיבּוּט (ז)

mackerel	kolyas	קוֹלְיָס (ז)
tuna	'tuna	טוּנָה (נ)
eel	tslofaχ	צְלוֹפָח (ז)

trout	forel	פּוֹרֶל (ז)
sardine	sardin	סַרְדִּין (ז)
pike	ze'ev 'mayim	זְאֵב מַיִם (ז)
herring	ma'liaχ	מָלִיחַ (ז)

bread	'leχem	לֶחֶם (ז)
cheese	gvina	גְּבִינָה (נ)
sugar	sukar	סוּכָּר (ז)
salt	'melaχ	מֶלַח (ז)

rice	'orez	אוֹרֶז (ז)
pasta (macaroni)	'pasta	פַּסְטָה (נ)
noodles	irtiyot	אַטְרִיּוֹת (נ"ר)

butter	χem'a	חֶמְאָה (נ)
vegetable oil	'ʃemen tsimχi	שֶׁמֶן צִמְחִי (ז)
sunflower oil	'ʃemen χamaniyot	שֶׁמֶן חַמָּנִיּוֹת (ז)
margarine	marga'rina	מַרְגָּרִינָה (נ)

| olives | zeitim | זֵיתִים (ז"ר) |
| olive oil | 'ʃemen 'zayit | שֶׁמֶן זַיִת (ז) |

milk	χalav	חָלָב (ז)
condensed milk	χalav merukaz	חָלָב מְרוּכָּז (ז)
yogurt	'yogurt	יוֹגוּרְט (ז)
soured cream	ʃa'menet	שַׁמֶּנֶת (נ)
cream (of milk)	ʃa'menet	שַׁמֶּנֶת (נ)

| mayonnaise | mayonez | מָיוֹנֵז (ז) |
| buttercream | ka'tsefet χem'a | קַצֶּפֶת חֶמְאָה (נ) |

groats (barley ~, etc.)	grisim	גְּרִיסִים (ז"ר)
flour	'kemaχ	קֶמַח (ז)
tinned food	ʃimurim	שִׁימּוּרִים (ז"ר)

cornflakes	ptitei 'tiras	פְּתִיתֵי תִּירָס (ז"ר)
honey	dvaʃ	דְּבַשׁ (ז)
jam	riba	רִיבָּה (נ)
chewing gum	'mastik	מַסְטִיק (ז)

42. Drinks

water	'mayim	מַיִם (ז"ר)
drinking water	mei ʃtiya	מֵי שְׁתִיָּה (ז"ר)
mineral water	'mayim mine'raliyim	מַיִם מִינֵרָלִיִּים (ז"ר)

still (adj)	lo mugaz	לֹא מוּגָז
carbonated (adj)	mugaz	מוּגָז
sparkling (adj)	mugaz	מוּגָז
ice	'keraχ	קֶרַח (ז)

with ice	im 'keraχ	עִם קֶרַח
non-alcoholic (adj)	natul alkohol	נְטוּל אַלְכּוֹהוֹל
soft drink	maʃke kal	מַשְׁקֶה קַל (ז)
refreshing drink	maʃke meraʼanen	מַשְׁקֶה מְרַעֲנֵן (ז)
lemonade	limo'nada	לִימוֹנָדָה (נ)
spirits	maʃka'ot χarifim	מַשְׁקָאוֹת חָרִיפִים (ז"ר)
wine	'yayin	יַיִן (ז)
white wine	'yayin lavan	יַיִן לָבָן (ז)
red wine	'yayin adom	יַיִן אָדוֹם (ז)
liqueur	liker	לִיקֶר (ז)
champagne	ʃam'panya	שַׁמְפַּנְיָה (נ)
vermouth	'vermut	וֶרְמוּט (ז)
whisky	'viski	וִיסְקִי (ז)
vodka	'vodka	וֹדְקָה (נ)
gin	dʒin	ג'ין (ז)
cognac	'konyak	קוֹנְיָאק (ז)
rum	rom	רוֹם (ז)
coffee	kafe	קָפֶּה (ז)
black coffee	kafe ʃaχor	קָפֶּה שָׁחוֹר (ז)
white coffee	kafe hafuχ	קָפֶּה הָפוּךְ (ז)
cappuccino	kapu'tʃino	קָפּוּצִ'ינוֹ (ז)
instant coffee	kafe names	קָפֶּה נָמֵס (ז)
milk	χalav	חָלָב (ז)
cocktail	kokteil	קוֹקְטֵיל (ז)
milkshake	'milkʃeik	מִילְקְשֵׁייק (ז)
juice	mits	מִיץ (ז)
tomato juice	mits agvaniyot	מִיץ עַגְבָנִיוֹת (ז)
orange juice	mits tapuzim	מִיץ תַּפּוּזִים (ז)
freshly squeezed juice	mits saχut	מִיץ סָחוּט (ז)
beer	'bira	בִּירָה (נ)
lager	'bira bahira	בִּירָה בָּהִירָה (נ)
bitter	'bira keha	בִּירָה כֵּהָה (נ)
tea	te	תֶּה (ז)
black tea	te ʃaχor	תֶּה שָׁחוֹר (ז)
green tea	te yarok	תֶּה יָרוֹק (ז)

43. Vegetables

vegetables	yerakot	יְרָקוֹת (ז"ר)
greens	'yerek	יֶרֶק (ז)
tomato	agvaniya	עַגְבָנִיָּה (נ)
cucumber	melafefon	מְלָפְפוֹן (ז)
carrot	'gezer	גֶּזֶר (ז)
potato	ta'puaχ adama	תַּפּוּחַ אֲדָמָה (ז)
onion	batsal	בָּצָל (ז)

garlic	ʃum	שׁוּם (ז)
cabbage	kruv	כְּרוּב (ז)
cauliflower	kruvit	כְּרוּבִית (נ)
Brussels sprouts	kruv nitsanim	כְּרוּב נִצָּנִים (ז)
broccoli	'brokoli	בְּרוֹקוֹלִי (ז)

beetroot	'selek	סֶלֶק (ז)
aubergine	χatsil	חָצִיל (ז)
courgette	kiʃu	קִישׁוּא (ז)
pumpkin	'dla'at	דְּלַעַת (נ)
turnip	'lefet	לֶפֶת (נ)

parsley	petro'zilya	פֶּטְרוֹזִילְיָה (נ)
dill	ʃamir	שָׁמִיר (ז)
lettuce	'χasa	חַסָּה (נ)
celery	'seleri	סֶלֶרִי (ז)
asparagus	aspa'ragos	אַסְפָּרָגוֹס (ז)
spinach	'tered	תֶּרֶד (ז)

pea	afuna	אֲפוּנָה (נ)
beans	pol	פּוֹל (ז)
maize	'tiras	תִּירָס (ז)
kidney bean	ʃu'it	שְׁעוּעִית (נ)

sweet paper	'pilpel	פִּלְפֵּל (ז)
radish	tsnonit	צְנוֹנִית (נ)
artichoke	artiʃok	אַרְטִישׁוֹק (ז)

44. Fruits. Nuts

fruit	pri	פְּרִי (ז)
apple	ta'puaχ	תַּפּוּחַ (ז)
pear	agas	אַגָּס (ז)
lemon	limon	לִימוֹן (ז)
orange	tapuz	תַּפּוּז (ז)
strawberry (garden ~)	tut sade	תּוּת שָׂדֶה (ז)

tangerine	klemen'tina	קְלֶמֶנְטִינָה (נ)
plum	ʃezif	שְׁזִיף (ז)
peach	afarsek	אֲפַרְסֵק (ז)
apricot	'miʃmeʃ	מִשְׁמֵשׁ (ז)
raspberry	'petel	פֶּטֶל (ז)
pineapple	'ananas	אֲנָנָס (ז)

banana	ba'nana	בַּנָנָה (נ)
watermelon	ava'tiaχ	אֲבַטִּיחַ (ז)
grape	anavim	עֲנָבִים (ז"ר)
sour cherry	duvdevan	דוּבְדְּבָן (ז)
sweet cherry	gudgedan	גּוּדְגְּדָן (ז)
melon	melon	מֶלוֹן (ז)

grapefruit	eʃkolit	אֶשְׁכּוֹלִית (נ)
avocado	avo'kado	אָבוֹקָדוֹ (ז)
papaya	pa'paya	פַּפָּאיָה (נ)

| mango | 'mango | מַנגוֹ (ז) |
| pomegranate | rimon | רִימוֹן (ז) |

redcurrant	dumdemanit aduma	דוּמדְמָנִית אֲדוּמָה (נ)
blackcurrant	dumdemanit ʃxora	דוּמדְמָנִית שחוֹרָה (נ)
gooseberry	xazarzar	חֲזַרזָר (ז)
bilberry	uxmanit	אוּכמָנִית (נ)
blackberry	'petel ʃaxor	פֶּטֶל שָחוֹר (ז)

raisin	tsimukim	צִימוּקִים (ז"ר)
fig	te'ena	תְאֵנָה (נ)
date	tamar	תָמָר (ז)

peanut	botnim	בּוֹטנִים (ז"ר)
almond	ʃaked	שָקֵד (ז)
walnut	egoz 'melex	אֱגוֹז מֶלֶך (ז)
hazelnut	egoz ilsar	אֱגוֹז אִלסָר (ז)
coconut	'kokus	קוֹקוּס (ז)
pistachios	'fistuk	פִּיסטוּק (ז)

45. Bread. Sweets

bakers' confectionery (pastry)	mutsrei kondi'torya	מוּצרֵי קוֹנדִיטוֹריָה (ז"ר)
bread	'lexem	לֶחֶם (ז)
biscuits	ugiya	עוּגִיָה (נ)

chocolate (n)	'ʃokolad	שוֹקוֹלָד (ז)
chocolate (as adj)	mi'ʃokolad	מְשוֹקוֹלָד
candy (wrapped)	sukariya	סוּכָּרִיָה (נ)
cake (e.g. cupcake)	uga	עוּגָה (נ)
cake (e.g. birthday ~)	uga	עוּגָה (נ)

| pie (e.g. apple ~) | pai | פַּאי (ז) |
| filling (for cake, pie) | milui | מִילוּי (ז) |

jam (whole fruit jam)	riba	רִיבָּה (נ)
marmalade	marme'lada	מַרמֶלָדָה (נ)
wafers	'vaflim	וַפלִים (ז"ר)
ice-cream	'glida	גלִידָה (נ)
pudding (Christmas ~)	'puding	פּוּדִינג (ז)

46. Cooked dishes

course, dish	mana	מָנָה (נ)
cuisine	mitbax	מִטבָּח (ז)
recipe	matkon	מַתכּוֹן (ז)
portion	mana	מָנָה (נ)

salad	salat	סָלָט (ז)
soup	marak	מָרָק (ז)
clear soup (broth)	marak tsax, tsir	מָרָק צַח, צִיר (ז)
sandwich (bread)	karix	כָּרִיך (ז)

fried eggs	beitsat ain	בֵּיצַת עַיִן (נ)
hamburger (beefburger)	'hamburger	הַמְבּוּרְגֶּר (ז)
beefsteak	umtsa, steik	אוּמְצָה (נ), סְטֵייק (ז)

side dish	to'sefet	תּוֹסֶפֶת (נ)
spaghetti	spa'geti	סְפָּגֶטִי (ז)
mash	meχit tapuχei adama	מְחִית תַּפּוּחֵי אֲדָמָה (נ)
pizza	'pitsa	פִּיצָה (נ)
porridge (oatmeal, etc.)	daysa	דַּייסָה (נ)
omelette	χavita	חֲבִיתָה (נ)

boiled (e.g. ~ beef)	mevuʃal	מְבוּשָׁל
smoked (adj)	meʿuʃan	מְעוּשָׁן
fried (adj)	metugan	מְטוּגָן
dried (adj)	meyubaʃ	מְיוּבָּשׁ
frozen (adj)	kafu	קָפוּא
pickled (adj)	kavuʃ	כָּבוּשׁ

sweet (sugary)	matok	מָתוֹק
salty (adj)	ma'luaχ	מָלוּחַ
cold (adj)	kar	קַר
hot (adj)	χam	חַם
bitter (adj)	marir	מָרִיר
tasty (adj)	ta'im	טָעִים

to cook in boiling water	levaʃel be'mayim rotχim	לְבַשֵּׁל בְּמַיִם רוֹתְחִים
to cook (dinner)	levaʃel	לְבַשֵּׁל
to fry (vt)	letagen	לְטַגֵּן
to heat up (food)	leχamem	לְחַמֵּם

to salt (vt)	leham'liaχ	לְהַמְלִיחַ
to pepper (vt)	lefalpel	לְפַלְפֵּל
to grate (vt)	lerasek	לְרַסֵּק
peel (n)	klipa	קְלִיפָה (נ)
to peel (vt)	lekalef	לְקַלֵּף

47. Spices

salt	'melaχ	מֶלַח (ז)
salty (adj)	ma'luaχ	מָלוּחַ
to salt (vt)	leham'liaχ	לְהַמְלִיחַ

black pepper	'pilpel ʃaχor	פִּלְפֵּל שָׁחוֹר (ז)
red pepper (milled ~)	'pilpel adom	פִּלְפֵּל אָדוֹם (ז)
mustard	χardal	חַרְדָּל (ז)
horseradish	χa'zeret	חֲזֶרֶת (נ)

condiment	'rotev	רוֹטֶב (ז)
spice	tavlin	תַּבְלִין (ז)
sauce	'rotev	רוֹטֶב (ז)
vinegar	'χomets	חוֹמֶץ (ז)

anise	kamnon	כַּמְנוֹן (ז)
basil	reχan	רֵיחָן (ז)

cloves	tsi'poren	צִיפּוֹרֶן (ז)
ginger	'dʒindʒer	ג׳ינג׳ר (ז)
coriander	'kusbara	כּוּסְבָּרָה (נ)
cinnamon	kinamon	קִינָמוֹן (ז)
sesame	'ʃumʃum	שׁוּמְשׁוֹם (ז)
bay leaf	ale dafna	עָלֵה דָפְנָה (ז)
paprika	'paprika	פַּפְּרִיקָה (נ)
caraway	'kimel	קִימֶל (ז)
saffron	ze'afran	זַעֲפְרָן (ז)

48. Meals

food	'oχel	אוֹכֶל (ז)
to eat (vi, vt)	le'eχol	לֶאֱכוֹל
breakfast	aruχat 'boker	אֲרוּחַת בּוֹקֶר (נ)
to have breakfast	le'eχol aruχat 'boker	לֶאֱכוֹל אֲרוּחַת בּוֹקֶר
lunch	aruχat tsaha'rayim	אֲרוּחַת צָהֳרַיִים (נ)
to have lunch	le'eχol aruχat tsaha'rayim	לֶאֱכוֹל אֲרוּחַת צָהֳרַיִים
dinner	aruχat 'erev	אֲרוּחַת עֶרֶב (נ)
to have dinner	le'eχol aruχat 'erev	לֶאֱכוֹל אֲרוּחַת עֶרֶב
appetite	te'avon	תֵּיאָבוֹן (ז)
Enjoy your meal!	betei'avon!	בְּתֵיאָבוֹן!
to open (~ a bottle)	lif'toaχ	לִפְתּוֹחַ
to spill (liquid)	liʃpoχ	לִשְׁפּוֹךְ
to spill out (vi)	lehiʃapeχ	לְהִישָׁפֵךְ
to boil (vi)	lir'toaχ	לִרְתּוֹחַ
to boil (vt)	lehar'tiaχ	לְהַרְתִּיחַ
boiled (~ water)	ra'tuaχ	רָתוּחַ
to chill, cool down (vt)	lekarer	לְקָרֵר
to chill (vi)	lehitkarer	לְהִתְקָרֵר
taste, flavour	'taʿam	טַעַם (ז)
aftertaste	'taʿam levai	טַעַם לְוַואי (ז)
to slim down (lose weight)	lirzot	לִרְזוֹת
diet	di''eta	דִיאָטָה (נ)
vitamin	vitamin	וִיטָמִין (ז)
calorie	ka'lorya	קָלוֹרִיָה (נ)
vegetarian (n)	tsimχoni	צִמְחוֹנִי (ז)
vegetarian (adj)	tsimχoni	צִמְחוֹנִי
fats (nutrient)	ʃumanim	שׁוּמָנִים (ז"ר)
proteins	χelbonim	חֶלְבּוֹנִים (ז"ר)
carbohydrates	paχmema	פַּחְמֵימָה (נ)
slice (of lemon, ham)	prusa	פְּרוּסָה (נ)
piece (of cake, pie)	χatiχa	חֲתִיכָה (נ)
crumb (of bread, cake, etc.)	perur	פֵּירוּר (ז)

49. Table setting

spoon	kaf	כַּף (ז)
knife	sakin	סַכִּין (ז, נ)
fork	mazleg	מַזְלֵג (ז)
cup (e.g., coffee ~)	'sefel	סֵפֶל (ז)
plate (dinner ~)	tsa'laxat	צַלַחַת (נ)
saucer	taxtit	תַּחְתִּית (נ)
serviette	mapit	מַפִּית (נ)
toothpick	keisam ʃi'nayim	קֵיסָם שִׁינַּיִים (ז)

50. Restaurant

restaurant	mis'ada	מִסְעָדָה (נ)
coffee bar	beit kafe	בֵּית קָפֶה (ז)
pub, bar	bar, pab	בָּר, פַּאבּ (ז)
tearoom	beit te	בֵּית תֵּה (ז)
waiter	meltsar	מֶלְצָר (ז)
waitress	meltsarit	מֶלְצָרִית (נ)
barman	'barmen	בַּרְמֶן (ז)
menu	tafrit	תַּפְרִיט (ז)
wine list	reʃimat yeynot	רְשִׁימַת יֵינוֹת (נ)
to book a table	lehazmin ʃulxan	לְהַזְמִין שׁוּלְחָן
course, dish	mana	מָנָה (נ)
to order (meal)	lehazmin	לְהַזְמִין
to make an order	lehazmin	לְהַזְמִין
aperitif	maʃke meta'aven	מַשְׁקֶה מְתַאֲבֵן (ז)
starter	meta'aven	מְתַאֲבֵן (ז)
dessert, pudding	ki'nuax	קִינּוּחַ (ז)
bill	xeʃbon	חֶשְׁבּוֹן (ז)
to pay the bill	leʃalem	לְשַׁלֵּם
to give change	latet 'odef	לָתֵת עוֹדֶף
tip	tip	טִיפּ (ז)

Family, relatives and friends

51. Personal information. Forms

name (first name)	ʃem	שֵׁם (ז)
surname (last name)	ʃem miʃpaχa	שֵׁם מִשְׁפָּחָה (ז)
date of birth	ta'ariχ leda	תַּאֲרִיך לֵידָה (ז)
place of birth	mekom leda	מְקוֹם לַידָה (ז)
nationality	le'om	לְאוֹם (ז)
place of residence	mekom megurim	מָקוֹם מְגוּרִים (ז)
country	medina	מְדִינָה (נ)
profession (occupation)	mik'tso'a	מִקְצוֹעַ (ז)
gender, sex	min	מִין (ז)
height	'gova	גּוֹבַהּ (ז)
weight	miʃkal	מִשְׁקָל (ז)

52. Family members. Relatives

mother	em	אֵם (נ)
father	av	אָב (ז)
son	ben	בֵּן (ז)
daughter	bat	בַּת (נ)
younger daughter	habat haktana	הַבַּת הַקְטַנָה (נ)
younger son	haben hakatan	הַבֵּן הַקָטָן (ז)
eldest daughter	habat habχora	הַבַּת הַבְּכוֹרָה (נ)
eldest son	haben habχor	הַבֵּן הַבְּכוֹר (ז)
brother	aχ	אָח (ז)
elder brother	aχ gadol	אָח גָדוֹל (ז)
younger brother	aχ katan	אָח קָטָן (ז)
sister	aχot	אָחוֹת (נ)
elder sister	aχot gdola	אָחוֹת גדוֹלָה (נ)
younger sister	aχot ktana	אָחוֹת קְטַנָה (נ)
cousin (masc.)	ben dod	בֵּן דוֹד (ז)
cousin (fem.)	bat 'doda	בַּת דוֹדָה (נ)
mummy	'ima	אִמָא (נ)
dad, daddy	'aba	אַבָּא (ז)
parents	horim	הוֹרִים (ז"ר)
child	'yeled	יֶלֶד (ז)
children	yeladim	יְלָדִים (ז"ר)
grandmother	'savta	סָבְתָא (נ)
grandfather	'saba	סָבָּא (ז)
grandson	'neχed	נֶכֶד (ז)

| granddaughter | neχda | נֶבְדָּה (נ) |
| grandchildren | neχadim | נְבָדִים (ז״ר) |

uncle	dod	דּוֹד (ז)
aunt	'doda	דּוֹדָה (נ)
nephew	aχyan	אַחְיָן (ז)
niece	aχyanit	אַחְיָנִית (נ)

mother-in-law (wife's mother)	χamot	חָמוֹת (נ)
father-in-law (husband's father)	χam	חָם (ז)
son-in-law (daughter's husband)	χatan	חָתָן (ז)

| stepmother | em χoreget | אֵם חוֹרֶגֶת (נ) |
| stepfather | av χoreg | אָב חוֹרֵג (ז) |

infant	tinok	תִּינוֹק (ז)
baby (infant)	tinok	תִּינוֹק (ז)
little boy, kid	pa'ot	פָּעוֹט (ז)

wife	iʃa	אִשָּׁה (נ)
husband	'ba'al	בַּעַל (ז)
spouse (husband)	ben zug	בֶּן זוּג (ז)
spouse (wife)	bat zug	בַּת זוּג (נ)

married (masc.)	nasui	נָשׂוּי
married (fem.)	nesu'a	נְשׂוּאָה
single (unmarried)	ravak	רַוָּק
bachelor	ravak	רַוָּק (ז)
divorced (masc.)	garuʃ	גָּרוּשׁ
widow	almana	אַלְמָנָה (נ)
widower	alman	אַלְמָן (ז)

relative	karov miʃpaχa	קָרוֹב מִשְׁפָּחָה (ז)
close relative	karov miʃpaχa	קָרוֹב מִשְׁפָּחָה (ז)
distant relative	karov raχok	קָרוֹב רָחוֹק (ז)
relatives	krovei miʃpaχa	קְרוֹבֵי מִשְׁפָּחָה (ז״ר)

orphan (boy)	yatom	יָתוֹם (ז)
orphan (girl)	yetoma	יְתוֹמָה (נ)
guardian (of a minor)	apo'tropos	אַפּוֹטְרוֹפּוֹס (ז)
to adopt (a boy)	le'amets	לְאַמֵּץ
to adopt (a girl)	le'amets	לְאַמֵּץ

53. Friends. Colleagues

friend (masc.)	χaver	חָבֵר (ז)
friend (fem.)	χavera	חֲבֵרָה (נ)
friendship	yedidut	יְדִידוּת (נ)
to be friends	lihyot yadidim	לִהְיוֹת יָדִידִים

| pal (masc.) | χaver | חָבֵר (ז) |
| pal (fem.) | χavera | חֲבֵרָה (נ) |

partner	ʃutaf	שׁוּתָף (ז)
chief (boss)	menahel, roʃ	מְנַהֵל (ז), רֹאשׁ (ז)
superior (n)	memune	מְמוּנֶה (ז)
owner, proprietor	beʿalim	בְּעָלִים (ז)
subordinate (n)	kafuf le	כָּפוּף ל (ז)
colleague	amit	עָמִית (ז)

acquaintance (person)	makar	מַכָּר (ז)
fellow traveller	ben levaya	בֶּן לְוָיָה (ז)
classmate	xaver lekita	חָבֵר לְכִּיתָה (ז)

neighbour (masc.)	ʃaxen	שָׁכֵן (ז)
neighbour (fem.)	ʃxena	שְׁכֵנָה (נ)
neighbours	ʃxenim	שְׁכֵנִים (ז"ר)

54. Man. Woman

woman	iʃa	אִשָׁה (נ)
girl (young woman)	baxura	בָּחוּרָה (נ)
bride	kala	כַּלָה (נ)

beautiful (adj)	yafa	יָפָה
tall (adj)	gvoha	גבוֹהָה
slender (adj)	tmira	תמִירָה
short (adj)	namux	נָמוּך

blonde (n)	blon'dinit	בּלוֹנדִינִית (נ)
brunette (n)	bru'netit	ברוּנֶטִית (נ)
ladies' (adj)	ʃel naʃim	שֶׁל נָשִׁים
virgin (girl)	betula	בְּתוּלָה (נ)
pregnant (adj)	hara	הָרָה

man (adult male)	'gever	גֶבֶר (ז)
blonde haired man	blon'dini	בּלוֹנדִינִי (ז)
dark haired man	ʃxarxar	שחַרחַר
tall (adj)	ga'voha	גָבוֹהַ
short (adj)	namux	נָמוּך
rude (rough)	gas	גַס
stocky (adj)	guʦ	גוּץ
robust (adj)	xason	חָסוֹן
strong (adj)	xazak	חָזָק
strength	'koax	כּוֹחַ (ז)

plump, fat (adj)	ʃamen	שָׁמֵן
swarthy (dark-skinned)	ʃaxum	שָׁחוּם
slender (well-built)	tamir	תָמִיר
elegant (adj)	ele'ganti	אֶלֶגַנטִי

55. Age

| age | gil | גִיל (ז) |
| youth (young age) | ne'urim | נְעוּרִים (ז"ר) |

young (adj)	tsa'ir	צָעִיר
younger (adj)	tsa'ir yoter	צָעִיר יוֹתֵר
older (adj)	mevugar yoter	מְבוּגָר יוֹתֵר

young man	baxur	בָּחוּר (ז)
teenager	'na'ar	נַעַר (ז)
guy, fellow	baxur	בָּחוּר (ז)

| old man | zaken | זָקֵן (ז) |
| old woman | zkena | זְקֵנָה (נ) |

adult (adj)	mevugar	מְבוּגָר (ז)
middle-aged (adj)	bagil ha'amida	בַּגִיל הָעֲמִידָה
elderly (adj)	zaken	זָקֵן
old (adj)	zaken	זָקֵן

retirement	'pensya	פֶּנסִיָה (נ)
to retire (from job)	latset legimla'ot	לָצֵאת לְגִימלָאוֹת
retiree, pensioner	pensyoner	פֶּנסִיוֹנֶר (ז)

56. Children

child	'yeled	יֶלֶד (ז)
children	yeladim	יְלָדִים (ז"ר)
twins	te'omim	תְאוֹמִים (ז"ר)

cradle	arisa	עֲרִיסָה (נ)
rattle	ra'aʃan	רַעֲשָן (ז)
nappy	xitul	חִיתוּל (ז)

dummy, comforter	motsets	מוֹצֵץ (ז)
pram	agala	עֲגָלָה (נ)
nursery	gan yeladim	גַן יְלָדִים (ז)
babysitter	beibi'siter	בֵּיבִּיסִיטֶר (ז, נ)

childhood	yaldut	יַלדוּת (נ)
doll	buba	בּוּבָּה (נ)
toy	tsa'a'tsu'a	צַעֲצוּע (ז)
construction set (toy)	misxak harkava	מִשׂחַק הַרכָּבָה (ז)
well-bred (adj)	mexunax	מְחוּנָך
ill-bred (adj)	lo mexunax	לֹא מְחוּנָך
spoilt (adj)	mefunak	מְפוּנָק

to be naughty	lehiʃtovev	לְהִשתוֹבֵב
mischievous (adj)	ʃovav	שוֹבָב
mischievousness	ma'ase 'kundes	מַעֲשֵׂה קוּנדֵס (ז)
mischievous child	'yeled ʃovav	יֶלֶד שוֹבָב (ז)

| obedient (adj) | tsaytan | צַייתָן |
| disobedient (adj) | lo memuʃma | לֹא מְמוּשמָע |

docile (adj)	ka'nu'a	כָּנוּעַ
clever (intelligent)	xaxam	חָכָם
child prodigy	'yeled 'pele	יֶלֶד פֶּלֶא (ז)

57. Married couples. Family life

to kiss (vt)	lenaʃek	לְנַשֵׁק
to kiss (vi)	lehitnaʃek	לְהִתְנַשֵׁק
family (n)	miʃpaχa	מִשְׁפָּחָה (נ)
family (as adj)	miʃpaχti	מִשְׁפַּחְתִּי
couple	zug	זוּג (ז)
marriage (state)	nisu'im	נִישׂוּאִים (ז"ר)
hearth (home)	aχ, ken	אָח (נ), קֵן (ז)
dynasty	ʃo'ʃelet	שׁוֹשֶׁלֶת (נ)
date	deit	דֵּייט (ז)
kiss	neʃika	נְשִׁיקָה (נ)
love (for sb)	ahava	אַהֲבָה (נ)
to love (sb)	le'ehov	לֶאֱהוֹב
beloved	ahuv	אָהוּב
tenderness	roχ	רוֹךְ (ז)
tender (affectionate)	adin, raχ	עָדִין, רַךְ
faithfulness	ne'emanut	נֶאֱמָנוּת (נ)
faithful (adj)	masur	מָסוּר
care (attention)	de'aga	דְּאָגָה (נ)
caring (~ father)	do'eg	דּוֹאֵג
newlyweds	zug tsa'ir	זוּג צָעִיר (ז)
honeymoon	ya'reaχ dvaʃ	יָרַח דְּבַשׁ (ז)
to get married (ab. woman)	lehitχaten	לְהִתְחַתֵּן
to get married (ab. man)	lehitχaten	לְהִתְחַתֵּן
wedding	χatuna	חֲתוּנָה (נ)
golden wedding	χatunat hazahav	חֲתוּנַת הַזָהָב (נ)
anniversary	yom nisu'in	יוֹם נִישׂוּאִין (ז)
lover (masc.)	me'ahev	מְאַהֵב (ז)
mistress (lover)	mea'hevet	מְאַהֶבֶת (נ)
adultery	bgida	בְּגִידָה (נ)
to cheat on ... (commit adultery)	livgod be...	לִבְגוֹד בְּ...
jealous (adj)	kanai	קַנַאי
to be jealous	lekane	לְקַנֵא
divorce	geruʃin	גֵרוּשִׁין (ז"ר)
to divorce (vi)	lehitgareʃ mi...	לְהִתְגָרֵשׁ מ...
to quarrel (vi)	lariv	לָרִיב
to be reconciled (after an argument)	lehitpayes	לְהִתְפַּייֵס
together (adv)	be'yaχad	בְּיַחַד
sex	min	מִין (ז)
happiness	'oʃer	אוֹשֶׁר (ז)
happy (adj)	me'uʃar	מְאוּשָׁר
misfortune (accident)	ason	אָסוֹן (ז)
unhappy (adj)	umlal	אוּמְלָל

Character. Feelings. Emotions

58. Feelings. Emotions

feeling (emotion)	'regeʃ	רֶגֶשׁ (ז)
feelings	regaʃot	רְגָשׁוֹת (ז״ר)
to feel (vt)	lehargiʃ	לְהַרְגִּישׁ
hunger	'ra'av	רָעָב (ז)
to be hungry	lihyot ra'ev	לִהְיוֹת רָעֵב
thirst	tsima'on	צִמָּאוֹן (ז)
to be thirsty	lihyot tsame	לִהְיוֹת צָמֵא
sleepiness	yaʃnuniyut	יַשְׁנוּנִיּוּת (נ)
to feel sleepy	lirtsot liʃon	לִרְצוֹת לִישׁוֹן
tiredness	ayefut	עֲיֵיפוּת (נ)
tired (adj)	ayef	עָיֵיף
to get tired	lehit'ayef	לְהִתְעַיֵּיף
mood (humour)	matsav 'ruaχ	מַצַּב רוּחַ (ז)
boredom	ʃi'amum	שִׁעֲמוּם (ז)
to be bored	lehiʃta'amem	לְהִשְׁתַּעֲמֵם
seclusion	hitbodedut	הִתְבּוֹדְדוּת (נ)
to seclude oneself	lehitboded	לְהִתְבּוֹדֵד
to worry (make anxious)	lehad'ig	לְהַדְאִיג
to be worried	lid'og	לִדְאוֹג
worrying (n)	de'aga	דְּאָגָה (נ)
anxiety	χarada	חֲרָדָה (נ)
preoccupied (adj)	mutrad	מוּטְרָד
to be nervous	lihyot atsbani	לִהְיוֹת עַצְבָּנִי
to panic (vi)	lehibahel	לְהִיבָּהֵל
hope	tikva	תִּקְוָה (נ)
to hope (vi, vt)	lekavot	לְקַוּוֹת
certainty	vada'ut	וַדָּאוּת (נ)
certain, sure (adj)	vada'i	וַדָּאִי
uncertainty	i vada'ut	אִי וַדָּאוּת (נ)
uncertain (adj)	lo ba'tuaχ	לֹא בָּטוּחַ
drunk (adj)	ʃikor	שִׁיכּוֹר
sober (adj)	pi'keaχ	פִּיכֵּחַ
weak (adj)	χalaʃ	חַלָּשׁ
happy (adj)	me'uʃar	מְאוּשָׁר
to scare (vt)	lehafχid	לְהַפְחִיד
fury (madness)	teruf	טֵירוּף
rage (fury)	'za'am	זַעַם (ז)
depression	dika'on	דִּיכָּאוֹן (ז)
discomfort (unease)	i noχut	אִי נוֹחוּת (נ)

comfort	noχut	נוֹחוּת (נ)
to regret (be sorry)	lehitsta'er	לְהִצְטַעֵר
regret	χarata	חֲרָטָה (נ)
bad luck	'χoser mazal	חוֹסֶר מַזָּל (ז)
sadness	'etsev	עֶצֶב (ז)

shame (remorse)	buʃa	בּוּשָׁה (נ)
gladness	simχa	שִׂמְחָה (נ)
enthusiasm, zeal	hitlahavut	הִתְלַהֲבוּת (נ)
enthusiast	mitlahev	מִתְלַהֵב
to show enthusiasm	lehitlahev	לְהִתְלַהֵב

59. Character. Personality

character	'ofi	אוֹפִי (ז)
character flaw	pgam be''ofi	פְּגַם בָּאוֹפִי (ז)
mind	'seχel	שֵׂכֶל (ז)
reason	bina	בִּינָה (נ)

conscience	matspun	מַצְפּוּן (ז)
habit (custom)	hergel	הֶרְגֵּל (ז)
ability (talent)	ye'χolet	יְכוֹלֶת (נ)
can (e.g. ~ swim)	la'da'at	לָדַעַת

patient (adj)	savlan	סַבְלָן
impatient (adj)	χasar savlanut	חֲסַר סַבְלָנוּת
curious (inquisitive)	sakran	סַקְרָן
curiosity	sakranut	סַקְרָנוּת (נ)

modesty	tsni'ut	צְנִיעוּת (נ)
modest (adj)	tsa'nu'a	צָנוּעַ
immodest (adj)	lo tsa'nu'a	לֹא צָנוּעַ

laziness	atslut	עַצְלוּת (נ)
lazy (adj)	atsel	עָצֵל
lazy person (masc.)	atslan	עַצְלָן (ז)

cunning (n)	armumiyut	עַרְמוּמִיוּת (נ)
cunning (as adj)	armumi	עַרְמוּמִי
distrust	'χoser emun	חוֹסֶר אֱמוּן (ז)
distrustful (adj)	χadʃani	חַדְשָׁנִי

generosity	nedivut	נְדִיבוּת (נ)
generous (adj)	nadiv	נָדִיב
talented (adj)	muxʃar	מוּכְשָׁר
talent	kiʃaron	כִּישָׁרוֹן (ז)

courageous (adj)	amits	אַמִּיץ
courage	'omets	אוֹמֶץ (ז)
honest (adj)	yaʃar	יָשָׁר
honesty	'yoʃer	יוֹשֶׁר (ז)

| careful (cautious) | zahir | זָהִיר |
| brave (courageous) | amits | אַמִּיץ |

| serious (adj) | retsini | רְצִינִי |
| strict (severe, stern) | χamur | חָמוּר |

decisive (adj)	neχrats	נֶחֱרָץ
indecisive (adj)	hasesan	הַסְּסָן
shy, timid (adj)	baiʃan	בַּיְישָׁן
shyness, timidity	baiʃanut	בַּיְישָׁנוּת (נ)

confidence (trust)	emun	אֵמוּן (ז)
to believe (trust)	leha'amin	לְהַאֲמִין
trusting (credulous)	tam	תָּם

sincerely (adv)	beχenut	בְּכֵנוּת
sincere (adj)	ken	כֵּן
sincerity	kenut	כֵּנוּת (נ)
open (person)	pa'tuaχ	פָּתוּחַ

calm (adj)	ʃalev	שָׁלֵו
frank (sincere)	glui lev	גְּלוּי לֵב
naïve (adj)	na''ivi	נָאִיבִי
absent-minded (adj)	mefuzar	מְפֻזָּר
funny (odd)	matsχik	מַצְחִיק

greed, stinginess	ta'avat 'betsa	תַּאֲוַת בֶּצַע (נ)
greedy, stingy (adj)	rodef 'betsa	רוֹדֵף בֶּצַע
stingy (adj)	kamtsan	קַמְצָן
evil (adj)	raʃa	רָשָׁע
stubborn (adj)	akʃan	עַקְשָׁן
unpleasant (adj)	lo na'im	לֹא נָעִים

selfish person (masc.)	ego'ist	אֶגוֹאִיסְט (ז)
selfish (adj)	anoχi	אָנוֹכִי
coward	paχdan	פַּחְדָן (ז)
cowardly (adj)	paχdani	פַּחְדָנִי

60. Sleep. Dreams

to sleep (vi)	liʃon	לִישׁוֹן
sleep, sleeping	ʃena	שֵׁינָה (נ)
dream	χalom	חֲלוֹם (ז)
to dream (in sleep)	laχalom	לַחֲלוֹם
sleepy (adj)	radum	רָדוּם

bed	mita	מִיטָה (נ)
mattress	mizran	מִזְרָן (ז)
blanket (eiderdown)	smiχa	שְׂמִיכָה (נ)
pillow	karit	כָּרִית (נ)
sheet	sadin	סָדִין (ז)

insomnia	nedudei ʃena	נְדוּדֵי שֵׁינָה (ז"ר)
sleepless (adj)	χasar ʃena	חֲסַר שֵׁינָה
sleeping pill	kadur ʃena	כַּדּוּר שֵׁינָה (ז)
to take a sleeping pill	la'kaχat kadur ʃena	לָקַחַת כַּדּוּר שֵׁינָה
to feel sleepy	lirtsot liʃon	לִרְצוֹת לִישׁוֹן

to yawn (vi)	lefahek	לְפַהֵק
to go to bed	la'leχet lifon	לָלֶכֶת לִישׁוֹן
to make up the bed	leha'tsi'a mita	לְהַצִּיעַ מִיטָה
to fall asleep	leheradem	לְהֵירָדֵם
nightmare	siyut	סִיוּט (ז)
snore, snoring	neχira	נְחִירָה (נ)
to snore (vi)	linχor	לִנְחוֹר
alarm clock	ʃa'on me'orer	שָׁעוֹן מְעוֹרֵר (ז)
to wake (vt)	leha'ir	לְהָעִיר
to wake up	lehit'orer	לְהִתְעוֹרֵר
to get up (vi)	lakum	לָקוּם
to have a wash	lehitraχets	לְהִתְרַחֵץ

61. Humour. Laughter. Gladness

humour (wit, fun)	humor	הוּמוֹר (ז)
sense of humour	χuʃ humor	חוּשׁ הוּמוֹר (ז)
to enjoy oneself	lehanot	לֵיהָנוֹת
cheerful (merry)	sa'meaχ	שָׂמֵחַ
merriment (gaiety)	alitsut	עֲלִיצוּת (נ)
smile	χiyuχ	חִיוּךְ (ז)
to smile (vi)	leχayeχ	לְחַיֵּךְ
to start laughing	lifrots bitsχok	לִפְרוֹץ בִּצְחוֹק
to laugh (vi)	litsχok	לִצְחוֹק
laugh, laughter	tsχok	צְחוֹק (ז)
anecdote	anek'dota	אֲנֶקְדוֹטָה (נ)
funny (anecdote, etc.)	matsχik	מַצְחִיק
funny (odd)	meʃa'a'ʃe'a	מְשַׁעֲשֵׁעַ
to joke (vi)	lehitba'deaχ	לְהִתְבַּדֵּחַ
joke (verbal)	bdiχa	בְּדִיחָה (נ)
joy (emotion)	simχa	שִׂמְחָה (נ)
to rejoice (vi)	lis'moaχ	לִשְׂמוֹחַ
joyful (adj)	sa'meaχ	שָׂמֵחַ

62. Discussion, conversation. Part 1

communication	'keʃer	קֶשֶׁר (ז)
to communicate	letakʃer	לְתַקְשֵׁר
conversation	siχa	שִׂיחָה (נ)
dialogue	du 'siaχ	דּוּ-שִׂיחַ (ז)
discussion (discourse)	diyun	דִּיּוּן (ז)
dispute (debate)	vi'kuaχ	וִיכּוּחַ (ז)
to dispute, to debate	lehitva'keaχ	לְהִתְוַוכֵּחַ
interlocutor	ben 'siaχ	בֶּן שִׂיחַ (ז)
topic (theme)	nose	נוֹשֵׂא (ז)

point of view	nekudat mabat	נְקוּדַת מַבָּט (נ)
opinion (point of view)	de'a	דֵעָה (נ)
speech (talk)	ne'um	נְאוּם (ז)

discussion (of a report, etc.)	diyun	דִיוּן (ז)
to discuss (vt)	ladun	לָדוּן
talk (conversation)	siχa	שִׂיחָה (נ)
to talk (to chat)	leso'χeaχ	לְשׂוֹחַ
meeting (encounter)	pgiſa	פְּגִישָׁה (נ)
to meet (vi, vt)	lehipageſ	לְהִיפָּגֵש

proverb	pitgam	פִּתְגָם (ז)
saying	pitgam	פִּתְגָם (ז)
riddle (poser)	χida	חִידָה (נ)
to pose a riddle	laχud χida	לָחוּד חִידָה
password	sisma	סִיסְמָה (נ)
secret	sod	סוֹד (ז)

oath (vow)	ſvu'a	שְׁבוּעָה (נ)
to swear (an oath)	lehiſava	לְהִישָּׁבַע
promise	havtaχa	הַבְטָחָה (נ)
to promise (vt)	lehav'tiaχ	לְהַבְטִיחַ

advice (counsel)	etsa	עֵצָה (נ)
to advise (vt)	leya'ets	לְיָעֵץ
to follow one's advice	lif'ol lefi ha'etsa	לִפְעוֹל לְפִי הָעֵצָה
to listen to ... (obey)	lehiſama	לְהִישָּׁמַע

news	χadaſot	חֲדָשׁוֹת (נ"ר)
sensation (news)	sen'satsya	סֶנְסַצְיָה (נ)
information (report)	meida	מֵידָע (ז)
conclusion (decision)	maskana	מַסְקָנָה (נ)
voice	kol	קוֹל (ז)
compliment	maχma'a	מַחְמָאָה (נ)
kind (nice)	adiv	אָדִיב

word	mila	מִילָה (נ)
phrase	miſpat	מִשְׁפָּט (ז)
answer	tſuva	תְשׁוּבָה (נ)

| truth | emet | אֱמֶת (נ) |
| lie | 'ſeker | שֶׁקֶר (ז) |

thought	maχſava	מַחְשָׁבָה (נ)
idea (inspiration)	ra'ayon	רַעְיוֹן (ז)
fantasy	fan'tazya	פַנְטַזְיָה (נ)

63. Discussion, conversation. Part 2

respected (adj)	meχubad	מְכוּבָּד
to respect (vt)	leχabed	לְכַבֵּד
respect	kavod	כָּבוֹד (ז)
Dear ... (letter)	hayakar ...	הַיָקָר ...
to introduce (sb to sb)	la'asot hekerut	לַעֲשׂוֹת הֶיכֵּרוּת

to make acquaintance	lehakir	לְהַכִּיר
intention	kavana	כַּוָונָה (נ)
to intend (have in mind)	lehitkaven	לְהִתְכַּוֵון
wish	iχul	אִיחוּל (ז)
to wish (~ good luck)	le'aχel	לְאַחֵל
surprise (astonishment)	hafta'a	הַפְתָּעָה (נ)
to surprise (amaze)	lehaf'ti'a	לְהַפְתִּיעַ
to be surprised	lehitpale	לְהִתְפַּלֵא
to give (vt)	latet	לָתֵת
to take (get hold of)	la'kaχat	לָקַחַת
to give back	lehaχzir	לְהַחֲזִיר
to return (give back)	lehaʃiv	לְהָשִׁיב
to apologize (vi)	lehitnatsel	לְהִתְנַצֵל
apology	hitnatslut	הִתְנַצְלוּת (נ)
to forgive (vt)	lis'loaχ	לִסְלוֹחַ
to talk (speak)	ledaber	לְדַבֵּר
to listen (vi)	lehakʃiv	לְהַקְשִׁיב
to hear out	liʃ'mo'a	לִשְׁמוֹעַ
to understand (vt)	lehavin	לְהָבִין
to show (to display)	lehar'ot	לְהַרְאוֹת
to look at …	lehistakel	לְהִסְתַּכֵּל
to call (yell for sb)	likro le…	לִקְרוֹא לְ...
to distract (disturb)	lehaf'ri'a	לְהַפְרִיעַ
to disturb (vt)	lehaf'ri'a	לְהַפְרִיעַ
to pass (to hand sth)	limsor	לִמְסוֹר
demand (request)	bakaʃa	בַּקָשָׁה (נ)
to request (ask)	levakeʃ	לְבַקֵש
demand (firm request)	driʃa	דְרִישָׁה (נ)
to demand (request firmly)	lidroʃ	לִדרוֹש
to tease (call names)	lehitgarot	לְהִתְגָרוֹת
to mock (make fun of)	lil'og	לִלְעוֹג
mockery, derision	'la'ag	לַעַג (ז)
nickname	kinui	כִּינוּי (ז)
insinuation	'remez	רֶמֶז (ז)
to insinuate (imply)	lirmoz	לִרמוֹז
to mean (vt)	lehitkaven le…	לְהִתְכַּוֵון לְ...
description	te'ur	תָיאוּר (ז)
to describe (vt)	leta'er	לְתָאֵר
praise (compliments)	'ʃevaχ	שֶבַח (ז)
to praise (vt)	leʃa'beaχ	לְשַבֵּחַ
disappointment	aχzava	אַכְזָבָה (נ)
to disappoint (vt)	le'aχzev	לְאַכֵזֵב
to be disappointed	lehit'aχzev	לְהִתְאַכֵזֵב
supposition	hanaχa	הַנָחָה (נ)
to suppose (assume)	leʃa'er	לְשַעֵר

| warning (caution) | azhara | אַזהָרָה (נ) |
| to warn (vt) | lehazhir | לְהַזהִיר |

64. Discussion, conversation. Part 3

| to talk into (convince) | leʃaχ'ne‘a | לְשַכנֵעַ |
| to calm down (vt) | lehar'gi‘a | לְהַרגִיעַ |

silence (~ is golden)	ʃtika	שתִיקָה (נ)
to be silent (not speaking)	liʃtok	לִשתוֹק
to whisper (vi, vt)	lilχoʃ	לִלחוֹש
whisper	leχiʃa	לְחִישָה (נ)

| frankly, sincerely (adv) | beχenut | בְּכֵנוּת |
| in my opinion ... | leda‘ati ... | לְדַעֲתִי ... |

detail (of the story)	prat	פּרָט (ז)
detailed (adj)	meforat	מְפוֹרָט
in detail (adv)	bimfurat	בְּמפוֹרָט

| hint, clue | 'remez | רֶמֶז (ז) |
| to give a hint | lirmoz | לִרמוֹז |

look (glance)	mabat	מַבָּט (ז)
to have a look	lehabit	לְהַבִּיט
fixed (look)	kafu	קָפוּא
to blink (vi)	lematsmets	לְמַצמֵץ
to wink (vi)	likrots	לִקרוֹץ
to nod (in assent)	lehanhen	לְהַנהֵן

sigh	anaχa	אֲנָחָה (נ)
to sigh (vi)	lehe’anaχ	לְהֵיאָנַח
to shudder (vi)	lir‘od	לִרעוֹד
gesture	meχva	מַחֲוָוה (נ)
to touch (one's arm, etc.)	la'ga‘at be...	לָגַעַת בְּ...
to seize (e.g., ~ by the arm)	litfos	לִתפוֹס
to tap (on the shoulder)	lit'poaχ	לִטפּוֹחַ

Look out!	zehirut!	זְהִירוּת!
Really?	be’emet?	בֶּאֱמֶת?
Are you sure?	ata ba'tuaχ?	אַתָה בָּטוּחַ?
Good luck!	behatslaχa!	בְּהַצלָחָה!
I see!	muvan!	מוּבָן!
What a pity!	χaval!	חֲבָל!

65. Agreement. Refusal

consent	haskama	הַסכָּמָה (נ)
to consent (vi)	lehaskim	לְהַסכִּים
approval	iʃur	אִישוּר (ז)
to approve (vt)	le’aʃer	לְאַשֵר
refusal	siruv	סֵירוּב (ז)

to refuse (vi, vt)	lesarev	לְסָרֵב
Great!	metsuyan!	מְצוּיָן!
All right!	tov!	טוֹב!
Okay! (I agree)	be'seder!	בְּסֵדֶר!

forbidden (adj)	asur	אָסוּר
it's forbidden	asur	אָסוּר
it's impossible	'bilti efʃari	בִּלְתִּי אֶפְשָׁרִי
incorrect (adj)	ʃagui	שָׁגוּי

to reject (~ a demand)	lidχot	לִדְחוֹת
to support (cause, idea)	litmoχ be...	לִתְמוֹךְ בְּ...
to accept (~ an apology)	lekabel	לְקַבֵּל

to confirm (vt)	le'aʃer	לְאַשֵׁר
confirmation	iʃur	אִישׁוּר (ז)
permission	reʃut	רְשׁוּת (נ)
to permit (vt)	leharʃot	לְהַרְשׁוֹת
decision	haχlata	הַחְלָטָה (נ)
to say nothing (hold one's tongue)	liʃtok	לִשְׁתּוֹק

condition (term)	tnai	תְּנַאי (ז)
excuse (pretext)	teruts	תֵּירוּץ (ז)
praise (compliments)	'ʃevaχ	שֶׁבַח (ז)
to praise (vt)	leʃa'beaχ	לְשַׁבֵּחַ

66. Success. Good luck. Failure

success	hatsala	הַצְלָחָה (נ)
successfully (adv)	behatslaχa	בְּהַצְלָחָה
successful (adj)	mutslaχ	מוּצְלָח

luck (good luck)	mazal	מַזָּל (ז)
Good luck!	behatslaχa!	בְּהַצְלָחָה!
lucky (e.g. ~ day)	mutslaχ	מוּצְלָח
lucky (fortunate)	bar mazal	בַּר מַזָּל

failure	kiʃalon	כִּישָׁלוֹן (ז)
misfortune	'χoser mazal	חוֹסֶר מַזָּל (ז)
bad luck	'χoser mazal	חוֹסֶר מַזָּל (ז)
unsuccessful (adj)	lo mutslaχ	לֹא מוּצְלָח
catastrophe	ason	אָסוֹן (ז)

pride	ga'ava	גַּאֲוָה (נ)
proud (adj)	ge'e	גֵּאֶה
to be proud	lehitga'ot	לְהִתְגָּאוֹת

winner	zoχe	זוֹכֶה (ז)
to win (vi)	lena'tseaχ	לְנַצֵּחַ
to lose (not win)	lehafsid	לְהַפְסִיד
try	nisayon	נִיסָיוֹן (ז)
to try (vi)	lenasot	לְנַסּוֹת
chance (opportunity)	hizdamnut	הִזְדַּמְנוּת (נ)

67. Quarrels. Negative emotions

shout (scream)	tseʿaka	צְעָקָה (נ)
to shout (vi)	litsʿok	לִצעוֹק
to start to cry out	lehatχil litsʿok	לְהַתחִיל לִצעוֹק
quarrel	riv	רִיב (ז)
to quarrel (vi)	lariv	לָרִיב
fight (squabble)	riv	רִיב (ז)
to make a scene	lariv	לָרִיב
conflict	siχsuχ	סִכסוּך (ז)
misunderstanding	i havana	אִי הֲבָנָה (נ)
insult	elbon	עֶלבּוֹן (ז)
to insult (vt)	lehaʿaliv	לְהַעֲלִיב
insulted (adj)	neʿelav	נֶעֱלָב
resentment	tina	טִינָה (נ)
to offend (vt)	lifˈgoʿa	לִפגוֹעַ
to take offence	lehipaga	לְהִיפָּגַע
indignation	hitmarmerut	הִתמַרמְרוּת (נ)
to be indignant	lehitraʿem	לְהִתרַעֵם
complaint	tluna	תלוּנָה (נ)
to complain (vi, vt)	lehitlonen	לְהִתלוֹנֵן
apology	hitnatslut	הִתנַצלוּת (נ)
to apologize (vi)	lehitnatsel	לְהִתנַצֵל
to beg pardon	levakeʃ sliχa	לְבַקֵש סלִיחָה
criticism	biˈkoret	בִּיקוֹרֶת (נ)
to criticize (vt)	levaker	לְבַקֵר
accusation (charge)	haʾaʃama	הַאֲשָמָה (נ)
to accuse (vt)	lehaʾaʃim	לְהַאֲשִים
revenge	nekama	נְקָמָה (נ)
to avenge (get revenge)	linkom	לִנקוֹם
to pay back	lehaχzir	לְהַחזִיר
disdain	zilzul	זִלזוּל (ז)
to despise (vt)	lezalzel be…	לְזַלזֵל בְּ...
hatred, hate	sinʾa	שִׂנאָה (נ)
to hate (vt)	lisno	לִשׂנוֹא
nervous (adj)	atsbani	עַצבָּנִי
to be nervous	lihyot atsbani	לִהיוֹת עַצבָּנִי
angry (mad)	kaʿus	כָּעוּס
to make angry	lehargiz	לְהַרגִיז
humiliation	haʃpala	הַשפָּלָה (נ)
to humiliate (vt)	lehaʃpil	לְהַשפִּיל
to humiliate oneself	lehaʃpil et atsmo	לְהַשפִּיל אֶת עַצמוֹ
shock	ˈhelem	הֶלֶם (ז)
to shock (vt)	lezaʿaˈzeʿa	לְזַעֲזֵעַ
trouble (e.g. serious ~)	tsara	צָרָה (נ)

unpleasant (adj)	lo na'im	לֹא נָעִים
fear (dread)	'paχad	פַּחַד (ז)
terrible (storm, heat)	nora	נוֹרָא
scary (e.g. ~ story)	mafχid	מַפְחִיד
horror	zva'a	זְוָעָה (נ)
awful (crime, news)	ayom	אָיֹם

to begin to tremble	lehera'ed	לְהֵירָעֵד
to cry (weep)	livkot	לִבְכּוֹת
to start crying	lehatχil livkot	לְהַתְחִיל לִבְכּוֹת
tear	dim'a	דְּמָעָה (נ)

fault	aʃma	אַשְׁמָה (נ)
guilt (feeling)	rigʃei aʃam	רִגְשֵׁי אָשָׁם (ז"ר)
dishonor (disgrace)	χerpa	חֶרְפָּה (נ)
protest	meχa'a	מְחָאָה (נ)
stress	'laχats	לַחַץ (ז)

to disturb (vt)	lehafri'a	לְהַפְרִיעַ
to be furious	liχ'os	לִכְעוֹס
angry (adj)	zo'em	זוֹעֵם
to end (~ a relationship)	lesayem	לְסַיֵּים
to swear (at sb)	lekalel	לְקַלֵּל

to scare (become afraid)	lehibahel	לְהִיבָּהֵל
to hit (strike with hand)	lehakot	לְהַכּוֹת
to fight (street fight, etc.)	lehitkotet	לְהִתְקוֹטֵט

to settle (a conflict)	lehasdir	לְהַסְדִּיר
discontented (adj)	lo merutse	לֹא מְרוּצֶה
furious (adj)	metoraf	מְטוֹרָף

| It's not good! | ze lo tov! | זֶה לֹא טוֹב! |
| It's bad! | ze ra! | זֶה רַע! |

Medicine

68. Diseases

illness	maxala	מַחֲלָה (נ)
to be ill	lihyot xole	לִהְיוֹת חוֹלֶה
health	bri'ut	בְּרִיאוּת (נ)
runny nose (coryza)	na'zelet	נַזֶּלֶת (נ)
tonsillitis	da'leket ʃkedim	דַּלֶּקֶת שְׁקֵדִים (נ)
cold (illness)	hitstanenut	הִצְטַנְּנוּת (נ)
to catch a cold	lehitstanen	לְהִצְטַנֵּן
bronchitis	bron'xitis	בְּרוֹנְכִיטִיס (ז)
pneumonia	da'leket re'ot	דַּלֶּקֶת רֵיאוֹת (נ)
flu, influenza	ʃa'pa'at	שַׁפַּעַת (נ)
shortsighted (adj)	ktsar re'iya	קְצַר רְאִיָּה
longsighted (adj)	rexok re'iya	רְחוֹק־רְאִיָּה
strabismus (crossed eyes)	pzila	פְּזִילָה (נ)
squint-eyed (adj)	pozel	פּוֹזֵל
cataract	katarakt	קָטָרַקְט (ז)
glaucoma	gla'u'koma	גְּלָאוּקוֹמָה (נ)
stroke	ʃavats moxi	שָׁבָץ מוֹחִי (ז)
heart attack	hetkef lev	הֶתְקֵף לֵב (ז)
myocardial infarction	'otem ʃrir halev	אוֹטֶם שְׁרִיר הַלֵּב (ז)
paralysis	ʃituk	שִׁיתּוּק (ז)
to paralyse (vt)	leʃatek	לְשַׁתֵּק
allergy	a'lergya	אָלֶרְגְיָה (נ)
asthma	'astma, ka'tseret	אַסְתְמָה, קַצֶּרֶת (נ)
diabetes	su'keret	סוּכֶּרֶת (נ)
toothache	ke'ev ʃi'nayim	כְּאֵב שִׁינַיִים (ז)
caries	a'ʃeʃet	עַשֶּׁשֶׁת (נ)
diarrhoea	ʃilʃul	שִׁלְשׁוּל (ז)
constipation	atsirut	עֲצִירוּת (נ)
stomach upset	kilkul keiva	קִלְקוּל קֵיבָה (ז)
food poisoning	har'alat mazon	הַרְעָלַת מָזוֹן (נ)
to get food poisoning	laxatof har'alat mazon	לַחֲטוֹף הַרְעָלַת מָזוֹן
arthritis	da'leket mifrakim	דַּלֶּקֶת מִפְרָקִים (נ)
rickets	ra'kexet	רַכֶּבֶת (נ)
rheumatism	ʃigaron	שִׁיגָּרוֹן (ז)
atherosclerosis	ar'teryo skle'rosis	אַרְטֶרְיוֹ־סְקְלֶרוֹסִיס (ז)
gastritis	da'leket keiva	דַּלֶּקֶת קֵיבָה (נ)
appendicitis	da'leket toseftan	דַּלֶּקֶת תּוֹסֶפְתָּן (נ)

| cholecystitis | da'leket kis hamara | דַּלֶּקֶת כִּיס הַמָּרָה (נ) |
| ulcer | 'ulkus, kiv | אוּלְקוּס, כִּיב (ז) |

measles	xa'tsevet	חַצֶּבֶת (נ)
rubella (German measles)	a'demet	אַדֶּמֶת (נ)
jaundice	tsa'hevet	צַהֶבֶת (נ)
hepatitis	da'leket kaved	דַּלֶּקֶת כָּבֵד (נ)

schizophrenia	sxizo'frenya	סְכִיזוֹפְרֶנְיָה (נ)
rabies (hydrophobia)	ka'levet	כַּלֶּבֶת (נ)
neurosis	noi'roza	נוֹירוֹזָה (נ)
concussion	za'a'zu'a 'moax	זַעֲזוּעַ מוֹחַ (ז)

cancer	sartan	סַרְטָן (ז)
sclerosis	ta'refet	טָרֶשֶׁת (נ)
multiple sclerosis	ta'refet nefotsa	טָרֶשֶׁת נְפוֹצָה (נ)

alcoholism	alkoholizm	אַלְכּוֹהוֹלִיזְם (ז)
alcoholic (n)	alkoholist	אַלְכּוֹהוֹלִיסְט (ז)
syphilis	a'gevet	עַגֶּבֶת (נ)
AIDS	eids	אֵיידְס (ז)

tumour	gidul	גִּידוּל (ז)
malignant (adj)	mam'ir	מַמְאִיר
benign (adj)	fapir	שָׁפִיר

fever	ka'daxat	קַדַּחַת (נ)
malaria	ma'larya	מָלַרְיָה (נ)
gangrene	gan'grena	גַּנְגְרֶנָה (נ)
seasickness	maxalat yam	מַחֲלַת יָם (נ)
epilepsy	maxalat hanefila	מַחֲלַת הַנְּפִילָה (נ)

epidemic	magefa	מַגֵּיפָה (נ)
typhus	'tifus	טִיפוּס (ז)
tuberculosis	fa'xefet	שַׁחֶפֶת (נ)
cholera	ko'lera	כּוֹלֵרָה (נ)
plague (bubonic ~)	davar	דֶּבֶר (ז)

69. Symptoms. Treatments. Part 1

symptom	simptom	סִימְפְּטוֹם (ז)
temperature	xom	חוֹם (ז)
high temperature (fever)	xom ga'voha	חוֹם גָּבוֹהַּ (ז)
pulse (heartbeat)	'dofek	דּוֹפֶק (ז)

dizziness (vertigo)	sxar'xoret	סְחַרְחוֹרֶת (נ)
hot (adj)	xam	חַם
shivering	tsmar'moret	צְמַרְמוֹרֶת (נ)
pale (e.g. ~ face)	xiver	חִיוֵּר

cough	fi'ul	שִׁיעוּל (ז)
to cough (vi)	lehifta'el	לְהִשְׁתַּעֵל
to sneeze (vi)	lehit'atef	לְהִתְעַטֵּשׁ
faint	ilafon	עִילָפוֹן (ז)

to faint (vi)	lehit'alef	לְהִתְעַלֵף
bruise (hématome)	χabura	חַבּוּרָה (נ)
bump (lump)	blita	בְּלִיטָה (נ)
to bang (bump)	lekabel maka	לְקַבֵּל מַכָּה
contusion (bruise)	maka	מַכָּה (נ)
to get a bruise	lekabel maka	לְקַבֵּל מַכָּה

to limp (vi)	lits'lo'a	לִצְלוֹעַ
dislocation	'neka	נֶקַע (ז)
to dislocate (vt)	lin'ko'a	לִנְקוֹעַ
fracture	'ʃever	שֶׁבֶר (ז)
to have a fracture	liʃbor	לִשְׁבּוֹר

cut (e.g. paper ~)	χataχ	חָתָך (ז)
to cut oneself	lehiχateχ	לְהֵיחָתֵך
bleeding	dimum	דִימוּם (ז)

burn (injury)	kviya	כְּווִייָה (נ)
to get burned	laχatof kviya	לַחֲטוֹף כְּווִייָה

to prick (vt)	lidkor	לִדְקוֹר
to prick oneself	lehidaker	לְהִידָקֵר
to injure (vt)	lif'tso'a	לִפְצוֹעַ
injury	ptsi'a	פְּצִיעָה (נ)
wound	'petsa	פֶּצַע (ז)
trauma	'tra'uma	טְרָאוּמָה (נ)

to be delirious	lahazot	לַהֲזוֹת
to stutter (vi)	legamgem	לְגַמְגֵם
sunstroke	makat 'ʃemeʃ	מַכַּת שֶׁמֶשׁ (נ)

70. Symptoms. Treatments. Part 2

pain, ache	ke'ev	כְּאֵב (ז)
splinter (in foot, etc.)	kots	קוֹץ (ז)

sweat (perspiration)	ze'a	זֵיעָה (נ)
to sweat (perspire)	leha'zi'a	לְהַזִיעַ
vomiting	haka'a	הֲקָאָה (נ)
convulsions	pirkusim	פִּירְכּוּסִים (ז"ר)

pregnant (adj)	hara	הָרָה
to be born	lehivaled	לְהִיווָלֵד
delivery, labour	leda	לֵידָה (נ)
to deliver (~ a baby)	la'ledet	לָלֶדֶת
abortion	hapala	הַפָּלָה (נ)

breathing, respiration	neʃima	נְשִׁימָה (נ)
in-breath (inhalation)	ʃe'ifa	שְׁאִיפָה (נ)
out-breath (exhalation)	neʃifa	נְשִׁיפָה (נ)
to exhale (breathe out)	linʃof	לִנְשׁוֹף
to inhale (vi)	liʃof	לִשְׁאוֹף
disabled person	naχe	נָכֶה (ז)
cripple	naχe	נָכֶה (ז)

drug addict	narkoman	נַרְקוֹמָן (ז)
deaf (adj)	xereʃ	חֵירֵשׁ
mute (adj)	ilem	אִילֵם
deaf mute (adj)	xereʃ-ilem	חֵירֵשׁ־אִילֵם
mad, insane (adj)	meʃuga	מְשׁוּגָּע
madman (demented person)	meʃuga	מְשׁוּגָּע (ז)
madwoman	meʃu'ga'at	מְשׁוּגַּעַת (נ)
to go insane	lehiʃta'ge'a	לְהִשְׁתַּגֵּעַ
gene	gen	גֵּן (ז)
immunity	xasinut	חֲסִינוּת (נ)
hereditary (adj)	toraʃti	תּוֹרַשְׁתִּי
congenital (adj)	mulad	מוּלָד
virus	'virus	וִירוּס (ז)
microbe	xaidak	חַיְדָּק (ז)
bacterium	bak'terya	בַּקְטֶרְיָה (נ)
infection	zihum	זִיהוּם (ז)

71. Symptoms. Treatments. Part 3

hospital	beit xolim	בֵּית חוֹלִים (ז)
patient	metupal	מְטוּפָּל (ז)
diagnosis	avxana	אַבְחָנָה (נ)
cure	ripui	רִיפּוּי (ז)
medical treatment	tipul refu'i	טִיפּוּל רְפוּאִי (ז)
to get treatment	lekabel tipul	לְקַבֵּל טִיפּוּל
to treat (~ a patient)	letapel be…	לְטַפֵּל בְּ…
to nurse (look after)	letapel be…	לְטַפֵּל בְּ…
care (nursing ~)	tipul	טִיפּוּל (ז)
operation, surgery	ni'tuax	נִיתוּחַ (ז)
to bandage (head, limb)	laxboʃ	לַחְבּוֹשׁ
bandaging	xaviʃa	חֲבִישָׁה (נ)
vaccination	xisun	חִיסּוּן (ז)
to vaccinate (vt)	lexasen	לְחַסֵּן
injection	zrika	זְרִיקָה (נ)
to give an injection	lehazrik	לְהַזְרִיק
attack	hetkef	הֶתְקֵף (ז)
amputation	kti'a	קְטִיעָה (נ)
to amputate (vt)	lik'to'a	לִקְטוֹעַ
coma	tar'demet	תַּרְדֶּמֶת (נ)
to be in a coma	lihyot betar'demet	לִהְיוֹת בְּתַרְדֶּמֶת
intensive care	tipul nimrats	טִיפּוּל נִמְרָץ (ז)
to recover (~ from flu)	lehaxlim	לְהַחְלִים
condition (patient's ~)	matsav	מַצָּב (ז)
consciousness	hakara	הַכָּרָה (נ)
memory (faculty)	zikaron	זִיכָּרוֹן (ז)

to pull out (tooth)	la'akor	לַעֲקוֹר
filling	stima	סְתִימָה (נ)
to fill (a tooth)	la'asot stima	לַעֲשׂוֹת סְתִימָה

| hypnosis | hip'noza | הִיפְנוֹזָה (נ) |
| to hypnotize (vt) | lehapnet | לְהַפְנֵט |

72. Doctors

doctor	rofe	רוֹפֵא (ז)
nurse	aχot	אָחוֹת (נ)
personal doctor	rofe iʃi	רוֹפֵא אִישִׁי (ז)

dentist	rofe ʃi'nayim	רוֹפֵא שִׁינַיִים (ז)
optician	rofe ei'nayim	רוֹפֵא עֵינַיִים (ז)
general practitioner	rofe pnimi	רוֹפֵא פְּנִימִי (ז)
surgeon	kirurg	כִּירוּרג (ז)

psychiatrist	psiχi''ater	פְּסִיכִיאָטֶר (ז)
paediatrician	rofe yeladim	רוֹפֵא יְלָדִים (ז)
psychologist	psiχolog	פְּסִיכוֹלוֹג (ז)
gynaecologist	rofe naʃim	רוֹפֵא נָשִׁים (ז)
cardiologist	kardyolog	קַרְדִיוֹלוֹג (ז)

73. Medicine. Drugs. Accessories

medicine, drug	trufa	תְרוּפָה (נ)
remedy	trufa	תְרוּפָה (נ)
to prescribe (vt)	lirʃom	לִרְשׁוֹם
prescription	mirʃam	מִרְשָׁם (ז)

tablet, pill	kadur	כַּדוּר (ז)
ointment	miʃχa	מִשְׁחָה (נ)
ampoule	'ampula	אַמְפּוּלָה (נ)
mixture, solution	ta'a'rovet	תַעֲרוֹבֶת (נ)
syrup	sirop	סִירוֹפ (ז)
capsule	gluya	גְלוּיָה (נ)
powder	avka	אַבְקָה (נ)

gauze bandage	taχ'boʃet 'gaza	תַחְבּוֹשֶׁת גָאזָה (ז)
cotton wool	'tsemer 'gefen	צֶמֶר גֶפֶן (ז)
iodine	yod	יוֹד (ז)

plaster	'plaster	פְּלַסְטֶר (ז)
eyedropper	taf'tefet	טַפְטֶפֶת (נ)
thermometer	madχom	מַדְחוֹם (ז)
syringe	mazrek	מַזְרֵק (ז)

wheelchair	kise galgalim	כִּיסֵא גַלְגַלִים (ז)
crutches	ka'bayim	קַבַּיִים (ז"ר)
painkiller	meʃakeχ ke'evim	מְשַׁכֵּךְ כְּאֵבִים (ז)
laxative	trufa meʃal'ʃelet	תְרוּפָה מְשַׁלְשֶׁלֶת (נ)

spirits (ethanol)	'kohal	כֹּוהַל (ז)
medicinal herbs	isvei marpe	עִשְׂבֵי מַרְפֵּא (ז"ר)
herbal (~ tea)	ʃel asavim	שֶׁל עֲשָׂבִים

74. Smoking. Tobacco products

tobacco	'tabak	טַבָּק (ז)
cigarette	si'garya	סִיגַרְיָה (נ)
cigar	sigar	סִיגָר (ז)
pipe	mik'teret	מִקְטֶרֶת (נ)
packet (of cigarettes)	χafisa	חֲפִיסָה (נ)
matches	gafrurim	גַּפְרוּרִים (ז"ר)
matchbox	kufsat gafrurim	קוּפְסַת גַּפְרוּרִים (נ)
lighter	maʦit	מַצִּית (ז)
ashtray	ma'afera	מַאֲפֵרָה (נ)
cigarette case	nartik lesi'garyot	נַרְתִּיק לְסִיגַרְיוֹת (ז)
cigarette holder	piya	פִּיָּה (נ)
filter (cigarette tip)	'filter	פִילְטֶר (ז)
to smoke (vi, vt)	le'aʃen	לְעַשֵּׁן
to light a cigarette	lehadlik si'garya	לְהַדְלִיק סִיגַרְיָה
smoking	iʃun	עִישּׁוּן (ז)
smoker	me'aʃen	מְעַשֵּׁן (ז)
cigarette end	bdal si'garya	בְּדַל סִיגַרְיָה (ז)
smoke, fumes	aʃan	עָשָׁן (ז)
ash	'efer	אֵפֶר (ז)

HUMAN HABITAT

City

city, town	ir	עִיר (נ)
capital city	ir bira	עִיר בִּירָה (נ)
village	kfar	כְּפָר (ז)
city map	mapat ha'ir	מַפַּת הָעִיר (נ)
city centre	merkaz ha'ir	מֶרְכַּז הָעִיר (ז)
suburb	parvar	פַּרְוָור (ז)
suburban (adj)	parvari	פַּרְוָורִי
outskirts	parvar	פַּרְוָור (ז)
environs (suburbs)	svivot	סְבִיבוֹת (נ"ר)
city block	ʃxuna	שְׁכוּנָה (נ)
residential block (area)	ʃxunat megurim	שְׁכוּנַת מְגוּרִים (נ)
traffic	tnu'a	תְּנוּעָה (נ)
traffic lights	ramzor	רַמְזוֹר (ז)
public transport	taxbura tsiburit	תַּחְבּוּרָה צִיבּוּרִית (נ)
crossroads	'tsomet	צוֹמֶת (ז)
zebra crossing	ma'avar xatsaya	מַעֲבַר חֲצָיָה (ז)
pedestrian subway	ma'avar tat karka'i	מַעֲבַר תַּת־קַרְקָעִי (ז)
to cross (~ the street)	laxatsot	לַחֲצוֹת
pedestrian	holex 'regel	הוֹלֵךְ רֶגֶל (ז)
pavement	midraxa	מִדְרָכָה (נ)
bridge	'geʃer	גֶּשֶׁר (ז)
embankment (river walk)	ta'yelet	טַיֶּלֶת (נ)
fountain	mizraka	מִזְרָקָה (נ)
allée (garden walkway)	sdera	שְׂדֵרָה (נ)
park	park	פַּארְק (ז)
boulevard	sdera	שְׂדֵרָה (נ)
square	kikar	כִּיכָּר (נ)
avenue (wide street)	rexov raʃi	רְחוֹב רָאשִׁי (ז)
street	rexov	רְחוֹב (ז)
side street	simta	סִמְטָה (נ)
dead end	mavoi satum	מָבוֹי סָתוּם (ז)
house	'bayit	בַּיִת (ז)
building	binyan	בִּנְיָן (ז)
skyscraper	gored ʃxakim	גּוֹרֵד שְׁחָקִים (ז)
facade	xazit	חֲזִית (נ)
roof	gag	גַּג (ז)

window	χalon	חַלּוֹן (ז)
arch	'keʃet	קֶשֶׁת (נ)
column	amud	עַמּוּד (ז)
corner	pina	פִּינָה (נ)

shop window	χalon ra'ava	חַלּוֹן רַאֲוָה (ז)
signboard (store sign, etc.)	'ʃelet	שֶׁלֶט (ז)
poster (e.g., playbill)	kraza	כְּרָזָה (נ)
advertising poster	'poster	פּוֹסְטֶר (ז)
hoarding	'luaχ pirsum	לוּחַ פִּרְסוּם (ז)

rubbish	'zevel	זֶבֶל (ז)
rubbish bin	paχ aʃpa	פַּח אַשְׁפָּה (ז)
to litter (vi)	lelaχleχ	לְלַכְלֵךְ
rubbish dump	mizbala	מִזְבָּלָה (נ)

telephone box	ta 'telefon	תָּא טֶלֶפוֹן (ז)
lamppost	amud panas	עַמּוּד פָּנָס (ז)
bench (park ~)	safsal	סַפְסָל (ז)

police officer	ʃoter	שׁוֹטֵר (ז)
police	miʃtara	מִשְׁטָרָה (נ)
beggar	kabtsan	קַבְּצָן (ז)
homeless (n)	χasar 'bayit	חֲסַר בַּיִת (ז)

76. Urban institutions

shop	χanut	חֲנוּת (נ)
chemist, pharmacy	beit mir'kaχat	בֵּית מִרְקַחַת (ז)
optician (spectacles shop)	χanut miʃka'fayim	חֲנוּת מִשְׁקָפַיִים (נ)
shopping centre	kanyon	קַנְיוֹן (ז)
supermarket	super'market	סוּפֶּרְמַרְקֶט (ז)

bakery	ma'afiya	מַאֲפִיָּיה (נ)
baker	ofe	אוֹפֶה (ז)
cake shop	χanut mamtakim	חֲנוּת מַמְתַּקִים (נ)
grocery shop	ma'kolet	מַכּוֹלֶת (נ)
butcher shop	itliz	אִטְלִיז (ז)

| greengrocer | χanut perot viyerakot | חֲנוּת פֵּירוֹת וִירָקוֹת (נ) |
| market | ʃuk | שׁוּק (ז) |

coffee bar	beit kafe	בֵּית קָפֶה (ז)
restaurant	mis'ada	מִסְעָדָה (נ)
pub, bar	pab	פָּאבּ (ז)
pizzeria	pi'tseriya	פִּיצֶרְיָיה (נ)

hairdresser	mispara	מִסְפָּרָה (נ)
post office	'do'ar	דּוֹאַר (ז)
dry cleaners	nikui yaveʃ	נִיקּוּי יָבֵשׁ (ז)
photo studio	'studyo letsilum	סְטוּדְיוֹ לְצִילוּם (ז)

| shoe shop | χanut na'a'layim | חֲנוּת נַעֲלַיִים (נ) |
| bookshop | χanut sfarim | חֲנוּת סְפָרִים (נ) |

sports shop	χanut sport	חֲנוּת סְפּוֹרְט (נ)
clothes repair shop	χanut tikun bgadim	חֲנוּת תִּיקוּן בְּגָדִים (נ)
formal wear hire	χanut haskarat bgadim	חֲנוּת הַשְׂכָּרַת בְּגָדִים (נ)
video rental shop	χanut haʃʃalat sratim	חֲנוּת הַשְׁאָלַת סְרָטִים (נ)

circus	kirkas	קִרְקָס (ז)
zoo	gan hayot	גַּן חַיּוֹת (ז)
cinema	kol'no'a	קוֹלְנוֹעַ (ז)
museum	muze'on	מוּזֵיאוֹן (ז)
library	sifriya	סִפְרִיָּה (נ)

theatre	te'atron	תֵּיאַטְרוֹן (ז)
opera (opera house)	beit 'opera	בֵּית אוֹפֵּרָה (ז)
nightclub	mo'adon 'laila	מוֹעֲדוֹן לַיְלָה (ז)
casino	ka'zino	קָזִינוֹ (ז)

mosque	misgad	מִסְגָּד (ז)
synagogue	beit 'kneset	בֵּית כְּנֶסֶת (ז)
cathedral	kated'rala	קָתֶדְרָלָה (נ)
temple	mikdaʃ	מִקְדָּשׁ (ז)
church	knesiya	כְּנֵסִיָּה (נ)

college	miχlala	מִכְלָלָה (נ)
university	uni'versita	אוּנִיבֶרְסִיטָה (נ)
school	beit 'sefer	בֵּית סֵפֶר (ז)

prefecture	maχoz	מָחוֹז (ז)
town hall	iriya	עִירִיָּה (נ)
hotel	beit malon	בֵּית מָלוֹן (ז)
bank	bank	בַּנְק (ז)

embassy	ʃagrirut	שַׁגְרִירוּת (נ)
travel agency	soχnut nesi'ot	סוֹכְנוּת נְסִיעוֹת (נ)
information office	modi'in	מוֹדִיעִין (ז)
currency exchange	misrad hamarat mat'be'a	מִשְׂרַד הֲמָרַת מַטְבֵּעַ (ז)

| underground, tube | ra'kevet taχtit | רַכֶּבֶת תַּחְתִּית (נ) |
| hospital | beit χolim | בֵּית חוֹלִים (ז) |

| petrol station | taχanat 'delek | תַּחֲנַת דֶּלֶק (נ) |
| car park | migraʃ χanaya | מִגְרַשׁ חֲנָיָה (ז) |

77. Urban transport

bus, coach	'otobus	אוֹטוֹבּוּס (ז)
tram	ra'kevet kala	רַכֶּבֶת קַלָּה (נ)
trolleybus	tro'leibus	טְרוֹלֵייבּוּס (ז)
route (bus ~)	maslul	מַסְלוּל (ז)
number (e.g. bus ~)	mispar	מִסְפָּר (ז)

to go by ...	lin'so'a be...	לִנְסוֹעַ בְּ...
to get on (~ the bus)	la'alot	לַעֲלוֹת
to get off ...	la'redet mi...	לָרֶדֶת מ...
stop (e.g. bus ~)	taχana	תַּחֲנָה (נ)

next stop	hataχana haba'a	הַתַּחֲנָה הַבָּאָה (נ)
terminus	hataχana ha'aχrona	הַתַּחֲנָה הָאַחֲרוֹנָה (נ)
timetable	'luaχ zmanim	לוּחַ זְמַנִּים (ז)
to wait (vt)	lehamtin	לְהַמְתִּין
ticket	kartis	כַּרְטִיס (ז)
fare	meχir hanesiya	מְחִיר הַנְּסִיעָה (ז)
cashier (ticket seller)	kupai	קוּפַּאי (ז)
ticket inspection	bi'koret kartisim	בִּיקּוֹרֶת כַּרְטִיסִים (נ)
ticket inspector	mevaker	מְבַקֵּר (ז)
to be late (for …)	le'aχer	לְאַחֵר
to miss (~ the train, etc.)	lefasfes	לְפַסְפֵּס
to be in a hurry	lemaher	לְמַהֵר
taxi, cab	monit	מוֹנִית (נ)
taxi driver	nahag monit	נֶהָג מוֹנִית (ז)
by taxi	bemonit	בְּמוֹנִית
taxi rank	taχanat moniyot	תַּחֲנַת מוֹנִיּוֹת (נ)
to call a taxi	lehazmin monit	לְהַזְמִין מוֹנִית
to take a taxi	la'kaχat monit	לָקַחַת מוֹנִית
traffic	tnu'a	תְּנוּעָה (נ)
traffic jam	pkak	פְּקָק (ז)
rush hour	ʃa'ot 'omes	שְׁעוֹת עוֹמֶס (נ"ר)
to park (vi)	laχanot	לַחֲנוֹת
to park (vt)	lehaχnot	לְהַחֲנוֹת
car park	χanaya	חֲנָיָה (נ)
underground, tube	ra'kevet taχtit	רַכֶּבֶת תַּחְתִּית (נ)
station	taχana	תַּחֲנָה (נ)
to take the tube	lin'so'a betaχtit	לִנְסוֹעַ בְּתַחְתִּית
train	ra'kevet	רַכֶּבֶת (נ)
train station	taχanat ra'kevet	תַּחֲנַת רַכֶּבֶת (נ)

78. Sightseeing

monument	an'darta	אַנְדַּרְטָה (נ)
fortress	mivtsar	מִבְצָר (ז)
palace	armon	אַרְמוֹן (ז)
castle	tira	טִירָה (נ)
tower	migdal	מִגְדָּל (ז)
mausoleum	ma'uzo'le'um	מָאוּזוֹלְיָאוּם (ז)
architecture	adriχalut	אַדְרִיכָלוּת (נ)
medieval (adj)	benaimi	בֵּינַיִימִי
ancient (adj)	atik	עַתִּיק
national (adj)	le'umi	לְאוּמִי
famous (monument, etc.)	mefursam	מְפוּרְסָם
tourist	tayar	תַּיָּיר (ז)
guide (person)	madriχ tiyulim	מַדְרִיךְ טִיּוּלִים (ז)
excursion, sightseeing tour	tiyul	טִיּוּל (ז)

to show (vt)	lehar'ot	לְהַרְאוֹת
to tell (vt)	lesaper	לְסַפֵּר
to find (vt)	limtso	לִמְצוֹא
to get lost (lose one's way)	la'leχet le'ibud	לָלֶכֶת לְאִיבּוּד
map (e.g. underground ~)	mapa	מַפָּה (נ)
map (e.g. city ~)	tarʃim	תַרְשִׁים (ז)
souvenir, gift	maz'keret	מַזְכֶּרֶת (נ)
gift shop	χanut matanot	חֲנוּת מַתָנוֹת (נ)
to take pictures	leʦalem	לְצַלֵם
to have one's picture taken	lehiʦtalem	לְהִצְטַלֵם

79. Shopping

to buy (purchase)	liknot	לִקְנוֹת
shopping	kniya	קְנִיָה (נ)
to go shopping	la'leχet lekniyot	לָלֶכֶת לִקְנִיוֹת
shopping	ariχat kniyot	עֲרִיכַת קְנִיוֹת (נ)
to be open (ab. shop)	pa'tuaχ	פָּתוּחַ
to be closed	sagur	סָגוּר
footwear, shoes	na'a'layim	נַעֲלַיִים (נ"ר)
clothes, clothing	bgadim	בְּגָדִים (ז"ר)
cosmetics	tamrukim	תַמְרוּקִים (ז"ר)
food products	muʦrei mazon	מוּצְרֵי מָזוֹן (ז"ר)
gift, present	matana	מַתָנָה (נ)
shop assistant (masc.)	moχer	מוֹכֵר (ז)
shop assistant (fem.)	mo'χeret	מוֹכֶרֶת (נ)
cash desk	kupa	קוּפָּה (נ)
mirror	mar'a	מַרְאָה (נ)
counter (shop ~)	duχan	דוּכָן (ז)
fitting room	'χeder halbaʃa	חֶדֶר הַלְבָּשָׁה (ז)
to try on	limdod	לִמְדוֹד
to fit (ab. dress, etc.)	lehat'im	לְהַתְאִים
to fancy (vt)	limtso χen be'ei'nayim	לִמְצוֹא חֵן בְּעֵינַיִים
price	meχir	מְחִיר (ז)
price tag	tag meχir	תַג מְחִיר (ז)
to cost (vt)	la'alot	לַעֲלוֹת
How much?	'kama?	כַּמָה?
discount	hanaχa	הֲנָחָה (נ)
inexpensive (adj)	lo yakar	לֹא יָקָר
cheap (adj)	zol	זוֹל
expensive (adj)	yakar	יָקָר
It's expensive	ze yakar	זֶה יָקָר
hire (n)	haskara	הַשְׂכָּרָה (נ)
to hire (~ a dinner jacket)	liskor	לִשְׂכּוֹר

| credit (trade credit) | aʃrai | (ז) אַשְׁרַאי |
| on credit (adv) | be'aʃrai | בְּאַשְׁרַאי |

80. Money

money	'kesef	(ז) כֶּסֶף
currency exchange	hamara	(נ) הַמָרָה
exchange rate	'ʃa'ar χalifin	(ז) שַׁעַר חֲלִיפִין
cashpoint	kaspomat	(ז) כַּסְפּוֹמָט
coin	mat'be'a	(ז) מַטְבֵּעַ

| dollar | 'dolar | (ז) דוֹלָר |
| euro | 'eiro | (ז) אֵירוֹ |

lira	'lira	(נ) לִירָה
Deutschmark	mark germani	(ז) מַרק גֶּרְמָנִי
franc	frank	(ז) פְרַנק
pound sterling	'lira 'sterling	(נ) לִירָה שְׁטֶרְלִינג
yen	yen	(ז) יֵן

debt	χov	(ז) חוֹב
debtor	'ba'al χov	(ז) בַּעַל חוֹב
to lend (money)	lehalvot	לְהַלְוֹות
to borrow (vi, vt)	lilvot	לִלְוֹות

bank	bank	(ז) בַּנק
account	χeʃbon	(ז) חֶשְׁבּוֹן
to deposit (vt)	lehafkid	לְהַפְקִיד
to deposit into the account	lehafkid leχeʃbon	לְהַפְקִיד לְחֶשְׁבּוֹן
to withdraw (vt)	limʃoχ meχeʃbon	לִמְשׁוֹךְ מֵחֶשְׁבּוֹן

credit card	kartis aʃrai	(ז) כַּרְטִיס אַשְׁרַאי
cash	mezuman	מְזוּמָן
cheque	tʃek	(ז) צֶ'ק
to write a cheque	liχtov tʃek	לִכְתוֹב צֶ'ק
chequebook	pinkas 'tʃekim	(ז) פִּנְקָס צֶ'קִים

wallet	arnak	(ז) אַרְנָק
purse	arnak lematbe''ot	(ז) אַרְנָק לְמַטְבְּעוֹת
safe	ka'sefet	(נ) כַּסֶּפֶת

heir	yoreʃ	(ז) יוֹרֵשׁ
inheritance	yeruʃa	(נ) יְרוּשָׁה
fortune (wealth)	'oʃer	(ז) עוֹשֶׁר

lease	χoze sχirut	(ז) חוֹזֶה שְׂכִירוּת
rent (money)	sχar dira	(ז) שְׂכַר דִירָה
to rent (sth from sb)	liskor	לִשְׂכּוֹר

price	meχir	(ז) מְחִיר
cost	alut	(נ) עֲלוּת
sum	sχum	(ז) סְכוּם
to spend (vt)	lehotsi	לְהוֹצִיא
expenses	hotsa'ot	(נ"ר) הוֹצָאוֹת

to economize (vi, vt)	laxasox	לַחְסוֹך
economical	xesxoni	חֶסְכוֹנִי

to pay (vi, vt)	leʃalem	לְשַׁלֵם
payment	taʃlum	תַּשְׁלוּם (ז)
change (give the ~)	'odef	עוֹדֶף (ז)

tax	mas	מַס (ז)
fine	knas	קְנָס (ז)
to fine (vt)	liknos	לִקְנוֹס

81. Post. Postal service

post office	'do'ar	דוֹאַר (ז)
post (letters, etc.)	'do'ar	דוֹאַר (ז)
postman	davar	דַּוָּר (ז)
opening hours	ʃa'ot avoda	שְׁעוֹת עֲבוֹדָה (נ״ר)

letter	mixtav	מִכְתָּב (ז)
registered letter	mixtav raʃum	מִכְתָּב רָשׁוּם (ז)
postcard	gluya	גְּלוּיָה (נ)
telegram	mivrak	מִבְרָק (ז)
parcel	xavila	חֲבִילָה (נ)
money transfer	ha'avarat ksafim	הַעֲבָרַת כְּסָפִים (נ)

to receive (vt)	lekabel	לְקַבֵּל
to send (vt)	liʃ'loax	לִשְׁלוֹחַ
sending	ʃlixa	שְׁלִיחָה (ז)

address	'ktovet	כְּתוֹבֶת (נ)
postcode	mikud	מִיקוּד (ז)
sender	ʃo'leax	שׁוֹלֵחַ (ז)
receiver	nim'an	נִמְעָן (ז)

name (first name)	ʃem prati	שֵׁם פְּרָטִי (ז)
surname (last name)	ʃem miʃpaxa	שֵׁם מִשְׁפָּחָה (ז)

postage rate	ta'arif	תַּעֲרִיף (ז)
standard (adj)	ragil	רָגִיל
economical (adj)	xesxoni	חֶסְכוֹנִי

weight	miʃkal	מִשְׁקָל (ז)
to weigh (~ letters)	liʃkol	לִשְׁקוֹל
envelope	ma'atafa	מַעֲטָפָה (נ)
postage stamp	bul 'do'ar	בּוּל דוֹאַר (ז)
to stamp an envelope	lehadbik bul	לְהַדְבִּיק בּוּל

Dwelling. House. Home

82. House. Dwelling

house	'bayit	בַּיִת (ז)
at home (adv)	ba'bayit	בַּבַּיִת
yard	χatser	חָצֵר (נ)
fence (iron ~)	gader	גָּדֵר (נ)
brick (n)	levena	לְבֵנָה (נ)
brick (as adj)	milevenim	מִלְבֵנִים
stone (n)	'even	אֶבֶן (נ)
stone (as adj)	me''even	מֵאֶבֶן
concrete (n)	beton	בֶּטוֹן (ז)
concrete (as adj)	mibeton	מִבֶּטוֹן
new (new-built)	χadaʃ	חָדָשׁ
old (adj)	yaʃan	יָשָׁן
decrepit (house)	balui	בָּלוּי
modern (adj)	mo'derni	מוֹדֶרְנִי
multistorey (adj)	rav komot	רַב־קוֹמוֹת
tall (~ building)	ga'voha	גָּבוֹהַ
floor, storey	'koma	קוֹמָה (נ)
single-storey (adj)	χad komati	חַד־קוֹמָתִי
ground floor	komat 'karka	קוֹמַת קַרְקַע (נ)
top floor	hakoma ha'elyona	הַקוֹמָה הָעֶלְיוֹנָה (נ)
roof	gag	גַּג (ז)
chimney	aruba	אֲרוּבָּה (נ)
roof tiles	'raʿaf	רַעַף (ז)
tiled (adj)	mereʿafim	מְרֻעָפִים
loft (attic)	aliyat gag	עֲלִיַּת גַּג (נ)
window	χalon	חַלוֹן (ז)
glass	zχuχit	זְכוּכִית (נ)
window ledge	'eden χalon	אֶדֶן חַלוֹן (ז)
shutters	trisim	תְּרִיסִים (ז"ר)
wall	kir	קִיר (ז)
balcony	mir'peset	מִרְפֶּסֶת (נ)
downpipe	marzev	מַרְזֵב (ז)
upstairs (to be ~)	le'mala	לְמַעְלָה
to go upstairs	la'alot bemadregot	לַעֲלוֹת בְּמַדְרֵגוֹת
to come down (the stairs)	la'redet bemadregot	לָרֶדֶת בְּמַדְרֵגוֹת
to move (to new premises)	la'avor	לַעֲבוֹר

83. House. Entrance. Lift

entrance	knisa	כְּנִיסָה (נ)
stairs (stairway)	madregot	מַדְרֵגוֹת (נ"ר)
steps	madregot	מַדְרֵגוֹת (נ"ר)
banisters	ma'ake	מַעֲקֶה (ז)
lobby (hotel ~)	'lobi	לוֹבִּי (ז)

postbox	teivat 'do'ar	תֵּיבַת דּוֹאַר (נ)
waste bin	paχ 'zevel	פַּח זֶבֶל (ז)
refuse chute	merik aʃpa	מֵרִיק אַשְׁפָּה (ז)

lift	ma'alit	מַעֲלִית (נ)
goods lift	ma'alit masa	מַעֲלִית מַשָּׂא (נ)
lift cage	ta ma'alit	תָּא מַעֲלִית (ז)
to take the lift	lin'so'a bema'alit	לִנְסוֹעַ בְּמַעֲלִית

flat	dira	דִּירָה (נ)
residents (~ of a building)	dayarim	דַּיָּירִים (ז"ר)
neighbour (masc.)	ʃaχen	שָׁכֵן (ז)
neighbour (fem.)	ʃχena	שְׁכֵנָה (נ)
neighbours	ʃχenim	שְׁכֵנִים (ז"ר)

84. House. Doors. Locks

door	'delet	דֶּלֶת (נ)
gate (vehicle ~)	'ʃa'ar	שַׁעַר (ז)
handle, doorknob	yadit	יָדִית (נ)
to unlock (unbolt)	lif'toaχ	לִפְתּוֹחַ
to open (vt)	lif'toaχ	לִפְתּוֹחַ
to close (vt)	lisgor	לִסְגּוֹר

| key | maf'teaχ | מַפְתֵּחַ (ז) |
| bunch (of keys) | tsror maftexot | צְרוֹר מַפְתְּחוֹת (ז) |

to creak (door, etc.)	laχarok	לַחֲרוֹק
creak	χarika	חֲרִיקָה (נ)
hinge (door ~)	tsir	צִיר (ז)
doormat	ʃtiχon	שְׁטִיחוֹן (ז)

door lock	man'ul	מַנְעוּל (ז)
keyhole	χor haman'ul	חוֹר הַמַּנְעוּל (ז)
crossbar (sliding bar)	'briaχ	בְּרִיחַ (ז)
door latch	'briaχ	בְּרִיחַ (ז)
padlock	man'ul	מַנְעוּל (ז)

to ring (~ the door bell)	letsaltsel	לְצַלְצֵל
ringing (sound)	tsiltsul	צִלְצוּל (ז)
doorbell	pa'amon	פַּעֲמוֹן (ז)
doorbell button	kaftor	כַּפְתּוֹר (ז)

| knock (at the door) | hakaʃa | הַקָּשָׁה (נ) |
| to knock (vi) | lehakiʃ | לְהַקִּישׁ |

code	kod	קוֹד (ז)
combination lock	man'ul kod	מַנְעוּל קוֹד (ז)
intercom	'interkom	אִינְטֶרְקוֹם (ז)
number (on the door)	mispar	מִסְפָּר (ז)
doorplate	luχit	לוּחִית (נ)
peephole	einit	עֵינִית (נ)

85. Country house

village	kfar	כְּפָר (ז)
vegetable garden	gan yarak	גַּן יָרָק (ז)
fence	gader	גָּדֵר (נ)
picket fence	gader yetedot	גָּדֵר יְתֵדוֹת (נ)
wicket gate	piʃpaʃ	פִּשְׁפָּשׁ (ז)

granary	asam	אָסָם (ז)
cellar	martef	מַרְתֵּף (ז)
shed (garden ~)	maχsan	מַחְסָן (ז)
water well	be'er	בְּאֵר (נ)

stove (wood-fired ~)	aχ	אָח (נ)
to stoke the stove	lehasik et ha'aχ	לְהַסִּיק אֶת הָאָח
firewood	atsei hasaka	עֲצֵי הַסָּקָה (ז"ר)
log (firewood)	bul ets	בּוּל עֵץ (ז)

veranda	mir'peset mekora	מִרְפֶּסֶת מְקוֹרָה (נ)
deck (terrace)	mir'peset	מִרְפֶּסֶת (נ)
stoop (front steps)	madregot ba'petaχ 'bayit	מַדְרֵגוֹת בְּפֶתַח בַּיִת (נ"ר)
swing (hanging seat)	nadneda	נַדְנֵדָה (נ)

86. Castle. Palace

castle	tira	טִירָה (נ)
palace	armon	אַרְמוֹן (ז)
fortress	mivtsar	מִבְצָר (ז)

wall (round castle)	χoma	חוֹמָה (נ)
tower	migdal	מִגְדָּל (ז)
keep, donjon	migdal merkazi	מִגְדָּל מֶרְכָּזִי (ז)

portcullis	ʃa'ar anaχi	שַׁעַר אֲנָכִי (ז)
subterranean passage	ma'avar tat karka'i	מַעֲבָר תַּת־קַרְקָעִי (ז)
moat	χafir	חָפִיר (ז)

| chain | ʃal'ʃelet | שַׁלְשֶׁלֶת (נ) |
| arrow loop | eʃnav 'yeri | אֶשְׁנָב יְרִי (ז) |

| magnificent (adj) | mefo'ar | מְפוֹאָר |
| majestic (adj) | malχuti | מַלְכוּתִי |

| impregnable (adj) | 'bilti χadir | בִּלְתִּי חָדִיר |
| medieval (adj) | benaimi | בֵּינַיְימִי |

87. Flat

flat	dira	דִּירָה (נ)
room	'xeder	חֶדֶר (ז)
bedroom	xadar ʃena	חֲדַר שֵׁינָה (ז)
dining room	pinat 'oxel	פִּינַת אוֹכֶל (נ)
living room	salon	סָלוֹן (ז)
study (home office)	xadar avoda	חֲדַר עֲבוֹדָה (ז)
entry room	prozdor	פְּרוֹזדוֹר (ז)
bathroom	xadar am'batya	חֲדַר אַמבַּטיָה (ז)
water closet	ʃerutim	שֵׁירוּתִים (ז"ר)
ceiling	tikra	תִקרָה (נ)
floor	ritspa	רִצפָּה (נ)
corner	pina	פִּינָה (נ)

88. Flat. Cleaning

to clean (vi, vt)	lenakot	לְנַקוֹת
to put away (to stow)	lefanot	לְפַנוֹת
dust	avak	אָבָק (ז)
dusty (adj)	me'ubak	מְאוּבָּק
to dust (vt)	lenakot avak	לְנַקוֹת אָבָק
vacuum cleaner	ʃo'ev avak	שׁוֹאֵב אָבָק (ז)
to vacuum (vt)	liʃ'ov avak	לִשׁאוֹב אָבָק
to sweep (vi, vt)	letate	לְטַאטֵא
sweepings	'psolet ti'tu	פְּסוֹלֶת טַאטוּא (נ)
order	'seder	סֵדֶר (ז)
disorder, mess	i 'seder	אִי סֵדֶר (ז)
mop	magev im smartut	מַגֵּב עִם סמַרטוּט (ז)
duster	smartut avak	סמַרטוּט אָבָק (ז)
short broom	mat'ate katan	מַטאַטֵא קָטָן (ז)
dustpan	ya'e	יָעֶה (ז)

89. Furniture. Interior

furniture	rehitim	רָהִיטִים (ז"ר)
table	ʃulxan	שׁוּלחָן (ז)
chair	kise	כָּסֵא (ז)
bed	mita	מִיטָה (נ)
sofa, settee	sapa	סַפָּה (נ)
armchair	kursa	כּוּרסָה (נ)
bookcase	aron sfarim	אָרוֹן סְפָרִים (ז)
shelf	madaf	מַדָף (ז)
wardrobe	aron bgadim	אָרוֹן בְּגָדִים (ז)
coat rack (wall-mounted ~)	mitle	מִתלֶה (ז)

coat stand	mitle	מִתלֶה (ז)
chest of drawers	ʃida	שִׁידָה (נ)
coffee table	ʃulχan itonim	שׁוּלחָן עִיתוֹנִים (ז)

mirror	mar'a	מַראָה (נ)
carpet	ʃa'tiaχ	שָׁטִיחַ (ז)
small carpet	ʃa'tiaχ	שָׁטִיחַ (ז)

fireplace	aχ	אָח (נ)
candle	ner	נֵר (ז)
candlestick	pamot	פָּמוֹט (ז)

drapes	vilonot	וִילוֹנוֹת (ז"ר)
wallpaper	tapet	טַפֶּט (ז)
blinds (jalousie)	trisim	תרִיסִים (ז"ר)

table lamp	menorat ʃulχan	מְנוֹרַת שׁוּלחָן (נ)
wall lamp (sconce)	menorat kir	מְנוֹרַת קִיר (נ)
standard lamp	menora o'medet	מְנוֹרָה עוֹמֶדֶת (נ)
chandelier	niv'reʃet	נִברֶשֶׁת (נ)

leg (of a chair, table)	'regel	רֶגֶל (נ)
armrest	miʃ'enet yad	מִשׁעֶנֶת יָד (נ)
back (backrest)	miʃ'enet	מִשׁעֶנֶת (נ)
drawer	megera	מְגֵירָה (נ)

90. Bedding

bedclothes	matsa'im	מַצָעִים (ז"ר)
pillow	karit	כָּרִית (נ)
pillowslip	tsipit	צִיפִּית (נ)
duvet	smiχa	שׂמִיכָה (נ)
sheet	sadin	סָדִין (ז)
bedspread	kisui mita	כִּיסוּי מִיטָה (ז)

91. Kitchen

kitchen	mitbaχ	מִטבָּח (ז)
gas	gaz	גָז (ז)
gas cooker	tanur gaz	תַנוּר גָז (ז)
electric cooker	tanur χaʃmali	תַנוּר חַשׁמַלִי (ז)
oven	tanur afiya	תַנוּר אֲפִייָה (ז)
microwave oven	mikrogal	מִיקרוֹגַל (ז)

refrigerator	mekarer	מְקָרֵר (ז)
freezer	makpi	מַקפִּיא (ז)
dishwasher	me'diaχ kelim	מֵדִיחַ כֵּלִים (ז)

mincer	matχenat basar	מַטחֲנַת בָּשָׂר (נ)
juicer	masχeta	מַסחֵטָה (נ)
toaster	'toster	טוֹסטֶר (ז)
mixer	'mikser	מִיקסֶר (ז)

coffee machine	meχonat kafe	מְכוֹנַת קָפֶה (נ)
coffee pot	findʒan	פִינגָ'אן (ז)
coffee grinder	matχenat kafe	מַטחֶנַת קָפֶה (נ)

kettle	kumkum	קוּמקוּם (ז)
teapot	kumkum	קוּמקוּם (ז)
lid	miχse	מִכסֶה (ז)
tea strainer	mis'nenet te	מְסַנֶנֶת תֵה (נ)

spoon	kaf	כַּף (נ)
teaspoon	kapit	כַּפִּית (נ)
soup spoon	kaf	כַּף (נ)
fork	mazleg	מַזלֵג (ז)
knife	sakin	סַכִּין (ז, נ)

tableware (dishes)	kelim	כֵּלִים (ז"ר)
plate (dinner ~)	tsa'laχat	צַלַחַת (נ)
saucer	taχtit	תַחתִית (נ)

shot glass	kosit	כּוֹסִית (נ)
glass (tumbler)	kos	כּוֹס (נ)
cup	'sefel	סֵפֶל (ז)

sugar bowl	mis'keret	מִסכֶּרֶת (נ)
salt cellar	milχiya	מִלחִייָה (נ)
pepper pot	pilpeliya	פִּלפְּלִייָה (נ)
butter dish	maχame'a	מַחמָאָה (ז)

stock pot (soup pot)	sir	סִיר (ז)
frying pan (skillet)	maχvat	מַחבַת (נ)
ladle	tarvad	תַרוַד (ז)
colander	mis'nenet	מְסַנֶנֶת (נ)
tray (serving ~)	magaʃ	מַגָש (ז)

bottle	bakbuk	בַּקבּוּק (ז)
jar (glass)	tsin'tsenet	צִנצֶנֶת (נ)
tin (can)	paχit	פַּחִית (נ)

bottle opener	potχan bakbukim	פּוֹתחָן בַּקבּוּקִים (ז)
tin opener	potχan kufsa'ot	פּוֹתחָן קוּפסָאוֹת (ז)
corkscrew	maχlets	מַחלֵץ (ז)
filter	'filter	פִילטֶר (ז)
to filter (vt)	lesanen	לְסַנֵן

waste (food ~, etc.)	'zevel	זֶבֶל (ז)
waste bin (kitchen ~)	paχ 'zevel	פַּח זֶבֶל (ז)

92. Bathroom

bathroom	χadar am'batya	חֲדַר אַמבַּטיָה (ז)
water	'mayim	מַיִם (ז"ר)
tap	'berez	בֶּרֶז (ז)
hot water	'mayim χamim	מַיִם חָמִים (ז"ר)
cold water	'mayim karim	מַיִם קָרִים (ז"ר)

toothpaste	miʃxat ʃi'nayim	מִשְׁחַת שִׁינַיִים (נ)
to clean one's teeth	leʦaxˈʦeax ʃi'nayim	לְצַחְצֵחַ שִׁינַיִים
toothbrush	miv'reʃet ʃi'nayim	מִבְרֶשֶׁת שִׁינַיִים (נ)

to shave (vi)	lehitga'leax	לְהִתְגַּלֵּחַ
shaving foam	'keʦef gi'luax	קֶצֶף גִּילּוּחַ (ז)
razor	'ta'ar	תַּעַר (ז)

to wash (one's hands, etc.)	liʃtof	לִשְׁטוֹף
to have a bath	lehitraxeʦ	לְהִתְרַחֵץ
shower	mik'laxat	מִקְלַחַת (נ)
to have a shower	lehitka'leax	לְהִתְקַלֵּחַ

bath	am'batya	אַמְבַּטְיָה (נ)
toilet (toilet bowl)	asla	אַסְלָה (נ)
sink (washbasin)	kiyor	כִּיּוֹר (ז)

| soap | sabon | סַבּוֹן (ז) |
| soap dish | saboniya | סַבּוֹנִיָּה (נ) |

sponge	sfog 'lifa	סְפוֹג לִיפָה (ז)
shampoo	ʃampu	שַׁמְפּוּ (ז)
towel	ma'gevet	מַגֶּבֶת (נ)
bathrobe	xaluk raxaʦa	חָלוּק רַחְצָה (ז)

laundry (laundering)	kvisa	כְּבִיסָה (נ)
washing machine	mexonat kvisa	מְכוֹנַת כְּבִיסָה (נ)
to do the laundry	lexabes	לְכַבֵּס
washing powder	avkat kvisa	אַבְקַת כְּבִיסָה (נ)

93. Household appliances

TV, telly	tele'vizya	טֵלֵוִויזְיָה (נ)
tape recorder	teip	טֵייפּ (ז)
video	maxʃir 'vide'o	מַכְשִׁיר וִידֵאוֹ (ז)
radio	'radyo	רָדִיוֹ (ז)
player (CD, MP3, etc.)	nagan	נַגָּן (ז)

video projector	makren	מַקְרֵן (ז)
home cinema	kol'no'a beiti	קוֹלְנוֹעַ בֵּיתִי (ז)
DVD player	nagan dividi	נַגָּן DVD (ז)
amplifier	magber	מַגְבֵּר (ז)
video game console	maxʃir plei'steiʃen	מַכְשִׁיר פְּלֵייסְטֵיישָׁן (ז)

video camera	maʦlemat 'vide'o	מַצְלֵמַת וִידֵאוֹ (נ)
camera (photo)	maʦlema	מַצְלֵמָה (נ)
digital camera	maʦlema digi'talit	מַצְלֵמָה דִיגִיטָלִית (נ)

vacuum cleaner	ʃo'ev avak	שׁוֹאֵב אָבָק (ז)
iron (e.g. steam ~)	magheʦ	מַגְהֵץ (ז)
ironing board	'kereʃ gihuʦ	קֶרֶשׁ גִיהוּץ (ז)

| telephone | 'telefon | טֶלֶפוֹן (ז) |
| mobile phone | 'telefon nayad | טֶלֶפוֹן נַיָּיד (ז) |

| typewriter | meχonat ktiva | מְכוֹנַת כְּתִיבָה (נ) |
| sewing machine | meχonat tfira | מְכוֹנַת תְּפִירָה (נ) |

microphone	mikrofon	מִיקְרוֹפוֹן (ז)
headphones	ozniyot	אוֹזְנִיוֹת (נ"ר)
remote control (TV)	ʃelet	שֶׁלֶט (ז)

CD, compact disc	taklitor	תַקְלִיטוֹר (ז)
cassette, tape	ka'letet	קַלֶטֶת (נ)
vinyl record	taklit	תַקְלִיט (ז)

94. Repairs. Renovation

renovations	ʃiputs	שִׁיפּוּץ (ז)
to renovate (vt)	leʃapets	לְשַׁפֵּץ
to repair, to fix (vt)	letaken	לְתַקֵן
to put in order	lesader	לְסַדֵר
to redo (do again)	la'asot meχadaʃ	לַעֲשׂוֹת מֵחָדָשׁ

paint	'tseva	צֶבַע (ז)
to paint (~ a wall)	lits'bo'a	לִצְבּוֹעַ
house painter	tsaba'i	צַבָּעִי (ז)
paintbrush	mikχol	מִכְחוֹל (ז)

| whitewash | sid | סִיד (ז) |
| to whitewash (vt) | lesayed | לְסַיֵּיד |

wallpaper	tapet	טַפֶּט (ז)
to wallpaper (vt)	lehadbik ta'petim	לְהַדְבִּיק טַפֶּטִים
varnish	'laka	לַכָּה (נ)
to varnish (vt)	lim'roaχ 'laka	לִמְרוֹחַ לַכָּה

95. Plumbing

water	'mayim	מַיִם (ז"ר)
hot water	'mayim χamim	מַיִם חָמִים (ז"ר)
cold water	'mayim karim	מַיִם קָרִים (ז"ר)
tap	'berez	בֶּרֶז (ז)

drop (of water)	tipa	טִיפָּה (נ)
to drip (vi)	letaftef	לְטַפְטֵף
to leak (ab. pipe)	lidlof	לִדְלוֹף
leak (pipe ~)	dlifa	דְלִיפָה (נ)
puddle	ʃlulit	שְׁלוּלִית (נ)

pipe	tsinor	צִינוֹר (ז)
valve (e.g., ball ~)	'berez	בֶּרֶז (ז)
to be clogged up	lehisatem	לְהִיסָתֵם

tools	klei avoda	כְּלֵי עֲבוֹדָה (ז"ר)
adjustable spanner	maf'teaχ mitkavnen	מַפְתֵּחַ מִתְכַּוְונֵן (ז)
to unscrew (lid, filter, etc.)	lif'toaχ	לִפְתוֹחַ

to screw (tighten)	lehavrig	לְהַבְרִיג
to unclog (vt)	lif'toaχ et hastima	לִפְתּוֹחַ אֶת הַסְּתִימָה
plumber	ʃravrav	שְׁרַבְרָב (ז)
basement	martef	מַרְתֵּף (ז)
sewerage (system)	biyuv	בִּיּוּב (ז)

96. Fire. Conflagration

fire (accident)	srefa	שְׂרֵיפָה (נ)
flame	lehava	לֶהָבָה (נ)
spark	nitsots	נִיצוֹץ (ז)
smoke (from fire)	aʃan	עָשָׁן (ז)
torch (flaming stick)	lapid	לַפִּיד (ז)
campfire	medura	מְדוּרָה (נ)

petrol	'delek	דֶּלֶק (ז)
paraffin	kerosin	קֵרוֹסִין (ז)
flammable (adj)	dalik	דָּלִיק
explosive (adj)	nafits	נָפִיץ
NO SMOKING	asur le'aʃen!	אָסוּר לְעַשֵּׁן!

safety	betiχut	בְּטִיחוּת (נ)
danger	sakana	סַכָּנָה (נ)
dangerous (adj)	mesukan	מְסוּכָּן

to catch fire	lehidalek	לְהִידָלֵק
explosion	pitsuts	פִּיצוּץ (ז)
to set fire	lehatsit	לְהַצִּית
arsonist	matsit	מַצִּית (ז)
arson	hatsata	הַצָּתָה (נ)

to blaze (vi)	liv'or	לִבְעוֹר
to burn (be on fire)	la'alot be'eʃ	לַעֲלוֹת בָּאֵשׁ
to burn down	lehisaref	לְהִישָׂרֵף

to call the fire brigade	lehazmin meχabei eʃ	לְהַזְמִין מְכַבֵּי אֵשׁ
firefighter, fireman	kabai	כַּבַּאי (ז)
fire engine	'reχev kibui	רֶכֶב כִּיבּוּי (ז)
fire brigade	meχabei eʃ	מְכַבֵּי אֵשׁ (ז"ר)
fire engine ladder	sulam kaba'im	סוּלָם כַּבָּאִים (ז)

fire hose	zarnuk	זַרְנוּק (ז)
fire extinguisher	mataf	מַטָּף (ז)
helmet	kasda	קַסְדָּה (נ)
siren	tsofar	צוֹפָר (ז)

to cry (for help)	lits'ok	לִצְעוֹק
to call for help	likro le'ezra	לִקְרוֹא לְעֶזְרָה
rescuer	matsil	מַצִּיל (ז)
to rescue (vt)	lehatsil	לְהַצִּיל

to arrive (vi)	leha'gi'a	לְהַגִּיעַ
to extinguish (vt)	leχabot	לְכַבּוֹת
water	'mayim	מַיִם (ז"ר)

sand	χol	חוֹל (ז)
ruins (destruction)	χoravot	חוֹרְבוֹת (נ"ר)
to collapse (building, etc.)	likros	לִקְרוֹס
to fall down (vi)	likros	לִקְרוֹס
to cave in (ceiling, floor)	lehitmotet	לְהִתְמוֹטֵט

| piece of debris | pisat χoravot | פִּיסַת חוֹרְבוֹת (נ) |
| ash | 'efer | אֵפֶר (ז) |

| to suffocate (die) | lehiχanek | לְהֵיחָנֵק |
| to be killed (perish) | lehihareg | לְהֵיהָרֵג |

HUMAN ACTIVITIES

Job. Business. Part 1

97. Banking

bank	bank	בַּנק (ז)
branch (of a bank)	snif	סנִיף (ז)
consultant	yo'ets	יוֹעֵץ (ז)
manager (director)	menahel	מְנַהֵל (ז)
bank account	χeʃbon	חֶשבּוֹן (ז)
account number	mispar χeʃbon	מִספַּר חֶשבּוֹן (ז)
current account	χeʃbon over vaʃav	חֶשבּוֹן עוֹבֵר וָשָב (ז)
deposit account	χeʃbon χisaχon	חֶשבּוֹן חִסָכוֹן (ז)
to open an account	lif'toaχ χeʃbon	לִפתוֹחַ חֶשבּוֹן
to close the account	lisgor χeʃbon	לִסגוֹר חֶשבּוֹן
to deposit into the account	lehafkid leχeʃbon	לְהַפקִיד לְחֶשבּוֹן
to withdraw (vt)	limʃoχ meχeʃbon	לִמשוֹך מֵחֶשבּוֹן
deposit	pikadon	פִּיקָדוֹן (ז)
to make a deposit	lehafkid	לְהַפקִיד
wire transfer	ha'avara banka'it	הַעֲבָרָה בַּנקָאִית (נ)
to wire, to transfer	leha'avir 'kesef	לְהַעֲבִיר כֶּסֶף
sum	sχum	סכום (ז)
How much?	'kama?	כַּמָה?
signature	χatima	חַתִימָה (נ)
to sign (vt)	laχtom	לַחתוֹם
credit card	kartis aʃrai	כַּרטִיס אַשרַאי (ז)
code (PIN code)	kod	קוֹד (ז)
credit card number	mispar kartis aʃrai	מִספַּר כַּרטִיס אַשרַאי (ז)
cashpoint	kaspomat	כַּספּוֹמָט (ז)
cheque	tʃek	צֶ'ק (ז)
to write a cheque	liχtov tʃek	לִכתוֹב צֶ'ק
chequebook	pinkas 'tʃekim	פִּנקָס צֶ'קִים (ז)
loan (bank ~)	halva'a	הַלוָואָה (נ)
to apply for a loan	levakeʃ halva'a	לְבַקֵש הַלוָואָה
to get a loan	lekabel halva'a	לְקַבֵּל הַלוָואָה
to give a loan	lehalvot	לְהַלווֹת
guarantee	arvut	עַרבוּת (נ)

98. Telephone. Phone conversation

telephone	'telefon	טֶלֶפוֹן (ז)
mobile phone	'telefon nayad	טֶלֶפוֹן נַיָּד (ז)
answerphone	meʃivon	מְשִׁיבוֹן (ז)
to call (by phone)	letsaltsel	לְצַלְצֵל
call, ring	siχat 'telefon	שִׂיחַת טֶלֶפוֹן (נ)
to dial a number	leχayeg mispar	לְחַיֵּג מִסְפָּר
Hello!	'halo!	הֶלוֹ!
to ask (vt)	liʃol	לִשְׁאוֹל
to answer (vi, vt)	la'anot	לַעֲנוֹת
to hear (vt)	liʃ'mo'a	לִשְׁמוֹעַ
well (adv)	tov	טוֹב
not well (adv)	lo tov	לֹא טוֹב
noises (interference)	hafra'ot	הַפְרָעוֹת (נ״ר)
receiver	ʃfo'feret	שְׁפוֹפֶרֶת (נ)
to pick up (~ the phone)	leharim ʃfo'feret	לְהָרִים שְׁפוֹפֶרֶת
to hang up (~ the phone)	leha'niaχ ʃfo'feret	לְהָנִיחַ שְׁפוֹפֶרֶת
busy (engaged)	tafus	תָּפוּס
to ring (ab. phone)	letsaltsel	לְצַלְצֵל
telephone book	'sefer tele'fonim	סֵפֶר טֶלֶפוֹנִים (ז)
local (adj)	mekomi	מְקוֹמִי
local call	siχa mekomit	שִׂיחָה מְקוֹמִית (נ)
trunk (e.g. ~ call)	bein ironi	בֵּין עִירוֹנִי
trunk call	siχa bein ironit	שִׂיחָה בֵּין עִירוֹנִית (נ)
international (adj)	benle'umi	בֵּינְלְאוּמִי
international call	siχa benle'umit	שִׂיחָה בֵּינְלְאוּמִית (נ)

99. Mobile telephone

mobile phone	'telefon nayad	טֶלֶפוֹן נַיָּד (ז)
display	masaχ	מָסָךְ (ז)
button	kaftor	כַּפְתּוֹר (ז)
SIM card	kartis sim	כַּרְטִיס סִים (ז)
battery	solela	סוֹלְלָה (נ)
to be flat (battery)	lehitroken	לְהִתְרוֹקֵן
charger	mit'an	מִטְעָן (ז)
menu	tafrit	תַּפְרִיט (ז)
settings	hagdarot	הַגְדָּרוֹת (נ״ר)
tune (melody)	mangina	מַנְגִּינָה (נ)
to select (vt)	livχor	לִבְחוֹר
calculator	maχʃevon	מַחְשְׁבוֹן (ז)
voice mail	ta koli	תָּא קוֹלִי (ז)
alarm clock	ʃa'on me'orer	שָׁעוֹן מְעוֹרֵר (ז)

contacts	anʃei 'keʃer	אַנְשֵׁי קֶשֶׁר (ז"ר)
SMS (text message)	misron	מִסְרוֹן (ז)
subscriber	manui	מָנוּי (ז)

100. Stationery

ballpoint pen	et kaduri	עֵט כַּדּוּרִי (ז)
fountain pen	et no've'a	עֵט נוֹבֵעַ (ז)
pencil	iparon	עִיפָּרוֹן (ז)
highlighter	'marker	מַרְקֵר (ז)
felt-tip pen	tuʃ	טוּשׁ (ז)
notepad	pinkas	פִּנְקָס (ז)
diary	yoman	יוֹמָן (ז)
ruler	sargel	סַרְגֵּל (ז)
calculator	maxʃevon	מַחְשְׁבוֹן (ז)
rubber	'maxak	מַחַק (ז)
drawing pin	'na'ats	נַעַץ (ז)
paper clip	mehadek	מְהַדֵּק (ז)
glue	'devek	דֶּבֶק (ז)
stapler	ʃadxan	שַׁדְכָן (ז)
hole punch	menakev	מְנַקֵּב (ז)
pencil sharpener	maxded	מַחְדֵּד (ז)

Job. Business. Part 2

101. Mass Media

newspaper	iton	עִיתוֹן (ז)
magazine	ʒurnal	ז'וּרנָל (ז)
press (printed media)	itonut	עִיתוֹנוּת (נ)
radio	'radyo	רַדְיוֹ (ז)
radio station	taχanat 'radyo	תַחֲנַת רַדְיוֹ (נ)
television	tele'vizya	טֶלֶוְוִיזְיָה (נ)
presenter, host	manχe	מַנְחֶה (ז)
newsreader	karyan	קַרְיָין (ז)
commentator	parʃan	פַּרְשָׁן (ז)
journalist	itonai	עִיתוֹנַאי (ז)
correspondent (reporter)	katav	כַּתָּב (ז)
press photographer	tsalam itonut	צַלָם עִיתוֹנוּת (ז)
reporter	katav	כַּתָּב (ז)
editor	oreχ	עוֹרֵךְ (ז)
editor-in-chief	oreχ raʃi	עוֹרֵךְ רָאשִׁי (ז)
to subscribe (to …)	lehasdir manui	לְהַסְדִיר מָנוּי
subscription	minui	מִנוּי (ז)
subscriber	manui	מָנוּי (ז)
to read (vi, vt)	likro	לִקְרוֹא
reader	kore	קוֹרֵא (ז)
circulation (of a newspaper)	tfutsa	תְפוּצָה (נ)
monthly (adj)	χodʃi	חוֹדְשִׁי
weekly (adj)	ʃvu'i	שְׁבוּעִי
issue (edition)	gilayon	גִילְיוֹן (ז)
new (~ issue)	tari	טָרִי
headline	ko'teret	כּוֹתֶרֶת (נ)
short article	katava ktsara	כַּתָּבָה קְצָרָה (נ)
column (regular article)	tur	טוּר (ז)
article	ma'amar	מַאֲמָר (ז)
page	amud	עָמוּד (ז)
reportage, report	katava	כַּתָּבָה (נ)
event (happening)	ei'ru'a	אֵירוּעַ (ז)
sensation (news)	sen'satsya	סֶנְסַצְיָה (נ)
scandal	ʃa'aruriya	שַׁעֲרוּרִיָה (נ)
scandalous (adj)	meviʃ	מֵבִישׁ
great (~ scandal)	gadol	גָדוֹל
programme (e.g. cooking ~)	toχnit	תוֹכְנִית (נ)
interview	ra'ayon	רַאֲיוֹן (ז)

| live broadcast | ʃidur χai | שִׁידוּר חַי (ז) |
| channel | aruts | עָרוּץ (ז) |

102. Agriculture

agriculture	χakla'ut	חַקְלָאוּת (נ)
peasant (masc.)	ikar	אִיכָּר (ז)
peasant (fem.)	χakla'ut	חַקְלָאִית (נ)
farmer	χavai	חַוַּאי (ז)

| tractor | 'traktor | טְרַקְטוֹר (ז) |
| combine, harvester | kombain | קוֹמְבַּיְין (ז) |

plough	maχreʃa	מַחְרֵשָׁה (נ)
to plough (vi, vt)	laχaroʃ	לַחֲרוֹשׁ
ploughland	sade χaruʃ	שָׂדֶה חָרוּשׁ (ז)
furrow (in field)	'telem	תֶּלֶם (ז)

to sow (vi, vt)	liz'ro'a	לִזְרוֹעַ
seeder	mazre'a	מַזְרֵעָה (ז)
sowing (process)	zri'a	זְרִיעָה (נ)

| scythe | χermeʃ | חֶרְמֵשׁ (ז) |
| to mow, to scythe | liktsor | לִקְצוֹר |

| spade (tool) | et | אֵת (ז) |
| to till (vt) | leta'teaχ | לְתַחֵחַ |

hoe	ma'ader	מַעְדֵּר (ז)
to hoe, to weed	lenakeʃ	לְנַכֵּשׁ
weed (plant)	'esev ʃote	עֵשֶׂב שׁוֹטֶה (ז)

watering can	maʃpeχ	מַשְׁפֵּךְ (ז)
to water (plants)	lehaʃkot	לְהַשְׁקוֹת
watering (act)	haʃkaya	הַשְׁקָיָה (נ)

| pitchfork | kilʃon | קִלְשׁוֹן (ז) |
| rake | magrefa | מַגְרֵפָה (נ) |

fertiliser	'deʃen	דֶשֶׁן (ז)
to fertilise (vt)	ledaʃen	לְדַשֵׁן
manure (fertiliser)	'zevel	זֶבֶל (ז)

field	sade	שָׂדֶה (ז)
meadow	aχu	אָחוּ (ז)
vegetable garden	gan yarak	גַּן יָרָק (ז)
orchard (e.g. apple ~)	bustan	בּוּסְתָּן (ז)

to graze (vt)	lir'ot	לִרְעוֹת
herdsman	ro'e tson	רוֹעֶה צֹאן (ז)
pasture	mir'e	מִרְעֶה (ז)

| cattle breeding | gidul bakar | גִּידּוּל בָּקָר (ז) |
| sheep farming | gidul kvasim | גִּידּוּל כְּבָשִׂים (ז) |

plantation	mata	מַטָּע (ז)
row (garden bed ~s)	aruga	עֲרוּגָה (נ)
hothouse	xamama	חֲמָמָה (נ)

| drought (lack of rain) | ba'tsoret | בַּצּוֹרֶת (נ) |
| dry (~ summer) | yavef | יָבֵשׁ |

grain	tvu'a	תְּבוּאָה (נ)
cereal crops	gidulei dagan	גִּידוּלֵי דָּגָן (ז"ר)
to harvest, to gather	liktof	לִקְטוֹף

miller (person)	toxen	טוֹחֵן (ז)
mill (e.g. gristmill)	taxanat 'kemax	טַחֲנַת קֶמַח (נ)
to grind (grain)	litxon	לִטְחוֹן
flour	'kemax	קֶמַח (ז)
straw	kaf	קַשׁ (ז)

103. Building. Building process

building site	atar bniya	אֲתַר בְּנִיָּה (ז)
to build (vt)	livnot	לִבְנוֹת
building worker	banai	בַּנַּאי (ז)

project	proyekt	פְּרוֹיֶיקְט (ז)
architect	adrixal	אַדְרִיכָל (ז)
worker	po'el	פּוֹעֵל (ז)

foundations (of a building)	yesodot	יְסוֹדוֹת (ז"ר)
roof	gag	גַּג (ז)
foundation pile	amud yesod	עַמּוּד יְסוֹד (ז)
wall	kir	קִיר (ז)

| reinforcing bars | mot xizuk | מוֹט חִיזּוּק (ז) |
| scaffolding | pigumim | פִּיגוּמִים (ז"ר) |

concrete	beton	בֶּטוֹן (ז)
granite	granit	גְּרָנִיט (ז)
stone	'even	אֶבֶן (נ)
brick	levena	לְבֵנָה (נ)

sand	xol	חוֹל (ז)
cement	'melet	מֶלֶט (ז)
plaster (for walls)	'tiax	טִיחַ (ז)
to plaster (vt)	leta'yeax	לְטַיֵּיחַ
paint	'tseva	צֶבַע (ז)
to paint (~ a wall)	lits'bo'a	לִצְבּוֹעַ
barrel	xavit	חָבִית (נ)

crane	aguran	עֲגוּרָן (ז)
to lift, to hoist (vt)	lehanif	לְהָנִיף
to lower (vt)	lehorid	לְהוֹרִיד

| bulldozer | daxpor | דַּחְפּוֹר (ז) |
| excavator | maxper | מַחְפֵּר (ז) |

scoop, bucket	ʃa'ov	שָׁאוֹב (ז)
to dig (excavate)	laχpor	לַחְפּוֹר
hard hat	kasda	קַסְדָה (נ)

Professions and occupations

job	avoda	עֲבוֹדָה (נ)
staff (work force)	'segel	סֶגֶל (ז)
personnel	'segel	סֶגֶל (ז)
career	kar'yera	קָרְיֶירָה (נ)
prospects (chances)	efʃaruyot	אֶפְשָׁרֻיּוֹת (נ"ר)
skills (mastery)	meyumanut	מְיֻמָּנוּת (נ)
selection (screening)	sinun	סִנּוּן (ז)
employment agency	soχnut 'koaχ adam	סוֹכְנוּת כֹּחַ אָדָם (נ)
curriculum vitae, CV	korot χayim	קוֹרוֹת חַיִּים (נ"ר)
job interview	ra'ayon avoda	רַאֲיוֹן עֲבוֹדָה (ז)
vacancy	misra pnuya	מִשְׂרָה פְּנוּיָה (נ)
salary, pay	mas'koret	מַשְׂכֹּרֶת (נ)
fixed salary	mas'koret kvu'a	מַשְׂכֹּרֶת קְבוּעָה (נ)
pay, compensation	taʃlum	תַּשְׁלוּם (ז)
position (job)	tafkid	תַּפְקִיד (ז)
duty (of an employee)	χova	חוֹבָה (נ)
range of duties	tχum aχrayut	תְּחוּם אַחְרָיוּת (ז)
busy (I'm ~)	asuk	עָסוּק
to fire (dismiss)	lefater	לְפַטֵּר
dismissal	pitur	פִּטּוּר (ז)
unemployment	avtala	אַבְטָלָה (נ)
unemployed (n)	muvtal	מוּבְטָל (ז)
retirement	'pensya	פֶּנְסְיָה (נ)
to retire (from job)	latset legimla'ot	לָצֵאת לְגִימְלָאוֹת

director	menahel	מְנַהֵל (ז)
manager (director)	menahel	מְנַהֵל (ז)
boss	bos	בּוֹס (ז)
superior	memune	מְמוּנֶּה (ז)
superiors	memunim	מְמוּנִּים (ז"ר)
president	nasi	נָשִׂיא (ז)
chairman	yoʃev roʃ	יוֹשֵׁב רֹאשׁ (ז)
deputy (substitute)	sgan	סְגָן (ז)
assistant	ozer	עוֹזֵר (ז)

| secretary | mazkir | מַזְכִּיר (ז) |
| personal assistant | mazkir iʃi | מַזְכִּיר אִישִׁי (ז) |

businessman	iʃ asakim	אִישׁ עֲסָקִים (ז)
entrepreneur	yazam	יָזָם (ז)
founder	meyased	מְיַיסֵד (ז)
to found (vt)	leyased	לְיַיסֵד

founding member	meχonen	מְכוֹנֵן (ז)
partner	ʃutaf	שׁוּתָף (ז)
shareholder	'ba'al menayot	בַּעַל מְנָיוֹת (ז)

millionaire	milyoner	מִילְיוֹנֵר (ז)
billionaire	milyarder	מִילְיַארְדֶּר (ז)
owner, proprietor	be'alim	בְּעָלִים (ז)
landowner	'ba'al adamot	בַּעַל אֲדָמוֹת (ז)

client	la'koaχ	לָקוֹחַ (ז)
regular client	la'koaχ ka'vu'a	לָקוֹחַ קָבוּעַ (ז)
buyer (customer)	kone	קוֹנֶה (ז)
visitor	mevaker	מְבַקֵּר (ז)

professional (n)	miktso'an	מִקְצוֹעָן (ז)
expert	mumχe	מוּמְחֶה (ז)
specialist	mumχe	מוּמְחֶה (ז)

| banker | bankai | בַּנְקַאי (ז) |
| broker | soχen | סוֹכֵן (ז) |

cashier	kupai	קוּפַּאי (ז)
accountant	menahel χeʃbonot	מְנַהֵל חֶשְׁבּוֹנוֹת (ז)
security guard	ʃomer	שׁוֹמֵר (ז)

investor	maʃki'a	מַשְׁקִיעַ (ז)
debtor	'ba'al χov	בַּעַל חוֹב (ז)
creditor	malve	מַלְוֶה (ז)
borrower	love	לוֹוֶה (ז)

| importer | yevu'an | יְבוּאָן (ז) |
| exporter | yetsu'an | יְצוּאָן (ז) |

manufacturer	yatsran	יַצְרָן (ז)
distributor	mefits	מֵפִיץ (ז)
middleman	metaveχ	מְתַוֵּוךְ (ז)

consultant	yo'ets	יוֹעֵץ (ז)
sales representative	natsig meχirot	נָצִיג מְכִירוֹת (ז)
agent	soχen	סוֹכֵן (ז)
insurance agent	soχen bi'tuaχ	סוֹכֵן בִּיטוּחַ (ז)

106. Service professions

| cook | tabaχ | טַבָּח (ז) |
| chef (kitchen chef) | ʃef | שֶׁף (ז) |

baker	ofe	אוֹפֶה (ז)
barman	'barmen	בַּרְמָן (ז)
waiter	meltsar	מֶלְצָר (ז)
waitress	meltsarit	מֶלְצָרִית (נ)
lawyer, barrister	orex din	עוֹרֵך דִין (ז)
lawyer (legal expert)	orex din	עוֹרֵך דִין (ז)
notary public	notaryon	נוֹטַרְיוֹן (ז)
electrician	xaʃmalai	חַשְׁמַלַאי (ז)
plumber	ʃravrav	שְׁרַבְרָב (ז)
carpenter	nagar	נַגָר (ז)
masseur	ma'ase	מְעַסֶה (ז)
masseuse	masa'ʒistit	מַסָז'יסְטִית (נ)
doctor	rofe	רוֹפֵא (ז)
taxi driver	nahag monit	נֶהַג מוֹנִית (ז)
driver	nahag	נֶהַג (ז)
delivery man	ʃa'liax	שָׁלִיחַ (ז)
chambermaid	xadranit	חַדְרָנִית (נ)
security guard	ʃomer	שׁוֹמֵר (ז)
flight attendant (fem.)	da'yelet	דַיֶילֶת (נ)
schoolteacher	more	מוֹרֶה (ז)
librarian	safran	סַפְרָן (ז)
translator	metargem	מְתַרְגֵם (ז)
interpreter	meturgeman	מְתוּרְגְמָן (ז)
guide	madrix tiyulim	מַדְרִיך טִיוּלִים (ז)
hairdresser	sapar	סַפָּר (ז)
postman	davar	דַוָור (ז)
salesman (store staff)	moxer	מוֹכֵר (ז)
gardener	ganan	גַנָן (ז)
domestic servant	meʃaret	מְשָׁרֵת (ז)
maid (female servant)	meʃa'retet	מְשָׁרֶתֶת (נ)
cleaner (cleaning lady)	menaka	מְנַקָה (נ)

107. Military professions and ranks

private	turai	טוּרַאי (ז)
sergeant	samal	סַמָל (ז)
lieutenant	'segen	סֶגֶן (ז)
captain	'seren	סֶרֶן (ז)
major	rav 'seren	רַב-סֶרֶן (ז)
colonel	aluf miʃne	אַלוּף מִשְׁנֶה (ז)
general	aluf	אַלוּף (ז)
marshal	'marʃal	מַרְשָׁל (ז)
admiral	admiral	אַדְמִירָל (ז)
military (n)	iʃ tsava	אִישׁ צָבָא (ז)
soldier	xayal	חַיָיל (ז)

officer	katsin	קָצִין (ז)
commander	mefaked	מְפַקֵד (ז)
border guard	ʃomer gvul	שׁוֹמֵר גְבוּל (ז)
radio operator	alχutai	אַלחוּטַאי (ז)
scout (searcher)	iʃ modi'in kravi	אִיש מוֹדִיעִין קְרָבִי (ז)
pioneer (sapper)	χablan	חַבְּלָן (ז)
marksman	tsalaf	צַלָף (ז)
navigator	navat	נַוָוט (ז)

108. Officials. Priests

king	'meleχ	מֶלֶךְ (ז)
queen	malka	מַלכָּה (נ)
prince	nasiχ	נָסִיך (ז)
princess	nesiχa	נְסִיכָה (נ)
czar	tsar	צָאר (ז)
czarina	tsa'rina	צָארִינָה (נ)
president	nasi	נָשִׂיא (ז)
Secretary (minister)	sar	שַׂר (ז)
prime minister	roʃ memʃala	רֹאש מֶמשָׁלָה (ז)
senator	se'nator	סֶנָאטוֹר (ז)
diplomat	diplomat	דִיפּלוֹמָט (ז)
consul	'konsul	קוֹנסוּל (ז)
ambassador	ʃagrir	שַׁגרִיר (ז)
counselor (diplomatic officer)	yo'ets	יוֹעֵץ (ז)
official, functionary (civil servant)	pakid	פָּקִיד (ז)
prefect	prefekt	פּרֶפֶקט (ז)
mayor	roʃ ha'ir	רֹאש הָעִיר (ז)
judge	ʃofet	שׁוֹפֵט (ז)
prosecutor	to've'a	תוֹבֵעַ (ז)
missionary	misyoner	מִיסיוֹנֶר (ז)
monk	nazir	נָזִיר (ז)
abbot	roʃ minzar ka'toli	רֹאש מִנזָר קָתוֹלִי (ז)
rabbi	rav	רַב (ז)
vizier	vazir	וָזִיר (ז)
shah	ʃaχ	שָׁאח (ז)
sheikh	ʃeiχ	שֵׁיח (ז)

109. Agricultural professions

| beekeeper | kavran | כַּווְרָן (ז) |
| shepherd | ro'e tson | רוֹעֶה צֹאן (ז) |

agronomist	agronom	אַגרוֹנוֹם (ז)
cattle breeder	megadel bakar	מְגַדֵל בָּקָר (ז)
veterinary surgeon	veterinar	וֶטֶרִינָר (ז)

farmer	χavai	חַוָאי (ז)
winemaker	yeinan	יֵינָן (ז)
zoologist	zo'olog	זוֹאוֹלוֹג (ז)
cowboy	'ka'uboi	קָאוּבּוֹי (ז)

110. Art professions

actor	saχkan	שַׂחקָן (ז)
actress	saχkanit	שַׂחקָנִית (נ)

singer (masc.)	zamar	זַמָר (ז)
singer (fem.)	za'meret	זַמֶרֶת (נ)

dancer (masc.)	rakdan	רַקדָן (ז)
dancer (fem.)	rakdanit	רַקדָנִית (נ)

performer (masc.)	saχkan	שַׂחקָן (ז)
performer (fem.)	saχkanit	שַׂחקָנִית (נ)

musician	muzikai	מוּזִיקָאי (ז)
pianist	psantran	פְּסַנתְרָן (ז)
guitar player	nagan gi'tara	נַגָן גִיטָרָה (ז)

conductor (orchestra ~)	mena'tseaχ	מְנַצֵחַ (ז)
composer	malχin	מַלחִין (ז)
impresario	amargan	אָמַרגָן (ז)

film director	bamai	בַּמַאי (ז)
producer	mefik	מֵפִיק (ז)
scriptwriter	tasritai	תַסרִיטַאי (ז)
critic	mevaker	מְבַקֵר (ז)

writer	sofer	סוֹפֵר (ז)
poet	meforer	מְשׁוֹרֵר (ז)
sculptor	pasal	פַּסָל (ז)
artist (painter)	tsayar	צַייָר (ז)

juggler	lahatutan	לַהֲטוּטָן (ז)
clown	leitsan	לֵיצָן (ז)
acrobat	akrobat	אַקרוֹבָּט (ז)
magician	kosem	קוֹסֵם (ז)

111. Various professions

doctor	rofe	רוֹפֵא (ז)
nurse	aχot	אָחוֹת (נ)
psychiatrist	psiχi''ater	פְּסִיכִיאָטֵר (ז)
dentist	rofe fi'nayim	רוֹפֵא שִׁינַיִים (ז)

surgeon	kirurg	כִּירוּרְג (ז)
astronaut	astro'na'ut	אַסטרוֹנָאוּט (ז)
astronomer	astronom	אַסטרוֹנוֹם (ז)
pilot	tayas	טַיָּס (ז)

driver (of a taxi, etc.)	nahag	נַהָג (ז)
train driver	nahag ra'kevet	נַהָג רַכֶּבֶת (ז)
mechanic	meχonai	מְכוֹנַאי (ז)

miner	kore	כּוֹרֶה (ז)
worker	po'el	פּוֹעֵל (ז)
locksmith	misgad	מַסגֵד (ז)
joiner (carpenter)	nagar	נַגָר (ז)
turner (lathe operator)	χarat	חָרָט (ז)
building worker	banai	בַּנַאי (ז)
welder	rataχ	רַתָּך (ז)

professor (title)	pro'fesor	פְּרוֹפֶסוֹר (ז)
architect	adriχal	אַדרִיכָל (ז)
historian	historyon	הִיסטוֹריוֹן (ז)
scientist	mad'an	מַדעָן (ז)
physicist	fizikai	פִיזִיקַאי (ז)
chemist (scientist)	χimai	כִימַאי (ז)

archaeologist	arχe'olog	אַרכֵיאוֹלוֹג (ז)
geologist	ge'olog	גֵיאוֹלוֹג (ז)
researcher (scientist)	χoker	חוֹקֵר (ז)

| babysitter | ʃmartaf | שׁמַרטַף (ז) |
| teacher, educator | more, meχaneχ | מוֹרֶה, מְחַנֵך (ז) |

editor	oreχ	עוֹרֵך (ז)
editor-in-chief	oreχ raʃi	עוֹרֵך רָאשִׁי (ז)
correspondent	katav	כַּתָב (ז)
typist (fem.)	kaldanit	קַלדָנִית (נ)

designer	me'atsev	מְעַצֵב (ז)
computer expert	mumχe maχʃevim	מוּמחֶה מַחשְׁבִים (ז)
programmer	metaχnet	מְתַכנֵת (ז)
engineer (designer)	mehandes	מְהַנדֵס (ז)

sailor	yamai	יַמַאי (ז)
seaman	malaχ	מַלָח (ז)
rescuer	matsil	מַצִיל (ז)

firefighter	kabai	כַּבַּאי (ז)
police officer	ʃoter	שׁוֹטֵר (ז)
watchman	ʃomer	שׁוֹמֵר (ז)
detective	balaʃ	בַּלָשׁ (ז)

customs officer	pakid 'meχes	פָּקִיד מֶכֶס (ז)
bodyguard	ʃomer roʃ	שׁוֹמֵר רֹאשׁ (ז)
prison officer	soher	סוֹהֵר (ז)
inspector	mefa'keaχ	מְפַקֵחַ (ז)
sportsman	sportai	ספוֹרטַאי (ז)
trainer, coach	me'amen	מְאַמֵן (ז)

butcher	katsav	קַצָּב (ז)
cobbler (shoe repairer)	sandlar	סַנְדְלָר (ז)
merchant	soχer	סוֹחֵר (ז)
loader (person)	sabal	סַבָּל (ז)

| fashion designer | me'atsev ofna | מְעַצֵּב אוֹפְנָה (ז) |
| model (fem.) | dugmanit | דוּגְמָנִית (נ) |

112. Occupations. Social status

| schoolboy | talmid | תַּלְמִיד (ז) |
| student (college ~) | student | סְטוּדֶנְט (ז) |

philosopher	filosof	פִּילוֹסוֹף (ז)
economist	kalkelan	כַּלְכְּלָן (ז)
inventor	mamtsi	מַמְצִיא (ז)

unemployed (n)	muvtal	מוּבְטָל (ז)
retiree, pensioner	pensyoner	פֶּנְסְיוֹנֶר (ז)
spy, secret agent	meragel	מְרַגֵּל (ז)

prisoner	asir	אָסִיר (ז)
striker	ʃovet	שׁוֹבֵת (ז)
bureaucrat	birokrat	בִּירוֹקְרָט (ז)
traveller (globetrotter)	metayel	מְטַיֵּל (ז)

gay, homosexual (n)	'lesbit, 'homo	לֶסְבִּית (נ), הוֹמוֹ (ז)
hacker	'haker	הָאקֶר (ז)
hippie	'hipi	הִיפִּי (ז)

bandit	ʃoded	שׁוֹדֵד (ז)
hit man, killer	ro'tseaχ saχir	רוֹצֵחַ שָׂכִיר (ז)
drug addict	narkoman	נַרְקוֹמָן (ז)
drug dealer	soχer samim	סוֹחֵר סַמִּים (ז)
prostitute (fem.)	zona	זוֹנָה (נ)
pimp	sarsur	סַרְסוּר (ז)

sorcerer	meχaʃef	מְכַשֵּׁף (ז)
sorceress (evil ~)	maχʃefa	מְכַשֵּׁפָה (נ)
pirate	ʃoded yam	שׁוֹדֵד יָם (ז)
slave	ʃifχa, 'eved	שִׁפְחָה (נ), עֶבֶד (ז)
samurai	samurai	סָמוּרַאי (ז)
savage (primitive)	'pere adam	פֶּרֶא אָדָם (ז)

Sports

sportsman	sportai	ספּוֹרְטָאי (ז)
kind of sport	anaf sport	עֲנַף ספּוֹרְט (ז)
basketball	kadursal	כַּדּוּרְסַל (ז)
basketball player	kadursalan	כַּדּוּרְסַלָן (ז)
baseball	'beisbol	בֵּייסְבּוֹל (ז)
baseball player	saχkan 'beisbol	שַׂחְקָן בֵּייסְבּוֹל (ז)
football	kadu'regel	כַּדּוּרֶגֶל (ז)
football player	kaduraglan	כַּדּוּרַגְלָן (ז)
goalkeeper	ʃo'er	שׁוֹעֵר (ז)
ice hockey	'hoki	הוֹקִי (ז)
ice hockey player	saχkan 'hoki	שַׂחְקָן הוֹקִי (ז)
volleyball	kadur'af	כַּדּוּרְעָף (ז)
volleyball player	saχkan kadur'af	שַׂחְקָן כַּדּוּרְעָף (ז)
boxing	igruf	אִיגְרוּף (ז)
boxer	mit'agref	מִתְאַגְרֵף (ז)
wrestling	heʼavkut	הֵיאָבְקוּת (נ)
wrestler	mitʼabek	מִתְאַבֵּק (ז)
karate	karate	קָרָטֶה (ז)
karate fighter	karatist	קָרָטִיסְט (ז)
judo	'dʒudo	ג'וּדוֹ (ז)
judo athlete	dʒudai	ג'וּדָאי (ז)
tennis	'tenis	טֶנִיס (ז)
tennis player	tenisai	טֶנִיסָאי (ז)
swimming	sχiya	שְׂחִייָה (נ)
swimmer	saχyan	שַׂחְיָין (ז)
fencing	'sayif	סַיִף (ז)
fencer	sayaf	סַיָּיף (ז)
chess	ʃaχmat	שַׁחְמָט (ז)
chess player	ʃaχmetai	שַׁחְמְטַאי (ז)
alpinism	tipus harim	טִיפּוּס הָרִים (ז)
alpinist	metapes harim	מְטַפֵּס הָרִים (ז)
running	ritsa	רִיצָה (נ)

runner	atsan	אָצָן (ז)
athletics	at'letika kala	אַתְלֶטִיקָה קַלָה (נ)
athlete	atlet	אַתְלֶט (ז)

| horse riding | reχiva al sus | רְכִיבָה עַל סוּס (נ) |
| horse rider | paraʃ | פָּרָשׁ (ז) |

figure skating	haχlaka omanutit	הַחְלָקָה אוֹמָנוּתִית (נ)
figure skater (masc.)	maχlik amanuti	מַחְלִיק אָמָנוּתִי (ז)
figure skater (fem.)	maχlika amanutit	מַחְלִיקָה אָמָנוּתִית (נ)

| powerlifting | haramat miʃkolot | הֲרָמַת מִשְׁקוֹלוֹת (נ) |
| powerlifter | miʃkolan | מִשְׁקוֹלָן (ז) |

| car racing | merots meχoniyot | מֵירוֹץ מְכוֹנִיוֹת (ז) |
| racer (driver) | nahag merotsim | נַהַג מֵרוֹצִים (ז) |

| cycling | reχiva al ofa'nayim | רְכִיבָה עַל אוֹפַנַּיִים (נ) |
| cyclist | roχev ofa'nayim | רוֹכֵב אוֹפַנַּיִים (ז) |

long jump	kfitsa la'roχav	קְפִיצָה לָרוֹחַק (נ)
pole vaulting	kfitsa bemot	קְפִיצָה בְּמוֹט (נ)
jumper	kofets	קוֹפֵץ (ז)

114. Kinds of sports. Miscellaneous

American football	'futbol	פוּטְבּוֹל (ז)
badminton	notsit	נוֹצִית (נ)
biathlon	bi'atlon	בִּיאַתְלוֹן (ז)
billiards	bilyard	בִּילְיַארְד (ז)

bobsleigh	miz'χelet	מִזְחֶלֶת (נ)
bodybuilding	pi'tuaχ guf	פִּיתּוּחַ גוּף (ז)
water polo	polo 'mayim	פּוֹלוֹ מַיִם (ז)
handball	kadur yad	כַּדּוּר-יָד (ז)
golf	golf	גוֹלְף (ז)

rowing	χatira	חֲתִירָה (נ)
scuba diving	tslila	צְלִילָה (נ)
cross-country skiing	ski bemiʃor	סְקִי בַּמִּישׁוֹר (ז)
table tennis (ping-pong)	'tenis ʃulχan	טֶנִיס שׁוּלְחָן (ז)

sailing	'ʃayit	שַׁיִט (ז)
rally	'rali	רָאלִי (ז)
rugby	'rogbi	רוֹגְבִּי (ז)
snowboarding	gliʃat 'ʃeleg	גְלִישַׁת שֶׁלֶג (נ)
archery	kaʃatut	קַשָׁתוּת (נ)

115. Gym

| barbell | miʃ'kolet | מְשְׁקוֹלָת (נ) |
| dumbbells | miʃkolot | מְשְׁקוֹלוֹת (נ״ר) |

training machine	maxʃir 'koʃer	מַכְשִׁיר כּוֹשֶׁר (ז)
exercise bicycle	ofanei 'koʃer	אוֹפַנֵּי כּוֹשֶׁר (ז"ר)
treadmill	halixon	הֲלִיכוֹן (ז)

horizontal bar	'metax	מַתָח (ז)
parallel bars	makbilim	מַקְבִּילִים (ז"ר)
vault (vaulting horse)	sus	סוּס (ז)
mat (exercise ~)	mizron	מִזְרוֹן (ז)

skipping rope	dalgit	דַלְגִית (נ)
aerobics	ei'robika	אֵירוֹבִּיקָה (ז)
yoga	'yoga	יוֹגָה (נ)

116. Sports. Miscellaneous

Olympic Games	hamisxakim ha'o'limpiyim	הַמִּשְׂחָקִים הָאוֹלִימְפִּיִים (ז"ר)
winner	mena'tseax	מְנַצֵּחַ (ז)
to be winning	lena'tseax	לְנַצֵּחַ
to win (vi)	lena'tseax	לְנַצֵּחַ

| leader | manhig | מַנְהִיג (ז) |
| to lead (vi) | lehovil | לְהוֹבִיל |

first place	makom riʃon	מָקוֹם רִאשׁוֹן (ז)
second place	makom ʃeni	מָקוֹם שֵׁנִי (ז)
third place	makom ʃliʃi	מָקוֹם שְׁלִישִׁי (ז)

medal	me'dalya	מֶדַלְיָה (נ)
trophy	pras	פְּרָס (ז)
prize cup (trophy)	ga'vi'a nitsaxon	גָּבִיעַ נִיצָחוֹן (ז)
prize (in game)	pras	פְּרָס (ז)
main prize	pras riʃon	פְּרָס רִאשׁוֹן (ז)

| record | si | שִׂיא (ז) |
| to set a record | lik'bo'a si | לִקְבּוֹעַ שִׂיא |

| final | gmar | גְּמָר (ז) |
| final (adj) | ʃel hagmar | שֶׁל הַגְּמָר |

| champion | aluf | אַלּוּף (ז) |
| championship | alifut | אֲלִיפוּת (נ) |

stadium	itstadyon	אִצְטַדְיוֹן (ז)
terrace	bama	בָּמָה (נ)
fan, supporter	ohed	אוֹהֵד (ז)
opponent, rival	yariv	יָרִיב (ז)

| start (start line) | kav zinuk | קַו זִינוּק (ז) |
| finish line | kav hagmar | קַו הַגְּמָר (ז) |

defeat	tvusa	תְּבוּסָה (נ)
to lose (not win)	lehafsid	לְהַפְסִיד
referee	ʃofet	שׁוֹפֵט (ז)
jury (judges)	xaver ʃoftim	חָבֵר שׁוֹפְטִים (ז)

T&P Books. Theme-based dictionary British English-Hebrew - 7000 words

score	totsa'a	תּוֹצָאָה (נ)
draw	'teku	תֵּיקוּ (ז)
to draw (vi)	lesayem be'teku	לְסַיֵּם בְּתֵיקוּ
point	nekuda	נְקוּדָה (נ)
result (final score)	totsa'a	תּוֹצָאָה (נ)

period	sivuv	סִיבוּב (ז)
half-time	hafsaka	הַפְסָקָה (נ)
doping	sam	סַם (ז)
to penalise (vt)	leha'aniʃ	לְהַעֲנִישׁ
to disqualify (vt)	lefsol	לִפְסוֹל

apparatus	maxʃir	מַכְשִׁיר (ז)
javelin	kidon	כִּידוֹן (ז)
shot (metal ball)	kadur barzel	כַּדּוּר בַּרְזֶל (ז)
ball (snooker, etc.)	kadur	כַּדּוּר (ז)

aim (target)	matara	מַטָּרָה (נ)
target	matara	מַטָּרָה (נ)
to shoot (vi)	lirot	לִירוֹת
accurate (~ shot)	meduyak	מְדוּיָק

trainer, coach	me'amen	מְאַמֵּן (ז)
to train (sb)	le'amen	לְאַמֵּן
to train (vi)	lehit'amen	לְהִתְאַמֵּן
training	imun	אִימוּן (ז)

gym	'xeder 'koʃer	חֲדַר כּוֹשֶׁר (ז)
exercise (physical)	imun	אִימוּן (ז)
warm-up (athlete ~)	ximum	חִימוּם (ז)

Education

school	beit 'sefer	בֵּית סֵפֶר (ז)
headmaster	menahel beit 'sefer	מְנַהֵל בֵּית סֵפֶר (ז)
student (m)	talmid	תַּלְמִיד (ז)
student (f)	talmida	תַּלְמִידָה (נ)
schoolboy	talmid	תַּלְמִיד (ז)
schoolgirl	talmida	תַּלְמִידָה (נ)
to teach (sb)	lelamed	לְלַמֵּד
to learn (language, etc.)	lilmod	לִלְמוֹד
to learn by heart	lilmod be'al pe	לִלְמוֹד בְּעַל פֶּה
to learn (~ to count, etc.)	lilmod	לִלְמוֹד
to be at school	lilmod	לִלְמוֹד
to go to school	la'leχet le'beit 'sefer	לָלֶכֶת לְבֵית סֵפֶר
alphabet	alefbeit	אָלֶפְבֵּית (ז)
subject (at school)	mik'tso'a	מִקְצוֹעַ (ז)
classroom	kita	כִּיתָה (נ)
lesson	ʃi'ur	שִׁיעוּר (ז)
playtime, break	hafsaka	הַפְסָקָה (נ)
school bell	pa'amon	פַּעֲמוֹן (ז)
school desk	ʃulχan limudim	שׁוּלְחַן לִימוּדִים (ז)
blackboard	'luaχ	לוּחַ (ז)
mark	tsiyun	צִיּוּן (ז)
good mark	tsiyun tov	צִיּוּן טוֹב (ז)
bad mark	tsiyun ga'ru'a	צִיּוּן גָּרוּעַ (ז)
to give a mark	latet tsiyun	לָתֵת צִיּוּן
mistake, error	ta'ut	טָעוּת (נ)
to make mistakes	la'asot ta'uyot	לַעֲשׂוֹת טָעוּיוֹת
to correct (an error)	letaken	לְתַקֵּן
crib	ʃlif	שְׁלִיף (ז)
homework	ʃi'urei 'bayit	שִׁיעוּרֵי בַּיִת (ז"ר)
exercise (in education)	targil	תַּרְגִּיל (ז)
to be present	lihyot no'χeaχ	לִהְיוֹת נוֹכֵחַ
to be absent	lehe'ader	לְהֵיעָדֵר
to miss school	lehaχsir	לְהַחְסִיר
to punish (vt)	leha'aniʃ	לְהַעֲנִישׁ
punishment	'oneʃ	עוֹנֶשׁ (ז)
conduct (behaviour)	hitnahagut	הִתְנַהֲגוּת (נ)

school report	yoman beit 'sefer	יוֹמָן בֵּית סֵפֶר (ז)
pencil	iparon	עִיפָּרוֹן (ז)
rubber	'maxak	מַחַק (ז)
chalk	gir	גִּיר (ז)
pencil case	kalmar	קַלְמָר (ז)

schoolbag	yalkut	יַלְקוּט (ז)
pen	et	עֵט (ז)
exercise book	max'beret	מַחְבֶּרֶת (נ)
textbook	'sefer limud	סֵפֶר לִימוּד (ז)
compasses	mexuga	מְחוּגָה (נ)

| to make technical drawings | lesartet | לְשַׂרְטֵט |
| technical drawing | sirtut | שִׂרְטוּט (ז) |

poem	ʃir	שִׁיר (ז)
by heart (adv)	be'al pe	בְּעַל פֶּה
to learn by heart	lilmod be'al pe	לִלְמוֹד בְּעַל פֶּה

school holidays	xuffa	חוּפְשָׁה (נ)
to be on holiday	lihyot bexuffa	לִהְיוֹת בְּחוּפְשָׁה
to spend holidays	leha'avir 'xofeʃ	לְהַעֲבִיר חוֹפֶשׁ

test (at school)	mivxan	מִבְחָן (ז)
essay (composition)	xibur	חִיבּוּר (ז)
dictation	haxtava	הַכְתָּבָה (נ)
exam (examination)	bxina	בְּחִינָה (נ)
to do an exam	lehibaxen	לְהִיבָּחֵן
experiment (e.g., chemistry ~)	nisui	נִיסוּי (ז)

118. College. University

academy	aka'demya	אָקָדָמְיָה (נ)
university	uni'versita	אוּנִיבֶרְסִיטָה (נ)
faculty (e.g., ~ of Medicine)	fa'kulta	פָקוּלְטָה (נ)

student (masc.)	student	סְטוּדֶנְט (ז)
student (fem.)	stu'dentit	סְטוּדֶנְטִית (נ)
lecturer (teacher)	martse	מַרְצֶה (ז)

| lecture hall, room | ulam hartsa'ot | אוּלַם הַרְצָאוֹת (ז) |
| graduate | boger | בּוֹגֵר (ז) |

| diploma | di'ploma | דִיפְלוֹמָה (נ) |
| dissertation | diser'tatsya | דִיסֶרְטַצְיָה (נ) |

| study (report) | mexkar | מֶחְקָר (ז) |
| laboratory | ma'abada | מַעֲבָּדָה (נ) |

lecture	hartsa'a	הַרְצָאָה (נ)
coursemate	xaver lelimudim	חָבֵר לְלִימוּדִים (ז)
scholarship, bursary	milga	מִלְגָה (נ)
academic degree	'to'ar aka'demi	תּוֹאַר אָקָדָמִי (ז)

119. Sciences. Disciplines

mathematics	mate'matika	מָתֶמָטִיקָה (נ)
algebra	'algebra	אַלְגֶבְּרָה (נ)
geometry	ge'o'metriya	גֵּיאוֹמֶטְרְיָה (נ)
astronomy	astro'nomya	אַסְטְרוֹנוֹמְיָה (נ)
biology	bio'logya	בִּיוֹלוֹגְיָה (נ)
geography	ge'o'grafya	גֵּיאוֹגְרַפְיָה (נ)
geology	ge'o'logya	גֵּיאוֹלוֹגְיָה (נ)
history	his'torya	הִיסְטוֹרְיָה (נ)
medicine	refu'a	רְפוּאָה (נ)
pedagogy	xinux	חִינוּךְ (ז)
law	mi∫patim	מִשְׁפָּטִים (ז"ר)
physics	'fizika	פִיזִיקָה (נ)
chemistry	'ximya	כִימְיָה (נ)
philosophy	filo'sofya	פִילוֹסוֹפְיָה (נ)
psychology	psixo'logya	פְּסִיכוֹלוֹגְיָה (נ)

120. Writing system. Orthography

grammar	dikduk	דִקדוּק (ז)
vocabulary	ot͡sar milim	אוֹצַר מִילִים (ז)
phonetics	torat ha'hege	תוֹרַת הַהֶגֶה (נ)
noun	∫em 'et͡sem	שֵׁם עֶצֶם (ז)
adjective	∫em 'to'ar	שֵׁם תּוֹאַר (ז)
verb	po'el	פּוֹעַל (ז)
adverb	'to'ar 'po'al	תּוֹאַר פּוֹעַל (ז)
pronoun	∫em guf	שֵׁם גוּף (ז)
interjection	milat kri'a	מִילַת קְרִיאָה (נ)
preposition	milat 'yaxas	מִילַת יַחַס (נ)
root	'∫ore∫	שׁוֹרֶשׁ (ז)
ending	si'yomet	סִיוֹמֶת (נ)
prefix	txilit	תְחִילִית (נ)
syllable	havara	הֲבָרָה (נ)
suffix	si'yomet	סִיוֹמֶת (נ)
stress mark	'ta'am	טַעַם (ז)
apostrophe	'gere∫	גֶרֶשׁ (ז)
full stop	nekuda	נְקוּדָה (נ)
comma	psik	פְּסִיק (ז)
semicolon	nekuda ufsik	נְקוּדָה וּפְסִיק (נ)
colon	nekudo'tayim	נְקוּדוֹתַיִם (נ"ר)
ellipsis	∫alo∫ nekudot	שְׁלוֹשׁ נְקוּדוֹת (נ"ר)
question mark	siman ∫e'ela	סִימָן שְׁאֵלָה (ז)
exclamation mark	siman kri'a	סִימָן קְרִיאָה (ז)

inverted commas	merχa'ot	מֵרְכָאוֹת (ז"ר)
in inverted commas	bemerχa'ot	בְּמֵרְכָאוֹת
parenthesis	sog'rayim	סוֹגְרַיִם (ז"ר)
in parenthesis	besog'rayim	בְּסוֹגְרַיִם

hyphen	makaf	מַקָּף (ז)
dash	kav mafrid	קַו מַפְרִיד (ז)
space (between words)	'revaχ	רֶוַח (ז)

| letter | ot | אוֹת (נ) |
| capital letter | ot gdola | אוֹת גְדוֹלָה (נ) |

| vowel (n) | tnu'a | תְנוּעָה (נ) |
| consonant (n) | itsur | עִיצוּר (ז) |

sentence	miʃpat	מִשְׁפָּט (ז)
subject	nose	נוֹשֵׂא (ז)
predicate	nasu	נָשׂוּא (ז)

line	ʃura	שׁוּרָה (נ)
on a new line	beʃura χadaʃa	בְּשׁוּרָה חֲדָשָׁה
paragraph	piska	פִּסְקָה (נ)

word	mila	מִילָה (נ)
group of words	tsiruf milim	צֵירוּף מִילִים (ז)
expression	bitui	בִּיטוּי (ז)
synonym	mila nir'defet	מִילָה נִרְדֶפֶת (נ)
antonym	'hefeχ	הֵפֶךְ (ז)

rule	klal	כְּלָל (ז)
exception	yotse min haklal	יוֹצֵא מִן הַכְּלָל (ז)
correct (adj)	naχon	נָכוֹן

conjugation	hataya	הַטָּיָיה (נ)
declension	hataya	הַטָּיָיה (נ)
nominal case	yaχasa	יַחֲסָה (נ)
question	ʃe'ela	שְׁאֵלָה (נ)
to underline (vt)	lehadgiʃ	לְהַדְגִּיש
dotted line	kav nakud	קַו נָקוּד (ז)

121. Foreign languages

language	safa	שָׂפָה (נ)
foreign (adj)	zar	זָר
foreign language	safa zara	שָׂפָה זָרָה (נ)
to study (vt)	lilmod	לִלְמוֹד
to learn (language, etc.)	lilmod	לִלְמוֹד

to read (vi, vt)	likro	לִקְרוֹא
to speak (vi, vt)	ledaber	לְדַבֵּר
to understand (vt)	lehavin	לְהָבִין
to write (vt)	liχtov	לִכְתוֹב
fast (adv)	maher	מַהֵר
slowly (adv)	le'at	לְאַט

fluently (adv)	χofʃi	חוֹפְשִׁי
rules	klalim	כְּלָלִים (ז"ר)
grammar	dikduk	דִּקְדּוּק (ז)
vocabulary	otsar milim	אוֹצַר מִילִים (ז)
phonetics	torat ha'hege	תוֹרַת הַהֶגֶה (נ)
textbook	'sefer limud	סֵפֶר לִימּוּד (ז)
dictionary	milon	מִילוֹן (ז)
teach-yourself book	'sefer lelimud atsmi	סֵפֶר לְלִימּוּד עַצְמִי (ז)
phrasebook	siχon	שִׂיחוֹן (ז)
cassette, tape	ka'letet	קַלֶּטֶת (נ)
videotape	ka'letet 'vide'o	קַלֶּטֶת וִידֵיאוֹ (נ)
CD, compact disc	taklitor	תַּקְלִיטוֹר (ז)
DVD	di vi di	דִּי. וִי. דִּי. (ז)
alphabet	alefbeit	אָלֶפְבֵּית (ז)
to spell (vt)	le'ayet	לְאַיֵּת
pronunciation	hagiya	הֲגִיָּה (נ)
accent	mivta	מִבְטָא (ז)
with an accent	im mivta	עִם מִבְטָא
without an accent	bli mivta	בְּלִי מִבְטָא
word	mila	מִילָה (נ)
meaning	maʃma'ut	מַשְׁמָעוּת (נ)
course (e.g. a French ~)	kurs	קוּרְס (ז)
to sign up	leheraʃem lekurs	לְהֵירָשֵׁם לְקוּרְס
teacher	more	מוֹרֶה (ז)
translation (process)	tirgum	תַּרְגּוּם (ז)
translation (text, etc.)	tirgum	תַּרְגּוּם (ז)
translator	metargem	מְתַרְגֵּם (ז)
interpreter	meturgeman	מְתוּרְגְּמָן (ז)
polyglot	poliglot	פּוֹלִיגְלוֹט (ז)
memory	zikaron	זִיכָּרוֹן (ז)

122. Fairy tale characters

Father Christmas	'santa 'kla'us	סַנְטָה קְלָאוּס (ז)
Cinderella	sinde'rela	סִינְדֶרֶלָה
mermaid	bat yam, betulat hayam	בַּת יָם, בְּתוּלַת הַיָּם (נ)
Neptune	neptun	נֶפְטוּן (ז)
magician, wizard	kosem	קוֹסֵם (ז)
fairy	'feya	פֵיָה (נ)
magic (adj)	kasum	קָסוּם
magic wand	ʃarvit 'kesem	שַׁרְבִיט קֶסֶם (ז)
fairy tale	agada	אַגָּדָה (נ)
miracle	nes	נֵס (ז)
dwarf	gamad	גַּמָּד (ז)

to turn into …	lahafoχ le…	לַהֲפוֹךְ לְ…
ghost	'ruaχ refa"im	רוּחַ רְפָאִים (ז)
phantom	'ruaχ refa"im	רוּחַ רְפָאִים (ז)
monster	mif'letset	מִפְלֶצֶת (נ)
dragon	drakon	דְרָקוֹן (ז)
giant	anak	עֲנָק (ז)

123. Zodiac Signs

Aries	tale	טָלֶה (ז)
Taurus	ʃor	שוֹר (ז)
Gemini	te'omim	תְאוֹמִים (ז"ר)
Cancer	sartan	סַרְטָן (ז)
Leo	arye	אַרְיֵה (ז)
Virgo	betula	בְּתוּלָה (נ)
Libra	moz'nayim	מֹאזְנַיִם (ז"ר)
Scorpio	akrav	עַקְרָב (ז)
Sagittarius	kaʃat	קַשָׁת (ז)
Capricorn	gdi	גְדִי (ז)
Aquarius	dli	דְלִי (ז)
Pisces	dagim	דָגִים (ז"ר)
character	'ofi	אוֹפִי (ז)
character traits	tχunot 'ofi	תְכוּנוֹת אוֹפִי (נ"ר)
behaviour	hitnahagut	הִתְנַהֲגוּת (נ)
to tell fortunes	lenabe et ha'atid	לְנַבֵּא אֶת הֶעָתִיד
fortune-teller	ma'gedet atidot	מַגֶדֶת עֲתִידוֹת (נ)
horoscope	horoskop	הוֹרוֹסְקוֹפ (ז)

Arts

theatre	te'atron	תֵּיאַטְרוֹן (ז)
opera	'opera	אוֹפֶּרָה (נ)
operetta	ope'reta	אוֹפֶּרֶטָה (נ)
ballet	balet	בָּלֶט (ז)
theatre poster	kraza	כְּרָזָה (נ)
theatre company	lahaka	לַהֲקָה (נ)
tour	masa hofa'ot	מַסַּע הוֹפָעוֹת (ז)
to be on tour	latset lemasa hofa'ot	לָצֵאת לְמַסַּע הוֹפָעוֹת
to rehearse (vi, vt)	la'aroχ χazara	לַעֲרוֹךְ חֲזָרָה
rehearsal	χazara	חֲזָרָה (נ)
repertoire	repertu'ar	רֶפֶּרְטוֹאָר (ז)
performance	hofa'a	הוֹפָעָה (נ)
theatrical show	hatsaga	הַצָּגָה (נ)
play	maχaze	מַחֲזֶה (ז)
ticket	kartis	כַּרְטִיס (ז)
booking office	kupa	קוּפָּה (נ)
lobby, foyer	'lobi	לוֹבִּי (ז)
coat check (cloakroom)	meltaχa	מֶלְתָּחָה (נ)
cloakroom ticket	mispar meltaχa	מִסְפַּר מֶלְתָּחָה (ז)
binoculars	miʃ'kefet	מִשְׁקֶפֶת (נ)
usher	sadran	סַדְרָן (ז)
stalls (orchestra seats)	parter	פַּרְטֶר (ז)
balcony	mir'peset	מִרְפֶּסֶת (נ)
dress circle	ya'tsi'a	יָצִיעַ (ז)
box	ta	תָּא (ז)
row	ʃura	שׁוּרָה (נ)
seat	moʃav	מוֹשָׁב (ז)
audience	'kahal	קָהָל (ז)
spectator	tsofe	צוֹפֶה (ז)
to clap (vi, vt)	limχo ka'payim	לִמְחוֹא כַּפַּיִים
applause	meχi'ot ka'payim	מְחִיאוֹת כַּפַּיִים (נ"ר)
ovation	tʃu'ot	תְּשׁוּאוֹת (נ"ר)
stage	bama	בָּמָה (נ)
curtain	masaχ	מָסָךְ (ז)
scenery	taf'ura	תַּפְאוּרָה (נ)
backstage	klayim	קְלָעִים
scene (e.g. the last ~)	'stsena	סְצֵינָה (נ)
act	ma'araχa	מַעֲרָכָה (נ)
interval	hafsaka	הַפְסָקָה (נ)

125. Cinema

actor	saχkan	שַׂחְקָן (ז)
actress	saχkanit	שַׂחְקָנִית (נ)
cinema (industry)	kol'noʻa	קוֹלְנוֹעַ (ז)
film	'seret	סֶרֶט (ז)
episode	epi'zoda	אֶפִּיזוֹדָה (נ)
detective film	'seret balaʃi	סֶרֶט בַּלָּשִׁי (ז)
action film	maʻarvon	מַעֲרְבוֹן (ז)
adventure film	'seret harpatkaʼot	סֶרֶט הַרְפַּתְקָאוֹת (ז)
science fiction film	'seret mada bidyoni	סֶרֶט מַדָע בְּדִיוֹנִי (ז)
horror film	'seret eima	סֶרֶט אֵימָה (ז)
comedy film	ko'medya	קוֹמֶדְיָה (נ)
melodrama	melo'drama	מֶלוֹדְרָמָה (נ)
drama	'drama	דְרָמָה (נ)
fictional film	'seret alilati	סֶרֶט עֲלִילָתִי (ז)
documentary	'seret tiʻudi	סֶרֶט תִיעוּדִי (ז)
cartoon	'seret ani'matsya	סֶרֶט אֲנִימַצְיָה (ז)
silent films	sratim ilmim	סְרָטִים אִילְמִים (ז"ר)
role (part)	tafkid	תַפְקִיד (ז)
leading role	tafkid raʃi	תַפְקִיד רָאשִׁי (ז)
to play (vi, vt)	lesaχek	לְשַׂחֵק
film star	koχav kol'noʻa	כּוֹכָב קוֹלְנוֹעַ (ז)
well-known (adj)	mefursam	מְפוּרְסָם
famous (adj)	mefursam	מְפוּרְסָם
popular (adj)	popu'lari	פּוֹפּוּלָרִי
script (screenplay)	tasrit	תַסְרִיט (ז)
scriptwriter	tasritai	תַסְרִיטָאי (ז)
film director	bamai	בַּמַאי (ז)
producer	mefik	מֵפִיק (ז)
assistant	ozer	עוֹזֵר (ז)
cameraman	tsalam	צַלָם (ז)
stuntman	paʻalulan	פַּעֲלוּלָן (ז)
double (body double)	saχkan maχlif	שַׂחְקָן מַחֲלִיף (ז)
to shoot a film	letsalem 'seret	לְצַלֵם סֶרֶט
audition, screen test	mivdak	מִבְדָק (ז)
shooting	hasrata	הַסְרָטָה (נ)
film crew	'tsevet ha'seret	צֶוֶות הַסֶרֶט (ז)
film set	atar hatsilum	אֲתַר הַצִילוּם (ז)
camera	matslema	מַצְלֵמָה (נ)
cinema	beit kol'noʻa	בֵּית קוֹלְנוֹעַ (ז)
screen (e.g. big ~)	masaχ	מָסָך (ז)
to show a film	leharʼot 'seret	לְהַרְאוֹת סֶרֶט
soundtrack	paskol	פַּסְקוֹל (ז)
special effects	e'fektim meyuχadim	אֶפֶּקְטִים מְיוּחָדִים (ז"ר)

subtitles	ktuviyot	כְּתוּבִיוֹת (נ"ר)
credits	ktuviyot	כְּתוּבִיוֹת (נ"ר)
translation	tirgum	תִּרְגּוּם (ז)

126. Painting

art	amanut	אָמָנוּת (נ)
fine arts	omanuyot yafot	אוֹמָנוּיוֹת יָפוֹת (נ"ר)
art gallery	ga'lerya le'amanut	גָּלֶרְיָה לְאָמָנוּת (נ)
art exhibition	ta'aruxat amanut	תַּעֲרוּכַת אָמָנוּת (נ)

painting (art)	tsiyur	צִיּוּר (ז)
graphic art	'grafika	גְּרָפִיקָה (נ)
abstract art	amanut muf'fetet	אָמָנוּת מוּפְשֶׁטֶת (נ)
impressionism	impresyonizm	אִימפְּרֶסְיוֹנִיזם (ז)

picture (painting)	tmuna	תְּמוּנָה (נ)
drawing	tsiyur	צִיּוּר (ז)
poster	'poster	פּוֹסְטֶר (ז)

illustration (picture)	iyur	אִיּוּר (ז)
miniature	minya'tura	מִינְיָאטוּרָה (נ)
copy (of painting, etc.)	he'etek	הֶעְתֵּק (ז)
reproduction	ʃi'atuk	שִׁיעָתוּק (ז)

mosaic	psefas	פְּסֵיפָס (ז)
stained glass window	vitraʒ	וִיטרָאז' (ז)
fresco	fresko	פְרֶסקוֹ (ז)
engraving	taxrit	תַּחרִיט (ז)

bust (sculpture)	pro'toma	פְּרוֹטוֹמָה (נ)
sculpture	'pesel	פֶּסֶל (ז)
statue	'pesel	פֶּסֶל (ז)
plaster of Paris	'geves	גֶּבֶס (ז)
plaster (as adj)	mi'geves	מִגֶּבֶס

portrait	dyukan	דְיוֹקָן (ז)
self-portrait	dyukan atsmi	דְיוֹקָן עַצמִי (ז)
landscape painting	tsiyur nof	צִיּוּר נוֹף (ז)
still life	'teva domem	טֶבַע דוֹמֵם (ז)
caricature	karika'tura	קָרִיקָטוּרָה (נ)
sketch	tarʃim	תַּרשִׁים (ז)

paint	'tseva	צֶבַע (ז)
watercolor paint	'tseva 'mayim	צֶבַע מַיִם (ז)
oil (paint)	'femen	שֶׁמֶן (ז)
pencil	iparon	עִיפָּרוֹן (ז)
Indian ink	tuʃ	טוּשׁ (ז)
charcoal	pexam	פֶּחָם (ז)

to draw (vi, vt)	letsayer	לְצַייֵר
to paint (vi, vt)	letsayer	לְצַייֵר
to pose (vi)	ledagmen	לְדַגמֵן
artist's model (masc.)	dugman eirom	דוּגמָן עֵירוֹם (ז)

artist's model (fem.)	dugmanit erom	דּוּגְמָנִית עֵירוֹם (נ)
artist (painter)	tsayar	צַיָּר (ז)
work of art	yetsirat amanut	יְצִירַת אָמָנוּת (נ)
masterpiece	yetsirat mofet	יְצִירַת מוֹפֵת (נ)
studio (artist's workroom)	'studyo	סְטוּדְיוֹ (ז)

canvas (cloth)	bad piʃtan	בַּד פִּשְׁתָּן (ז)
easel	kan tsiyur	כַּן צִיּוּר (ז)
palette	'plata	פַּלֶטָה (נ)

frame (picture ~, etc.)	mis'geret	מִסְגֶּרֶת (נ)
restoration	ʃixzur	שִׁחְזוּר (ז)
to restore (vt)	leʃaxzer	לְשַׁחְזֵר

127. Literature & Poetry

literature	sifrut	סִפְרוּת (נ)
author (writer)	sofer	סוֹפֵר (ז)
pseudonym	ʃem badui	שֵׁם בָּדוּי (ז)

book	'sefer	סֵפֶר (ז)
volume	'kerex	כֶּרֶךְ (ז)
table of contents	'toxen inyanim	תּוֹכֶן עִנְיָנִים (ז)
page	amud	עַמּוּד (ז)
main character	hagibor haraʃi	הַגִּיבּוֹר הָרָאשִׁי (ז)
autograph	xatima	חֲתִימָה (נ)

short story	sipur katsar	סִיפּוּר קָצָר (ז)
story (novella)	sipur	סִיפּוּר (ז)
novel	roman	רוֹמָן (ז)
work (writing)	xibur	חִיבּוּר (ז)
fable	maʃal	מָשָׁל (ז)
detective novel	roman balaʃi	רוֹמָן בַּלָשִׁי (ז)

poem (verse)	ʃir	שִׁיר (ז)
poetry	ʃira	שִׁירָה (נ)
poem (epic, ballad)	po''ema	פּוֹאֶמָה (נ)
poet	meʃorer	מְשׁוֹרֵר (ז)

fiction	sifrut yafa	סִפְרוּת יָפָה (נ)
science fiction	mada bidyoni	מַדָּע בְּדִיוֹנִי (ז)
adventures	harpatka'ot	הַרְפַּתְקָאוֹת (נ"ר)
educational literature	sifrut limudit	סִפְרוּת לִימוּדִית (נ)
children's literature	sifrut yeladim	סִפְרוּת יְלָדִים (נ)

128. Circus

circus	kirkas	קִרְקָס (ז)
travelling circus	kirkas nayad	קִרְקָס נַיָּד (ז)
programme	toxnit	תּוֹכְנִית (נ)
performance	hofa'a	הוֹפָעָה (נ)
act (circus ~)	hofa'a	הוֹפָעָה (נ)

circus ring	zira	זִירָה (נ)
pantomime (act)	panto'mima	פַּנטוֹמִימָה (נ)
clown	leitsan	לֵיצָן (ז)
acrobat	akrobat	אַקרוֹבָּט (ז)
acrobatics	akro'batika	אַקרוֹבָּטִיקָה (נ)
gymnast	mit'amel	מִתעַמֵל (ז)
acrobatic gymnastics	hit'amlut	הִתעַמלוּת (נ)
somersault	'salta	סַלטָה (נ)
strongman	atlet	אַתלֵט (ז)
tamer (e.g., lion ~)	me'alef	מְאַלֵף (ז)
rider (circus horse ~)	roxev	רוֹכֵב (ז)
assistant	ozer	עוֹזֵר (ז)
stunt	pa'alul	פַּעֲלוּל (ז)
magic trick	'kesem	קֶסֶם (ז)
conjurer, magician	kosem	קוֹסֵם (ז)
juggler	lahatutan	לַהֲטוּטָן (ז)
to juggle (vi, vt)	lelahtet	לְלַהֲטֵט
animal trainer	me'alef hayot	מְאַלֵף חַיוֹת (ז)
animal training	iluf xayot	אִילוּף חַיוֹת (ז)
to train (animals)	le'alef	לְאַלֵף

129. Music. Pop music

music	'muzika	מוּזִיקָה (נ)
musician	muzikai	מוּזִיקַאי (ז)
musical instrument	kli negina	כּלִי נְגִינָה (ז)
to play ...	lenagen be...	לְנַגֵן בְּ...
guitar	gi'tara	גִיטָרָה (נ)
violin	kinor	כִּינוֹר (ז)
cello	'tʃelo	צֶ'לוֹ (ז)
double bass	kontrabas	קוֹנטרַבָּס (ז)
harp	'nevel	נֵבֶל (ז)
piano	psanter	פְּסַנתֵר (ז)
grand piano	psanter kanaf	פְּסַנתֵר כָּנָף (ז)
organ	ugav	עוּגָב (ז)
wind instruments	klei neʃifa	כּלֵי נְשִיפָה (ז"ר)
oboe	abuv	אַבּוּב (ז)
saxophone	saksofon	סַקסוֹפוֹן (ז)
clarinet	klarinet	קלָרִינֶט (ז)
flute	xalil	חָלִיל (ז)
trumpet	xatsotsra	חֲצוֹצרָה (נ)
accordion	akordyon	אָקוֹרדִיוֹן (ז)
drum	tof	תוֹף (ז)
duo	'du'o	דוּאוֹ (ז)
trio	ʃliʃiya	שלִישִיָה (נ)

quartet	revi'iya	רְבִיעִיָּה (נ)
choir	makhela	מַקְהֵלָה (נ)
orchestra	tiz'moret	תִּזְמֹרֶת (נ)
pop music	'muzikat pop	מוּזִיקַת פּוֹפ (נ)
rock music	'muzikat rok	מוּזִיקַת רוֹק (נ)
rock group	lehakat rok	לַהֲקַת רוֹק (נ)
jazz	dʒez	ג'ז (ז)
idol	koχav	כּוֹכָב (ז)
admirer, fan	ohed	אוֹהֵד (ז)
concert	kontsert	קוֹנְצֶרְט (ז)
symphony	si'fonya	סִימְפוֹנְיָה (נ)
composition	yetsira	יְצִירָה (נ)
to compose (write)	leχaber	לְחַבֵּר
singing (n)	ʃira	שִׁירָה (נ)
song	ʃir	שִׁיר (ז)
tune (melody)	mangina	מַנְגִּינָה (נ)
rhythm	'ketsev	קֶצֶב (ז)
blues	bluz	בְּלוּז (ז)
sheet music	tavim	תָּוִים (ז"ר)
baton	ʃarvit ni'tsuaχ	שַׁרְבִיט נִיצּוּחַ (ז)
bow	'keʃet	קֶשֶׁת (נ)
string	meitar	מֵיתָר (ז)
case (e.g. guitar ~)	nartik	נַרְתִּיק (ז)

Rest. Entertainment. Travel

130. Trip. Travel

tourism, travel	tayarut	תַּיָּירוּת (נ)
tourist	tayar	תַּיָּיר (ז)
trip, voyage	tiyul	טִיוּל (ז)
adventure	harpatka	הַרְפַּתְקָה (נ)
trip, journey	nesi'a	נְסִיעָה (נ)
holiday	χuʃʃa	חוּפְשָׁה (נ)
to be on holiday	lihyot beχuʃʃa	לִהְיוֹת בְּחוּפְשָׁה
rest	menuχa	מְנוּחָה (נ)
train	ra'kevet	רַכֶּבֶת (נ)
by train	bera'kevet	בְּרַכֶּבֶת
aeroplane	matos	מָטוֹס (ז)
by aeroplane	bematos	בְּמָטוֹס
by car	bemeχonit	בְּמְכוֹנִית
by ship	be'oniya	בְּאוֹנִייָּה
luggage	mit'an	מִטְעָן (ז)
suitcase	mizvada	מִזְוָודָה (נ)
luggage trolley	eglat mit'an	עֲגָלַת מִטְעָן (נ)
passport	darkon	דַּרְכּוֹן (ז)
visa	'viza, aʃra	וִיזָה, אַשְׁרָה (נ)
ticket	kartis	כַּרְטִיס (ז)
air ticket	kartis tisa	כַּרְטִיס טִיסָה (ז)
guidebook	madriχ	מַדְרִיךְ (ז)
map (tourist ~)	mapa	מַפָּה (נ)
area (rural ~)	ezor	אָזוֹר (ז)
place, site	makom	מָקוֹם (ז)
exotica (n)	ek'zotika	אֶקְזוֹטִיקָה (נ)
exotic (adj)	ek'zoti	אֶקְזוֹטִי
amazing (adj)	nifla	נִפְלָא
group	kvutsa	קְבוּצָה (נ)
excursion, sightseeing tour	tiyul	טִיוּל (ז)
guide (person)	madriχ tiyulim	מַדְרִיךְ טִיוּלִים (ז)

131. Hotel

hotel	malon	מָלוֹן (ז)
motel	motel	מוֹטֵל (ז)
three-star (~ hotel)	ʃloʃa koχavim	שְׁלוֹשָׁה כּוֹכָבִים

| five-star | χamiʃa koχavim | חֲמִישָׁה כּוֹכָבִים |
| to stay (in a hotel, etc.) | lehit'aχsen | לְהִתְאַכְסֵן |

room	'χeder	חֶדֶר (ז)
single room	'χeder yaχid	חֶדֶר יָחִיד (ז)
double room	'χeder zugi	חֶדֶר זוּגִי (ז)
to book a room	lehazmin 'χeder	לְהַזְמִין חֶדֶר

| half board | χatsi pensiyon | חֲצִי פֶּנְסִיוֹן (ז) |
| full board | pensyon male | פֶּנְסִיוֹן מָלֵא (ז) |

with bath	im am'batya	עִם אַמְבַּטְיָה
with shower	im mik'laχat	עִם מִקְלַחַת
satellite television	tele'vizya bekvalim	טֶלֶוִיזְיָה בְּכְבָלִים (נ)
air-conditioner	mazgan	מַזְגָן (ז)
towel	ma'gevet	מַגֶבֶת (נ)
key	maf'teaχ	מַפְתֵחַ (ז)

administrator	amarkal	אֲמַרְכָּל (ז)
chambermaid	χadranit	חַדְרָנִית (נ)
porter	sabal	סַבָּל (ז)
doorman	pakid kabala	פְּקִיד קַבָּלָה (ז)

restaurant	mis'ada	מִסְעָדָה (נ)
pub, bar	bar	בָּר (ז)
breakfast	aruχat 'boker	אֲרוּחַת בּוֹקֶר (נ)
dinner	aruχat 'erev	אֲרוּחַת עֶרֶב (נ)
buffet	miznon	מִזְנוֹן (ז)

| lobby | 'lobi | לוֹבִּי (ז) |
| lift | ma'alit | מַעֲלִית (נ) |

| DO NOT DISTURB | lo lehaf'ri'a | לֹא לְהַפְרִיעַ |
| NO SMOKING | asur le'aʃen! | אָסוּר לְעַשֵׁן! |

132. Books. Reading

book	'sefer	סֵפֶר (ז)
author	sofer	סוֹפֵר (ז)
writer	sofer	סוֹפֵר (ז)
to write (~ a book)	liχtov	לִכְתוֹב

reader	kore	קוֹרֵא (ז)
to read (vi, vt)	likro	לִקְרוֹא
reading (activity)	kri'a	קְרִיאָה (נ)

| silently (to oneself) | belev, be'ʃeket | בְּלֵב, בְּשֶׁקֶט |
| aloud (adv) | bekol ram | בְּקוֹל רָם |

to publish (vt)	lehotsi la'or	לְהוֹצִיא לָאוֹר
publishing (process)	hotsa'a la'or	הוֹצָאָה לָאוֹר (נ)
publisher	motsi le'or	מוֹצִיא לָאוֹר (ז)
publishing house	hotsa'a la'or	הוֹצָאָה לָאוֹר (נ)
to come out (be released)	latset le'or	לָצֵאת לָאוֹר

release (of a book)	hafatsa	הַפָּצָה (נ)
print run	tfutsa	תפוצָה (נ)
bookshop	χanut sfarim	חֲנוּת סְפָרִים (נ)
library	sifriya	סִפְרִיָּה (נ)
story (novella)	sipur	סִיפּוּר (ז)
short story	sipur katsar	סִיפּוּר קָצָר (ז)
novel	roman	רוֹמָן (ז)
detective novel	roman balaʃi	רוֹמָן בַּלָשִי (ז)
memoirs	ziχronot	זִיכרוֹנוֹת (ז״ר)
legend	agada	אַגָּדָה (נ)
myth	'mitos	מִיתוֹס (ז)
poetry, poems	ʃirim	שִירִים (ז״ר)
autobiography	otobio'grafya	אוֹטוֹבִּיוֹגרַפיָה (נ)
selected works	mivχar ktavim	מִבחַר כּתָבִים (ז)
science fiction	mada bidyoni	מַדָע בְּדִיוֹנִי (ז)
title	kotar	כּוֹתָר (ז)
introduction	mavo	מָבוֹא (ז)
title page	amud ha'ʃa'ar	עַמוּד הַשַעַר (ז)
chapter	'perek	פֶּרֶק (ז)
extract	'keta	קֶטַע (ז)
episode	epi'zoda	אֶפִּיזוֹדָה (נ)
plot (storyline)	alila	עֲלִילָה (נ)
contents	'toχen	תוֹכֶן (ז)
table of contents	'toχen inyanim	תוֹכֶן עִנייָנִים (ז)
main character	hagibor haraʃi	הַגִיבּוֹר הָרָאשִי (ז)
volume	'kereχ	כֶּרֶך (ז)
cover	kriχa	כּרִיכָה (נ)
binding	kriχa	כּרִיכָה (נ)
bookmark	simaniya	סִימָנִייָה (נ)
page	amud	עַמוּד (ז)
to page through	ledafdef	לְדַפּדֵף
margins	ʃu'layim	שוּלַייִם (ז״ר)
annotation (marginal note, etc.)	he'ara	הֶעָרָה (נ)
footnote	he'arat ʃu'layim	הֶעָרַת שוּלַייִם (נ)
text	tekst	טֶקסט (ז)
type, fount	gufan	גוּפָן (ז)
misprint, typo	ta'ut dfus	טָעוּת דפוּס (נ)
translation	tirgum	תַרגוּם (ז)
to translate (vt)	letargem	לְתַרגֵם
original (n)	makor	מָקוֹר (ז)
famous (adj)	mefursam	מְפוּרסָם
unknown (not famous)	lo ya'du'a	לא יָדוּעַ
interesting (adj)	me'anyen	מְעַניֵין

121

bestseller	rav 'mexer	רַב-מֶכֶר (ז)
dictionary	milon	מִילוֹן (ז)
textbook	'sefer limud	סֵפֶר לִימוּד (ז)
encyclopedia	entsiklo'pedya	אֶנצִיקלוֹפֶּדיָה (נ)

133. Hunting. Fishing

hunting	'tsayid	צַיִד (ז)
to hunt (vi, vt)	latsud	לָצוּד
hunter	tsayad	צַיָד (ז)
to shoot (vi)	lirot	לִירוֹת
rifle	rove	רוֹבֶה (ז)
bullet (shell)	kadur	כַּדוּר (ז)
shot (lead balls)	kaduriyot	כַּדוּרִיוֹת (נ"ר)
steel trap	mal'kodet	מַלכּוֹדֶת (נ)
snare (for birds, etc.)	mal'kodet	מַלכּוֹדֶת (נ)
to fall into the steel trap	lehilaxed bemal'kodet	לְהִילָכֵד בְּמַלכּוֹדֶת
to lay a steel trap	leha'niax mal'kodet	לְהָנִיחַ מַלכּוֹדֶת
poacher	tsayad lelo refut	צַיָד לְלֹא רְשׁוּת (ז)
game (in hunting)	xayot bar	חַיוֹת בַּר (נ"ר)
hound dog	'kelev 'tsayid	כֶּלֶב צַיִד (ז)
safari	sa'fari	סָפָארִי (ז)
mounted animal	puxlats	פּוּחלָץ (ז)
fisherman	dayag	דַיָג (ז)
fishing (angling)	'dayig	דַיִג (ז)
to fish (vi)	ladug	לָדוּג
fishing rod	xaka	חַכָּה (נ)
fishing line	xut haxaka	חוּט הַחַכָּה (ז)
hook	'keres	קֶרֶס (ז)
float	matsof	מָצוֹף (ז)
bait	pitayon	פִּיתָיוֹן (ז)
to cast a line	lizrok et haxaka	לִזרוֹק אֶת הַחַכָּה
to bite (ab. fish)	liv'lo‘a pitayon	לִבלוֹע פִּיתָיוֹן
catch (of fish)	ʃlal 'dayig	שְׁלַל דַיִג (ז)
ice-hole	mivka 'kerax	מִבקָע קֶרַח (ז)
fishing net	'refet dayagim	רֶשֶׁת דַיָגִים (נ)
boat	sira	סִירָה (נ)
to net (to fish with a net)	ladug be'refet	לָדוּג בְּרֶשֶׁת
to cast[throw] the net	lizrok 'refet	לִזרוֹק רֶשֶׁת
to haul the net in	ligror 'refet	לִגרוֹר רֶשֶׁת
to fall into the net	lehilaxed be'refet	לְהִילָכֵד בְּרֶשֶׁת
whaler (person)	tsayad livyatanim	צַיָד לְווִיתָנִים (ז)
whaleboat	sfinat tseid livyetanim	סְפִינַת צַיד לְווִיתָנִית (נ)
harpoon	tsiltsal	צִלצָל (ז)

134. Games. Billiards

billiards	bilyard	בִּילְיַארְד (ז)
billiard room, hall	'xeder bilyard	חֲדַר בִּילְיַארְד (ז)
ball (snooker, etc.)	kadur bilyard	כַּדּוּר בִּילְיַארְד (ז)
to pocket a ball	lehaxnis kadur lekis	לְהַכְנִיס כַּדּוּר לְכִּיס
cue	makel bilyard	מַקֵּל בִּילְיַארְד (ז)
pocket	kis	כִּיס (ז)

135. Games. Playing cards

diamonds	yahalom	יַהֲלוֹם (ז)
spades	ale	עָלֶה (ז)
hearts	lev	לֵב (ז)
clubs	tiltan	תִּלְתָּן (ז)
ace	as	אָס (ז)
king	'melex	מֶלֶךְ (ז)
queen	malka	מַלְכָּה (נ)
jack, knave	nasix	נָסִיךְ (ז)
playing card	klaf	קְלָף (ז)
cards	klafim	קְלָפִים (ז"ר)
trump	klaf nitsaxon	קְלָף נִיצָחוֹן (ז)
pack of cards	xafisat klafim	חֲפִיסַת קְלָפִים (נ)
point	nekuda	נְקוּדָה (נ)
to deal (vi, vt)	lexalek klafim	לְחַלֵּק קְלָפִים
to shuffle (cards)	litrof	לִטְרוֹף
lead, turn (n)	tor	תּוֹר (ז)
cardsharp	noxel klafim	נוֹכֵל קְלָפִים (ז)

136. Rest. Games. Miscellaneous

to stroll (vi, vt)	letayel ba'regel	לְטַיֵּל בָּרֶגֶל
stroll (leisurely walk)	tiyul ragli	טִיּוּל רַגְלִי (ז)
car ride	nesi'a bamexonit	נְסִיעָה בָּמְכוֹנִית (נ)
adventure	harpatka	הַרְפַּתְקָה (נ)
picnic	'piknik	פִּיקְנִיק (ז)
game (chess, etc.)	misxak	מִשְׂחָק (ז)
player	saxkan	שַׂחְקָן (ז)
game (one ~ of chess)	misxak	מִשְׂחָק (ז)
collector (e.g. philatelist)	asfan	אַסְפָן (ז)
to collect (stamps, etc.)	le'esof	לֶאֱסוֹף
collection	'osef	אוֹסֶף (ז)
crossword puzzle	ta∫bets	תַּשְׁבֵּץ (ז)
racecourse (hippodrome)	hipodrom	הִיפּוֹדְרוֹם (ז)

disco (discotheque)	diskotek	דִיסקוֹטֶק (ז)
sauna	'sa'una	סָאוּנָה (נ)
lottery	'loto	לוֹטוֹ (ז)

camping trip	tiyul maxana'ut	טִיוּל מַחֲנָאוּת (ז)
camp	maxane	מַחֲנֶה (ז)
tent (for camping)	'ohel	אוֹהֶל (ז)
compass	matspen	מַצְפֵּן (ז)
camper	maxnai	מַחְנַאי (ז)

to watch (film, etc.)	lir'ot	לִרְאוֹת
viewer	tsofe	צוֹפֶה (ז)
TV show (TV program)	toxnit tele'vizya	תוֹכְנִית טֶלֶוִיזְיָה (נ)

137. Photography

camera (photo)	matslema	מַצְלֵמָה (נ)
photo, picture	tmuna	תְמוּנָה (נ)

photographer	tsalam	צַלָּם (ז)
photo studio	'studyo letsilum	סְטוּדְיוֹ לְצִילוּם (ז)
photo album	albom tmunot	אַלְבּוֹם תְמוּנוֹת (ז)

camera lens	adaʃa	עֲדָשָׁה (נ)
telephoto lens	a'defet teleskop	עֲדֶשֶׁת טֶלֶסְקוֹפ (נ)
filter	masnen	מַסְנֵן (ז)
lens	adaʃa	עֲדָשָׁה (נ)

optics (high-quality ~)	'optika	אוֹפְּטִיקָה (נ)
diaphragm (aperture)	tsamtsam	צַמְצָם (ז)
exposure time (shutter speed)	zman hahe'ara	זְמַן הַהֶאָרָה (ז)
viewfinder	einit	עֵינִית (נ)
digital camera	matslema digi'talit	מַצְלֵמָה דִיגִיטָלִית (נ)
tripod	xatsuva	חֲצוּבָה (נ)
flash	mavzek	מַבְזֵק (ז)

to photograph (vt)	letsalem	לְצַלֵם
to take pictures	letsalem	לְצַלֵם
to have one's picture taken	lehitstalem	לְהִצְטַלֵם

focus	moked	מוֹקֵד (ז)
to focus	lemaked	לְמַקֵד
sharp, in focus (adj)	xad, memukad	חַד, מְמוּקָד
sharpness	xadut	חַדוּת (נ)

contrast	nigud	נִיגוּד (ז)
contrast (as adj)	menugad	מְנוּגָד

picture (photo)	tmuna	תְמוּנָה (נ)
negative (n)	taʃlil	תַשְׁלִיל (ז)
film (a roll of ~)	'seret	סֶרֶט (ז)
frame (still)	freim	פְרֵיים (ז)
to print (photos)	lehadpis	לְהַדְפִּיס

138. Beach. Swimming

beach	χof yam	חוֹף יָם (ז)
sand	χol	חוֹל (ז)
deserted (beach)	ʃomem	שׁוֹמֵם
suntan	ʃizuf	שִׁיזוּף (ז)
to get a tan	lehiʃtazef	לְהִשְׁתַּזֵף
tanned (adj)	ʃazuf	שָׁזוּף
sunscreen	krem hagana	קְרֶם הֲגָנָה (ז)
bikini	bi'kini	בִּיקִינִי (ז)
swimsuit, bikini	'beged yam	בֶּגֶד יָם (ז)
swim trunks	'beged yam	בֶּגֶד יָם (ז)
swimming pool	breχa	בְּרֵיכָה (נ)
to swim (vi)	lisχot	לִשְׂחוֹת
shower	mik'laχat	מִקְלַחַת (נ)
to change (one's clothes)	lehaχlif bgadim	לְהַחֲלִיף בְּגָדִים
towel	ma'gevet	מַגֶּבֶת (נ)
boat	sira	סִירָה (נ)
motorboat	sirat ma'no'a	סִירַת מָנוֹעַ (נ)
water ski	ski 'mayim	סְקִי מַיִם (ז)
pedalo	sirat pe'dalim	סִירַת פְּדָלִים (נ)
surfing	gliʃat galim	גלִישַׁת גַלִים
surfer	goleʃ	גוֹלֵשׁ (ז)
scuba set	'skuba	סקוּבָּה (נ)
flippers (swim fins)	snapirim	סַנַפִּירִים (ז"ר)
mask (diving ~)	maseχa	מַסֵכָה (נ)
diver	tsolelan	צוֹלְלָן (ז)
to dive (vi)	litslol	לִצְלוֹל
underwater (adv)	mi'taχat lifnei ha'mayim	מִתַּחַת לִפְנֵי הַמַיִם
beach umbrella	ʃimʃiya	שִׁמְשִׁיָה (נ)
beach chair (sun lounger)	kise 'noaχ	כִּיסֵא נוֹחַ (ז)
sunglasses	miʃkefei 'ʃemeʃ	מִשׁקְפֵי שֶׁמֶשׁ (ז"ר)
air mattress	mizron mitna'peaχ	מִזְרוֹן מִתְנַפֵּחַ (ז)
to play (amuse oneself)	lesaχek	לְשַׂחֵק
to go for a swim	lehitraχets	לְהִתְרַחֵץ
beach ball	kadur yam	כַּדוּר יָם (ז)
to inflate (vt)	lena'peaχ	לְנַפֵּחַ
inflatable, air (adj)	menupaχ	מְנוּפָּח
wave	gal	גַל (ז)
buoy (line of ~s)	matsof	מָצוֹף (ז)
to drown (ab. person)	lit'bo'a	לִטְבּוֹעַ
to save, to rescue	lehatsil	לְהַצִיל
life jacket	χagorat hatsala	חֲגוֹרַת הַצָלָה (נ)
to observe, to watch	litspot, lehaʃkif	לִצְפּוֹת, לְהַשְׁקִיף
lifeguard	matsil	מַצִיל (ז)

TECHNICAL EQUIPMENT. TRANSPORT

Technical equipment

139. Computer

computer	maxſev	(ז) מַחְשֵׁב
notebook, laptop	maxſev nayad	(ז) מַחְשֵׁב נַיָּד
to turn on	lehadlik	לְהַדְלִיק
to turn off	lexabot	לְכַבּוֹת
keyboard	mik'ledet	(נ) מִקְלֶדֶת
key	makaſ	(ז) מַקָּשׁ
mouse	axbar	(ז) עַכְבָּר
mouse mat	ſa'tiax le'axbar	(ז) שָׁטִיחַ לְעַכְבָּר
button	kaftor	(ז) כַּפְתּוֹר
cursor	saman	(ז) סַמָּן
monitor	masax	(ז) מָסָךְ
screen	tsag	(ז) צַג
hard disk	disk ka'ſiax	(ז) דִּיסְק קָשִׁיחַ
hard disk capacity	'nefax disk ka'ſiax	(ז) נֶפַח דִּיסְק קָשִׁיחַ
memory	zikaron	(ז) זִכָּרוֹן
random access memory	zikaron giſa akra'it	(ז) זִכָּרוֹן גִּישָׁה אַקְרָאִית
file	'kovets	(ז) קוֹבֶץ
folder	tikiya	(נ) תִּיקִיָּה
to open (vt)	lif'toax	לִפְתּוֹחַ
to close (vt)	lisgor	לִסְגּוֹר
to save (vt)	liſmor	לִשְׁמוֹר
to delete (vt)	limxok	לִמְחוֹק
to copy (vt)	leha'atik	לְהַעְתִּיק
to sort (vt)	lemayen	לְמַיֵּן
to transfer (copy)	leha'avir	לְהַעֲבִיר
programme	toxna	(נ) תּוֹכְנָה
software	toxna	(נ) תּוֹכְנָה
programmer	metaxnet	(ז) מְתַכְנֵת
to program (vt)	letaxnet	לְתַכְנֵת
hacker	'haker	(ז) הָאקֶר
password	sisma	(נ) סִיסְמָה
virus	'virus	(ז) וִירוּס
to find, to detect	limtso, le'ater	לִמְצוֹא, לְאַתֵּר
byte	bait	(ז) בַּיְט

megabyte	megabait	מֶגָבַּייט (ז)
data	netunim	נְתוּנִים (ז"ר)
database	bsis netunim	בְּסִיס נְתוּנִים (ז)

cable (USB, etc.)	'kevel	כֶּבֶל (ז)
to disconnect (vt)	lenatek	לְנַתֵק
to connect (sth to sth)	lexaber	לְחַבֵּר

140. Internet. E-mail

Internet	'internet	אִינטֶרנֶט (ז)
browser	dafdefan	דַפדְפָן (ז)
search engine	ma'no'a xipus	מָנוֹעַ חִיפּוּשׂ (ז)
provider	sapak	סַפָּק (ז)

webmaster	menahel ha'atar	מְנַהֵל הָאַתָר (ז)
website	atar	אַתָר (ז)
web page	daf 'internet	דַף אִינטֶרנֶט (ז)

| address (e-mail ~) | 'ktovet | כְּתוֹבֶת (נ) |
| address book | 'sefer ktovot | סֵפֶר כְּתוֹבוֹת (ז) |

postbox	teivat 'do'ar	תֵיבַת דוֹאַר (נ)
post	'do'ar, 'do'al	דוֹאַר (ז), דוֹאַ"ל (ז)
full (adj)	gaduʃ	גָדוּשׁ

message	hoda'a	הוֹדָעָה (נ)
incoming messages	hoda'ot nixnasot	הוֹדָעוֹת נִכנָסוֹת (נ"ר)
outgoing messages	hoda'ot yots'ot	הוֹדָעוֹת יוֹצאוֹת (נ"ר)
sender	ʃo'leax	שׁוֹלֵחַ (ז)
to send (vt)	liʃ'loax	לִשׁלוֹחַ
sending (of mail)	ʃlixa	שְׁלִיחָה (נ)
receiver	nim'an	נִמעָן (ז)
to receive (vt)	lekabel	לְקַבֵּל

| correspondence | hitkatvut | הִתכַּתְבוּת (נ) |
| to correspond (vi) | lehitkatev | לְהִתכַּתֵב |

file	'kovets	קוֹבֶץ (ז)
to download (vt)	lehorid	לְהוֹרִיד
to create (vt)	litsor	לִיצוֹר
to delete (vt)	limxok	לִמחוֹק
deleted (adj)	maxuk	מָחוּק

connection (ADSL, etc.)	xibur	חִיבּוּר (ז)
speed	mehirut	מְהִירוּת (נ)
modem	'modem	מוֹדֶם (ז)
access	giʃa	גִישָׁה (נ)
port (e.g. input ~)	port	פּוֹרט (ז)

connection (make a ~)	xibur	חִיבּוּר (ז)
to connect to ... (vi)	lehitxaber	לְהִתחַבֵּר
to select (vt)	livxor	לִבחוֹר
to search (for ...)	lexapes	לְחַפֵּשׂ

Transport

aeroplane	matos	מָטוֹס (ז)
air ticket	kartis tisa	כַּרְטִיס טִיסָה (ז)
airline	xevrat teʻufa	חֶבְרַת תְּעוּפָה (נ)
airport	nemal teʻufa	נְמַל תְּעוּפָה (ז)
supersonic (adj)	al koli	עַל קוֹלִי
captain	kabarnit	קַבַּרְנִיט (ז)
crew	'tsevet	צֶוֶת (ז)
pilot	tayas	טַיָּס (ז)
stewardess	da'yelet	דַיֶּלֶת (נ)
navigator	navat	נַוָּט (ז)
wings	kna'fayim	כְּנָפַיִם (נ"ר)
tail	zanav	זָנָב (ז)
cockpit	'kokpit	קוֹקְפִּיט (ז)
engine	ma'no'a	מָנוֹעַ (ז)
undercarriage (landing gear)	kan nesi'a	כַּן נְסִיעָה (ז)
turbine	tur'bina	טוּרְבִּינָה (נ)
propeller	madxef	מַדְחֵף (ז)
black box	kufsa ʃxora	קוּפְסָה שְׁחוֹרָה (נ)
yoke (control column)	'hege	הֶגֶה (ז)
fuel	'delek	דֶּלֶק (ז)
safety card	hora'ot betixut	הוֹרָאוֹת בְּטִיחוּת (נ"ר)
oxygen mask	masexat xamtsan	מַסֵּיכַת חַמְצָן (נ)
uniform	madim	מַדִּים (ז"ר)
lifejacket	xagorat hatsala	חֲגוֹרַת הַצָּלָה (נ)
parachute	mitsnax	מִצְנָח (ז)
takeoff	hamra'a	הַמְרָאָה (נ)
to take off (vi)	lehamri	לְהַמְרִיא
runway	maslul hamra'a	מַסְלוּל הַמְרָאָה (ז)
visibility	re'ut	רְאוּת (נ)
flight (act of flying)	tisa	טִיסָה (נ)
altitude	'gova	גּוֹבַה (ז)
air pocket	kis avir	כִּיס אֲוִויר (ז)
seat	moʃav	מוֹשָׁב (ז)
headphones	ozniyot	אוֹזְנִיּוֹת (נ"ר)
folding tray (tray table)	magaʃ mitkapel	מַגָּשׁ מִתְקַפֵּל (ז)
airplane window	tsohar	צוֹהַר (ז)
aisle	ma'avar	מַעֲבָר (ז)

142. Train

train	ra'kevet	רַכֶּבֶת (נ)
commuter train	ra'kevet parvarim	רַכֶּבֶת פַּרְבָרִים (נ)
express train	ra'kevet mehira	רַכֶּבֶת מְהִירָה (נ)
diesel locomotive	katar 'dizel	קַטָּר דִיזֶל (ז)
steam locomotive	katar	קַטָּר (ז)
coach, carriage	karon	קָרוֹן (ז)
buffet car	kron mis'ada	קְרוֹן מִסְעָדָה (ז)
rails	mesilot	מְסִילוֹת (נ"ר)
railway	mesilat barzel	מְסִילַת בַּרְזֶל (נ)
sleeper (track support)	'eden	אֶדֶן (ז)
platform (railway ~)	ratsif	רָצִיף (ז)
platform (~ 1, 2, etc.)	mesila	מְסִילָה (נ)
semaphore	ramzor	רַמְזוֹר (ז)
station	taxana	תַחֲנָה (נ)
train driver	nahag ra'kevet	נֶהָג רַכֶּבֶת (ז)
porter (of luggage)	sabal	סַבָּל (ז)
carriage attendant	sadran ra'kevet	סַדְרָן רַכֶּבֶת (ז)
passenger	no'se'a	נוֹסֵעַ (ז)
ticket inspector	bodek	בּוֹדֵק (ז)
corridor (in train)	prozdor	פְּרוֹזְדוֹר (ז)
emergency brake	ma'atsar xirum	מַעֲצָר חִירוּם (ז)
compartment	ta	תָּא (ז)
berth	dargaʃ	דַרְגָשׁ (ז)
upper berth	dargaʃ elyon	דַרְגָשׁ עֶלְיוֹן (ז)
lower berth	dargaʃ taxton	דַרְגָשׁ תַחְתוֹן (ז)
bed linen, bedding	matsa'im	מַצָעִים (ז"ר)
ticket	kartis	כַּרְטִיס (ז)
timetable	'luax zmanim	לוּחַ זְמַנִים (ז)
information display	ʃelet meida	שֶׁלֶט מֵידָע (ז)
to leave, to depart	latset	לָצֵאת
departure (of a train)	yetsi'a	יְצִיאָה (נ)
to arrive (ab. train)	leha'gi'a	לְהַגִיעַ
arrival	haga'a	הַגָעָה (נ)
to arrive by train	leha'gi'a bera'kevet	לְהַגִיעַ בְּרַכֶּבֶת
to get on the train	la'alot lera'kevet	לַעֲלוֹת לְרַכֶּבֶת
to get off the train	la'redet mehara'kevet	לָרֶדֶת מֵהַרַכֶּבֶת
train crash	hitraskut	הִתְרַסְקוּת (נ)
to derail (vi)	la'redet mipasei ra'kevet	לָרֶדֶת מִפַּסֵי רַכֶּבֶת
steam locomotive	katar	קַטָּר (ז)
stoker, fireman	masik	מַסִיק (ז)
firebox	kivʃan	כִּבְשָׁן (ז)
coal	pexam	פֶּחָם (ז)

143. Ship

ship	sfina	סְפִינָה (נ)
vessel	sfina	סְפִינָה (נ)
steamship	oniyat kitor	אוֹנִיַת קִיטוֹר (נ)
riverboat	sfinat nahar	סְפִינַת נָהָר (נ)
cruise ship	oniyat ta'anugot	אוֹנִיַת תַעֲנוּגוֹת (נ)
cruiser	sa'yeret	סַיֶירֶת (נ)
yacht	'yaχta	יַכְטָה (נ)
tugboat	go'reret	גוֹרֶרֶת (נ)
barge	arba	אַרְבָּה (נ)
ferry	ma'a'boret	מַעֲבּוֹרֶת (נ)
sailing ship	sfinat mifras	סְפִינַת מִפְרָשׂ (נ)
brigantine	briganit	בְּרִיגָנִית (נ)
ice breaker	ʃo'veret 'keraχ	שׁוֹבֶרֶת קֶרַח (נ)
submarine	tso'lelet	צוֹלֶלֶת (נ)
boat (flat-bottomed ~)	sira	סִירָה (נ)
dinghy (lifeboat)	sira	סִירָה (נ)
lifeboat	sirat hatsala	סִירַת הַצָּלָה (נ)
motorboat	sirat ma'no'a	סִירַת מָנוֹעַ (נ)
captain	rav χovel	רַב־חוֹבֵל (ז)
seaman	malaχ	מַלָח (ז)
sailor	yamai	יַמַאי (ז)
crew	'tsevet	צֶוֶת (ז)
boatswain	rav malaχim	רַב־מַלָחִים (ז)
ship's boy	'na'ar sipun	נַעַר סִיפּוּן (ז)
cook	tabaχ	טַבָּח (ז)
ship's doctor	rofe ha'oniya	רוֹפֵא הָאוֹנִיָה (ז)
deck	sipun	סִיפּוּן (ז)
mast	'toren	תוֹרֶן (ז)
sail	mifras	מִפְרָשׂ (ז)
hold	'beten oniya	בֶּטֶן אוֹנִיָה (נ)
bow (prow)	χartom	חַרְטוֹם (ז)
stern	yarketei hasfina	יַרְכְּתֵי הַסְפִינָה (ז"ר)
oar	maʃot	מָשׁוֹט (ז)
screw propeller	madχef	מַדְחֵף (ז)
cabin	ta	תָא (ז)
wardroom	mo'adon ktsinim	מוֹעֲדוֹן קְצִינִים (ז)
engine room	χadar meχonot	חֲדַר מְכוֹנוֹת (ז)
bridge	'geʃer hapikud	גֶשֶׁר הַפִּיקוּד (ז)
radio room	ta alχutan	תָא אַלְחוּטָן (ז)
wave (radio)	'teder	תֶדֶר (ז)
logbook	yoman ha'oniya	יוֹמַן הָאוֹנִיָה (ז)
spyglass	miʃ'kefet	מִשְׁקֶפֶת (נ)
bell	pa'amon	פַּעֲמוֹן (ז)

flag	'degel	דֶּגֶל (ז)
hawser (mooring ~)	avot ha'oniya	עֲבוֹת הָאוֹנִיָּה (נ)
knot (bowline, etc.)	'keʃer	קֶשֶׁר (ז)

| deckrails | ma'ake hasipun | מַעֲקֶה הַסִּיפּוּן (ז) |
| gangway | 'keveʃ | כֶּבֶשׁ (ז) |

anchor	'ogen	עוֹגֶן (ז)
to weigh anchor	leharim 'ogen	לְהָרִים עוֹגֶן
to drop anchor	la'agon	לַעֲגוֹן
anchor chain	ʃar'ʃeret ha'ogen	שַׁרְשֶׁרֶת הָעוֹגֶן (נ)

port (harbour)	namal	נָמֵל (ז)
quay, wharf	'mezaχ	מֶזַח (ז)
to berth (moor)	la'agon	לַעֲגוֹן
to cast off	lehaflig	לְהַפְלִיג

trip, voyage	masa, tiyul	מַסָּע (ז), טִיּוּל (ז)
cruise (sea trip)	'ʃayit	שַׁיִט (ז)
course (route)	kivun	כִּיווּן (ז)
route (itinerary)	nativ	נָתִיב (ז)

fairway (safe water channel)	nativ 'ʃayit	נָתִיב שַׁיִט (ז)
shallows	sirton	שִׂרְטוֹן (ז)
to run aground	la'alot al hasirton	לַעֲלוֹת עַל הַשִּׂרְטוֹן

storm	sufa	סוּפָה (נ)
signal	ot	אוֹת (ז)
to sink (vi)	lit'bo'a	לִטְבּוֹעַ
Man overboard!	adam ba'mayim!	אָדָם בַּמַּיִם!
SOS (distress signal)	kri'at hatsala	קְרִיאַת הַצָּלָה
ring buoy	galgal hatsala	גַּלְגַּל הַצָּלָה (ז)

144. Airport

airport	nemal te'ufa	נְמֵל תְּעוּפָה (ז)
aeroplane	matos	מָטוֹס (ז)
airline	χevrat te'ufa	חֶבְרַת תְּעוּפָה (נ)
air traffic controller	bakar tisa	בַּקָּר טִיסָה (ז)

departure	hamra'a	הַמְרָאָה (נ)
arrival	neχita	נְחִיתָה (נ)
to arrive (by plane)	leha'gi'a betisa	לְהַגִּיעַ בְּטִיסָה

| departure time | zman hamra'a | זְמַן הַמְרָאָה (ז) |
| arrival time | zman neχita | זְמַן נְחִיתָה (ז) |

| to be delayed | lehit'akev | לְהִתְעַכֵּב |
| flight delay | ikuv hatisa | עִיכּוּב הַטִּיסָה (ז) |

information board	'luaχ meida	לוּחַ מֵידָע (ז)
information	meida	מֵידָע (ז)
to announce (vt)	leho'dia	לְהוֹדִיעַ
flight (e.g. next ~)	tisa	טִיסָה (נ)

| customs | 'meχes | מֶכֶס (ז) |
| customs officer | pakid 'meχes | פְּקִיד מֶכֶס (ז) |

customs declaration	hatsharat meχes	הַצהָרַת מֶכֶס (נ)
to fill in (vt)	lemale	לְמַלֵא
to fill in the declaration	lemale 'tofes hatshara	לְמַלֵא טוֹפֶס הַצהָרָה
passport control	bdikat darkonim	בְּדִיקַת דַרכּוֹנִים (נ)

luggage	kvuda	כְּבוּדָה (נ)
hand luggage	kvudat yad	כְּבוּדַת יָד (נ)
luggage trolley	eglat kvuda	עֶגלַת כְּבוּדָה (נ)

landing	neχita	נְחִיתָה (נ)
landing strip	maslul neχita	מַסלוּל נְחִיתָה (ז)
to land (vi)	linχot	לִנחוֹת
airstair (passenger stair)	'keveʃ	כֶּבֶש (ז)

check-in	tʃek in	צֶ'ק אִין (ז)
check-in counter	dalpak tʃek in	דַלפַּק צֶ'ק אִין (ז)
to check-in (vi)	leva'tse'a tʃek in	לְבַצֵעַ צֶ'ק אִין
boarding card	kartis aliya lematos	כַּרטִיס עֲלִיָה לְמָטוֹס (ז)
departure gate	'ʃa'ar yetsi'a	שַעַר יְצִיאָה (ז)

transit	ma'avar	מַעֲבָר (ז)
to wait (vt)	lehamtin	לְהַמתִין
departure lounge	traklin tisa	טרַקלִין טִיסָה (ז)
to see off	lelavot	לְלַווֹת
to say goodbye	lomar lehitra'ot	לוֹמַר לְהִתרָאוֹת

145. Bicycle. Motorcycle

bicycle	ofa'nayim	אוֹפַנַּיִים (ז"ר)
scooter	kat'no'a	קַטנוֹעַ (ז)
motorbike	ofno'a	אוֹפנוֹעַ (ז)

to go by bicycle	lirkov al ofa'nayim	לִרכּוֹב עַל אוֹפַנַּיִים
handlebars	kidon	כִּידוֹן (ז)
pedal	davʃa	דַוושָה (נ)
brakes	blamim	בּלָמִים (ז"ר)
bicycle seat (saddle)	ukaf	אוּכָּף (ז)

pump	maʃeva	מַשאֵבָה (נ)
pannier rack	sabal	סַבָּל (ז)
front lamp	panas kidmi	פָּנָס קִדמִי (ז)
helmet	kasda	קַסדָה (נ)

wheel	galgal	גַלגַל (ז)
mudguard	kanaf	כָּנָף (נ)
rim	χiʃuk	חִישוּק (ז)
spoke	χiʃur	חִישוּר (ז)

Cars

146. Types of cars

car	meχonit	מְכוֹנִית (נ)
sports car	meχonit sport	מְכוֹנִית סְפּוֹרְט (נ)
limousine	limu'zina	לִימוּזִינָה (נ)
off-road vehicle	'reχev 'ʃetaχ	רֶכֶב שֶׁטַח (ז)
drophead coupé (convertible)	meχonit gag niftaχ	מְכוֹנִית גַג נִפְתָּח (נ)
minibus	'minibus	מִינִיבּוּס (ז)
ambulance	'ambulans	אַמְבּוּלַנְס (ז)
snowplough	maf'leset 'ʃeleg	מַפְלֶסֶת שֶׁלֶג (נ)
lorry	masa'it	מַשָׂאִית (נ)
road tanker	meχalit 'delek	מֵיכָלִית דֶלֶק (נ)
van (small truck)	masa'it kala	מַשָׂאִית קַלָּה (נ)
tractor unit	gorer	גוֹרֵר (ז)
trailer	garur	גָרוּר (ז)
comfortable (adj)	'noaχ	נוֹחַ
used (adj)	meʃumaʃ	מְשׁוּמָשׁ

147. Cars. Bodywork

bonnet	miχse hama'no'a	מִכְסֶה הַמָנוֹעַ (ז)
wing	kanaf	כָּנָף (נ)
roof	gag	גַג (ז)
windscreen	ʃimʃa kidmit	שִׁמְשָׁה קִדְמִית (נ)
rear-view mirror	mar'a aχorit	מַרְאָה אֲחוֹרִית (נ)
windscreen washer	mataz	מַתָז (ז)
windscreen wipers	magev	מַגֵב (ז)
side window	ʃimʃat tsad	שִׁמְשַׁת צַד (נ)
electric window	χalon χaʃmali	חַלוֹן חַשְׁמַלִי (ז)
aerial	an'tena	אַנְטֶנָה (נ)
sunroof	χalon gag	חַלוֹן גַג (ז)
bumper	pagoʃ	פָּגוֹשׁ (ז)
boot	ta mit'an	תָא מִטְעָן (ז)
roof luggage rack	gagon	גָגוֹן (ז)
door	'delet	דֶלֶת (נ)
door handle	yadit	יָדִית (נ)
door lock	man'ul	מַנְעוּל (ז)
number plate	luχit riʃui	לוּחִית רִישׁוּי (נ)
silencer	am'am	עַמְעָם (ז)

| petrol tank | meixal 'delek | מֵיכָל דֶּלֶק (ז) |
| exhaust pipe | maflet | מַפְלֵט (ז) |

accelerator	gaz	גָּז (ז)
pedal	davʃa	דַּוְושָׁה (נ)
accelerator pedal	davʃat gaz	דַּוְושַׁת גָּז (נ)

brake	'belem	בֶּלֶם (ז)
brake pedal	davʃat hablamim	דַּוְושַׁת הַבְּלָמִים (נ)
to brake (use the brake)	livlom	לִבְלוֹם
handbrake	'belem xaniya	בֶּלֶם חֲנָיָה (ז)

clutch	matsmed	מַצְמֵד (ז)
clutch pedal	davʃat hamatsmed	דַּוְושַׁת הַמַּצְמֵד (נ)
clutch disc	luxit hamatsmed	לוּחִית הַמַּצְמֵד (נ)
shock absorber	bolem za'a'zu'a	בּוֹלֵם זַעֲזוּעִים (ז)

wheel	galgal	גַּלְגַּל (ז)
spare tyre	galgal xilufi	גַּלְגַּל חִילוּפִי (ז)
tyre	tsmig	צְמִיג (ז)
wheel cover (hubcap)	tsa'laxat galgal	צַלַּחַת גַּלְגַּל (נ)

driving wheels	galgalim meni'im	גַּלְגַּלִּים מְנִיעִים (ז"ר)
front-wheel drive (as adj)	shel hana'a kidmit	שֶׁל הֲנָעָה קִדְמִית
rear-wheel drive (as adj)	shel hana'a axorit	שֶׁל הֲנָעָה אֲחוֹרִית
all-wheel drive (as adj)	shel hana'a male'a	שֶׁל הֲנָעָה מָלְאָה

gearbox	teivat hiluxim	תֵּיבַת הִילוּכִים (נ)
automatic (adj)	oto'mati	אוֹטוֹמָטִי
mechanical (adj)	me'xani	מֵכָנִי
gear lever	yadit hiluxim	יָדִית הִילוּכִים (נ)

| headlamp | panas kidmi | פָּנָס קִדְמִי (ז) |
| headlights | panasim | פָּנָסִים (ז"ר) |

dipped headlights	or namux	אוֹר נָמוּךְ (ז)
full headlights	or ga'voha	אוֹר גָּבוֹהַּ (ז)
brake light	or 'belem	אוֹר בֶּלֶם (ז)

sidelights	orot xanaya	אוֹרוֹת חֲנָיָה (ז"ר)
hazard lights	orot xerum	אוֹרוֹת חֵירוּם (ז"ר)
fog lights	orot arafel	אוֹרוֹת עֲרָפֶל (ז"ר)
turn indicator	panas itut	פָּנָס אִיתּוּת (ז)
reversing light	orot revers	אוֹרוֹת רֶבֶרְס (ז"ר)

148. Cars. Passenger compartment

car interior	ta hanos'im	תָּא הַנּוֹסְעִים (ז)
leather (as adj)	asui me'or	עָשׂוּי מֵעוֹר
velour (as adj)	ktifati	קְטִיפָתִי
upholstery	ripud	רִיפּוּד (ז)

| instrument (gage) | maxven | מַכְוֵון (ז) |
| dashboard | 'luax maxvenim | לוּחַ מַכְוֵונִים (ז) |

speedometer	mad mehirut	מַד מְהִירוּת (ז)
needle (pointer)	'maxat	מַחַט (נ)
mileometer	mad merxak	מַד מֶרְחָק (ז)
indicator (sensor)	xaifan	חַיְישָׁן (ז)
level	ramat mi'lui	רָמַת מִילוּי (נ)
warning light	nurat azhara	נוּרַת אַזְהָרָה (נ)
steering wheel	'hege	הֶגֶה (ז)
horn	tsofar	צוֹפָר (ז)
button	kaftor	כַּפְתוֹר (ז)
switch	'meteg	מֶתֶג (ז)
seat	mofav	מוֹשָׁב (ז)
backrest	mif''enet	מִשְׁעֶנֶת (נ)
headrest	mif''enet rof	מִשְׁעֶנֶת רֹאשׁ (נ)
seat belt	xagorat betixut	חֲגוֹרַת בְּטִיחוּת (נ)
to fasten the belt	lehadek xagora	לְהַדֵּק חֲגוֹרָה
adjustment (of seats)	kivnun	כִּיווּנוּן (ז)
airbag	karit avir	כָּרִית אֲווִיר (נ)
air-conditioner	mazgan	מַזְגָן (ז)
radio	'radyo	רָדִיוֹ (ז)
CD player	'diskmen	דִיסְקְמָן (ז)
to turn on	lehadlik	לְהַדְלִיק
aerial	an'tena	אַנְטֶנָה (נ)
glove box	ta kfafot	תָא כְּפָפוֹת (ז)
ashtray	ma'afera	מַאֲפֵרָה (נ)

149. Cars. Engine

engine, motor	ma'no'a	מָנוֹעַ (ז)
diesel (as adj)	shel 'dizel	שֶׁל דִיזֶל
petrol (as adj)	'delek	דֶלֶק
engine volume	'nefax ma'no'a	נֶפַח מָנוֹעַ (ז)
power	otsma	עוֹצְמָה (נ)
horsepower	'koax sus	כּוֹחַ סוּס (ז)
piston	buxna	בּוּכְנָה (נ)
cylinder	tsi'linder	צִילִינְדֶר (ז)
valve	fastom	שַׁסְתוֹם (ז)
injector	mazrek	מַזְרֵק (ז)
generator (alternator)	mexolel	מְחוֹלֵל (ז)
carburettor	me'ayed	מְאַייֵד (ז)
motor oil	'femen mano'im	שֶׁמֶן מָנוֹעִים (ז)
radiator	matsnen	מַצְנֵן (ז)
coolant	nozel kirur	נוֹזֶל קִירוּר (ז)
cooling fan	me'avrer	מְאַווְרֵר (ז)
battery (accumulator)	matsber	מַצְבֵּר (ז)
starter	mat'ne'a	מַתְנֵעַ (ז)

| ignition | hatsata | הַצָּתָה (נ) |
| sparking plug | matset | מַצֵּת (ז) |

terminal (battery ~)	'hedek	הֶדֶק (ז)
positive terminal	'hedek χiyuvi	הֶדֶק חִיּוּבִי (ז)
negative terminal	'hedek ʃlili	הֶדֶק שְׁלִילִי (ז)
fuse	natiχ	נָתִיך (ז)

air filter	masnen avir	מַסְנֵן אֲוִיר (ז)
oil filter	masnen 'ʃemen	מַסְנֵן שֶׁמֶן (ז)
fuel filter	masnen 'delek	מַסְנֵן דֶּלֶק (ז)

150. Cars. Crash. Repair

car crash	te'una	תְּאוּנָה (נ)
traffic accident	te'unat draχim	תְּאוּנַת דְּרָכִים (נ)
to crash (into the wall, etc.)	lehitnageʃ	לְהִתְנַגֵּשׁ
to get smashed up	lehima'eχ	לְהִימָעֵך
damage	'nezek	נֶזֶק (ז)
intact (unscathed)	ʃalem	שָׁלֵם

breakdown	takala	תַּקָּלָה (נ)
to break down (vi)	lehitkalkel	לְהִתְקַלְקֵל
towrope	'χevel grar	חֶבֶל גְּרָר (ז)

puncture	'teker	תֶּקֶר (ז)
to have a puncture	lehitpantʃer	לְהִתְפַּנְצֵ'ר
to pump up	lena'peaχ	לְנַפֵּחַ
pressure	'laχats	לַחַץ (ז)
to check (to examine)	livdok	לִבְדּוֹק

repair	ʃiputs	שִׁפּוּץ (ז)
garage (auto service shop)	musaχ	מוּסָך (ז)
spare part	'χelek χiluf	חֵלֶק חִילּוּף (ז)
part	'χelek	חֵלֶק (ז)

bolt (with nut)	'boreg	בּוֹרֶג (ז)
screw (fastener)	'boreg	בּוֹרֶג (ז)
nut	om	אוֹם (ז)
washer	diskit	דִיסְקִית (נ)
bearing (e.g. ball ~)	mesav	מֵסַב (ז)

tube	tsinorit	צִינּוֹרִית (נ)
gasket (head ~)	'etem	אֶטֶם (ז)
cable, wire	χut	חוּט (ז)

jack	dʒek	גֵ'ק (ז)
spanner	maf'teaχ bragim	מַפְתֵּחַ בְּרָגִים (ז)
hammer	patiʃ	פַּטִּישׁ (ז)
pump	maʃeva	מַשְׁאֵבָה (נ)
screwdriver	mavreg	מַבְרֵג (ז)

| fire extinguisher | mataf | מַטָּף (ז) |
| warning triangle | meʃulaʃ χirum | מְשׁוּלָּשׁ חֵירוּם (ז) |

to stall (vi)	ledomem	לְדוֹמֵם
stall (n)	hadmama	הַדְמָמָה (נ)
to be broken	lihyot ʃavur	לִהְיוֹת שָׁבוּר
to overheat (vi)	lehitχamem yoter midai	לְהִתְחַמֵם יוֹתֵר מִדַי
to be clogged up	lehisatem	לְהִיסָתֵם
to freeze up (pipes, etc.)	likpo	לִקְפּוֹא
to burst (vi, ab. tube)	lehitpa'ke'a	לְהִתְפַּקֵעַ
pressure	'laχaʦ	לַחַץ (ז)
level	ramat mi'lui	רָמַת מִילוּי (נ)
slack (~ belt)	rafe	רָפֶּה
dent	dfika	דְפִיקָה (נ)
knocking noise (engine)	'ra'aʃ	רַעַש (ז)
crack	'sedek	סֶדֶק (ז)
scratch	srita	שְׂרִיטָה (נ)

151. Cars. Road

road	'dereχ	דֶרֶךְ (נ)
motorway	kviʃ mahir	כְּבִיש מָהִיר (ז)
highway	kviʃ mahir	כְּבִיש מָהִיר (ז)
direction (way)	kivun	כִּיווּן (ז)
distance	merχak	מֶרְחָק (ז)
bridge	'geʃer	גֶשֶׁר (ז)
car park	χanaya	חֲנָיָה (נ)
square	kikar	כִּיכָּר (נ)
road junction	meχlaf	מֶחְלָף (ז)
tunnel	minhara	מִנְהָרָה (נ)
petrol station	taχanat 'delek	תַחֲנַת דֶלֶק (נ)
car park	migraʃ χanaya	מִגְרַש חֲנָיָה (ז)
petrol pump	maʃevat 'delek	מַשְׁאֵבַת דֶלֶק (נ)
auto repair shop	musaχ	מוּסָךְ (ז)
to fill up	letadlek	לְתַדְלֵק
fuel	'delek	דֶלֶק (ז)
jerrycan	'dʒerikan	גִ'רִיקָן (ז)
asphalt, tarmac	asfalt	אַסְפַלְט (ז)
road markings	simun	סִימוּן (ז)
kerb	sfat midraχa	שְׂפַת מִדְרָכָה (נ)
crash barrier	ma'ake betiχut	מַעֲקֶה בְּטִיחוּת (ז)
ditch	te'ala	תְעָלָה (נ)
roadside (shoulder)	ʃulei ha'dereχ	שׁוּלֵי הַדֶרֶךְ (ז"ר)
lamppost	amud te'ura	עַמוּד תְאוֹרָה (ז)
to drive (a car)	linhog	לִנְהוֹג
to turn (e.g., ~ left)	lifnot	לִפְנוֹת
to make a U-turn	leva'ʦe'a pniyat parsa	לְבַצֵעַ פְּנִיַית פַּרְסָה
reverse (~ gear)	hiluχ aχori	הִילוּךְ אֲחוֹרִי (ז)
to honk (vi)	liʦpor	לִצְפּוֹר
honk (sound)	ʦfira	צְפִירָה (נ)

to get stuck (in the mud, etc.)	lehitaka	לְהִיתָקַע
to spin the wheels	lesovev et hagalgal al rek	לְסוֹבֵב אֶת הַגַּלְגַּלִים עַל רֵיק
to cut, to turn off (vt)	ledomem	לְדוֹמֵם
speed	mehirut	מְהִירוּת (נ)
to exceed the speed limit	linhog bemehirut muf'rezet	לִנְהוֹג בִּמְהִירוּת מוּפְרֶזֶת
to give a ticket	liknos	לִקְנוֹס
traffic lights	ramzor	רַמְזוֹר (ז)
driving licence	riʃyon nehiga	רִשְׁיוֹן נְהִיגָה (ז)
level crossing	ma'avar pasei ra'kevet	מַעֲבַר פַּסֵי רַכֶּבֶת (ז)
crossroads	'tsomet	צוֹמֶת (ז)
zebra crossing	ma'avar xatsaya	מַעֲבַר חֲצָיָה (ז)
bend, curve	pniya	פְּנִיָיה (נ)
pedestrian precinct	midreχov	מִדְרְחוֹב (ז)

PEOPLE. LIFE EVENTS

152. Holidays. Event

celebration, holiday	χagiga	חֲגִיגָה (נ)
national day	χag le'umi	חַג לְאוּמִי (ז)
public holiday	yom χag	יוֹם חַג (ז)
to commemorate (vt)	laχgog	לַחְגּוֹג
event (happening)	hitraχaʃut	הִתְרַחֲשׁוּת (נ)
event (organized activity)	ei'ru'a	אֵירוּעַ (ז)
banquet (party)	se'uda χagigit	סְעוּדָה חֲגִיגִית (נ)
reception (formal party)	ei'ruaχ	אֵירוּחַ (ז)
feast	miʃte	מִשְׁתָּה (ז)
anniversary	yom haʃana	יוֹם הַשָּׁנָה (ז)
jubilee	χag hayovel	חַג הַיּוֹבֵל (ז)
to celebrate (vt)	laχgog	לַחְגּוֹג
New Year	ʃana χadaʃa	שָׁנָה חֲדָשָׁה (נ)
Happy New Year!	ʃana tova!	שָׁנָה טוֹבָה!
Father Christmas	'santa 'kla'us	סַנְטָה קלָאוּס
Christmas	χag hamolad	חַג הַמּוֹלָד (ז)
Merry Christmas!	χag hamolad sa'meaχ!	חַג הַמּוֹלָד שָׂמֵחַ!
Christmas tree	ets χag hamolad	עֵץ חַג הַמּוֹלָד (ז)
fireworks (fireworks show)	zikukim	זִיקוּקִים (ז"ר)
wedding	χatuna	חֲתוּנָה (נ)
groom	χatan	חָתָן (ז)
bride	kala	כַּלָּה (נ)
to invite (vt)	lehazmin	לְהַזְמִין
invitation card	hazmana	הַזְמָנָה (נ)
guest	o'reaχ	אוֹרֵחַ (ז)
to visit (~ your parents, etc.)	levaker	לְבַקֵּר
to meet the guests	lekabel orχim	לְקַבֵּל אוֹרְחִים
gift, present	matana	מַתָּנָה (נ)
to give (sth as present)	latet matana	לָתֵת מַתָּנָה
to receive gifts	lekabel matanot	לְקַבֵּל מַתָּנוֹת
bouquet (of flowers)	zer	זֵר (ז)
congratulations	braχa	בְּרָכָה (נ)
to congratulate (vt)	levareχ	לְבָרֵך
greetings card	kartis braχa	כַּרְטִיס בְּרָכָה (ז)
to send a postcard	liʃloaχ gluya	לִשְׁלוֹחַ גלוּיָה
to get a postcard	lekabel gluya	לְקַבֵּל גלוּיָה

toast	leharim kosit	לְהָרִים כּוֹסִית
to offer (a drink, etc.)	leχabed	לְכַבֵּד
champagne	ʃam'panya	שַׁמְפַּנְיָה (נ)

to enjoy oneself	lehanot	לֵיהָנוֹת
merriment (gaiety)	alitsut	עֲלִיצוּת (נ)
joy (emotion)	simχa	שִׂמְחָה (נ)

| dance | rikud | רִיקוּד (ז) |
| to dance (vi, vt) | lirkod | לִרְקוֹד |

| waltz | vals | וַלְס (ז) |
| tango | 'tango | טַנְגוֹ (ז) |

153. Funerals. Burial

cemetery	beit kvarot	בֵּית קְבָרוֹת (ז)
grave, tomb	'kever	קֶבֶר (ז)
cross	tslav	צְלָב (ז)
gravestone	matseva	מַצֵּבָה (נ)
fence	gader	גָּדֵר (נ)
chapel	beit tfila	בֵּית תְּפִילָה (ז)

death	'mavet	מָוֶת (ז)
to die (vi)	lamut	לָמוּת
the deceased	niftar	נִפְטָר (ז)
mourning	'evel	אֵבֶל (ז)

to bury (vt)	likbor	לִקְבּוֹר
undertakers	beit levayot	בֵּית לְוָיוֹת (ז)
funeral	levaya	לְוָיָה (נ)

wreath	zer	זֵר (ז)
coffin	aron metim	אֲרוֹן מֵתִים (ז)
hearse	kron hamet	קְרוֹן הַמֵּת (ז)
shroud	taχriχim	תַּכְרִיכִים (ז"ר)

funeral procession	tahaluχat 'evel	תַּהֲלוּכַת אֵבֶל (נ)
funerary urn	kad 'efer	כַּד אֶפֶר (ז)
crematorium	misrafa	מִשְׂרָפָה (נ)

obituary	moda'at 'evel	מוֹדָעַת אֵבֶל (נ)
to cry (weep)	livkot	לִבְכּוֹת
to sob (vi)	lehitya'peaχ	לְהִתְיַפֵּחַ

154. War. Soldiers

platoon	maχlaka	מַחְלָקָה (נ)
company	pluga	פְּלוּגָה (נ)
regiment	χativa	חֲטִיבָה (נ)
army	tsava	צָבָא (ז)
division	ugda	אוּגְדָּה (נ)

| section, squad | kita | פִּיתָה (נ) |
| host (army) | 'χayil | חַיִל (ז) |

| soldier | χayal | חַיָּיל (ז) |
| officer | katsin | קָצִין (ז) |

private	turai	טוּרָאי (ז)
sergeant	samal	סַמָל (ז)
lieutenant	'segen	סֶגֶן (ז)
captain	'seren	סֶרֶן (ז)
major	rav 'seren	רַב־סֶרֶן (ז)
colonel	aluf miʃne	אַלוּף מִשְׁנֶה (ז)
general	aluf	אַלוּף (ז)

sailor	yamai	יַמַאי (ז)
captain	rav χovel	רַב־חוֹבֵל (ז)
boatswain	rav malaχim	רַב־מַלָּחִים (ז)

artilleryman	totχan	תוֹתְחָן (ז)
paratrooper	tsanχan	צַנְחָן (ז)
pilot	tayas	טַיָּיס (ז)
navigator	navat	נַוָּוט (ז)
mechanic	meχonai	מְכוֹנַאי (ז)

pioneer (sapper)	χablan	חַבְּלָן (ז)
parachutist	tsanχan	צַנְחָן (ז)
reconnaissance scout	iʃ modi'in kravi	אִישׁ מוֹדִיעִין קְרָבִי (ז)
sniper	tsalaf	צַלָּף (ז)
patrol (group)	siyur	סִיוּר (ז)
to patrol (vt)	lefatrel	לְפַטְרֵל
sentry, guard	zakif	זָקִיף (ז)

warrior	loχem	לוֹחֵם (ז)
patriot	patriyot	פַּטְרִיוֹט (ז)
hero	gibor	גִיבּוֹר (ז)
heroine	gibora	גִיבּוֹרָה (נ)

traitor	boged	בּוֹגֵד (ז)
to betray (vt)	livgod	לִבְגוֹד
deserter	arik	עָרִיק (ז)
to desert (vi)	la'arok	לַעֲרוֹק

mercenary	sχir 'χerev	שְׂכִיר חֶרֶב (ז)
recruit	tiron	טִירוֹן (ז)
volunteer	mitnadev	מִתְנַדֵב (ז)

dead (n)	harug	הָרוּג (ז)
wounded (n)	pa'tsu'a	פָּצוּעַ (ז)
prisoner of war	ʃavui	שָׁבוּי (ז)

155. War. Military actions. Part 1

| war | milχama | מִלְחָמָה (נ) |
| to be at war | lehilaχem | לְהִילָחֵם |

civil war	mil'xemet ezraxim	מִלְחֶמֶת אֶזְרָחִים (נ)
treacherously (adv)	bogdani	בּוֹגְדָנִי
declaration of war	haxrazat milxama	הַכְרָזַת מִלְחָמָה (נ)
to declare (~ war)	lehaxriz	לְהַכְרִיז
aggression	tokfanut	תּוֹקְפָּנוּת (נ)
to attack (invade)	litkof	לִתְקוֹף

to invade (vt)	lixboʃ	לִכְבּוֹש
invader	koveʃ	כּוֹבֵש (ז)
conqueror	koveʃ	כּוֹבֵש (ז)

defence	hagana	הֲגָנָה (נ)
to defend (a country, etc.)	lehagen al	לְהָגֵן עַל
to defend (against …)	lehitgonen	לְהִתְגּוֹנֵן

enemy	oyev	אוֹיֵב (ז)
foe, adversary	yariv	יָרִיב (ז)
enemy (as adj)	ʃel oyev	שֶׁל אוֹיֵב

strategy	astra'tegya	אַסְטְרָטֶגְיָה (נ)
tactics	'taktika	טַקְטִיקָה (נ)

order	pkuda	פְּקוּדָה (נ)
command (order)	pkuda	פְּקוּדָה (נ)
to order (vt)	lifkod	לִפְקוֹד
mission	mesima	מְשִׂימָה (נ)
secret (adj)	sodi	סוֹדִי

battle	maʻaraxa	מַעֲרָכָה (נ)
combat	krav	קְרָב (ז)

attack	hatkafa	הַתְקָפָה (נ)
charge (assault)	histaʻarut	הִסְתַּעֲרוּת (נ)
to storm (vt)	lehistaʻer	לְהִסְתַּעֵר
siege (to be under ~)	matsor	מָצוֹר (ז)

offensive (n)	mitkafa	מִתְקָפָה (נ)
to go on the offensive	latset lemitkafa	לָצֵאת לְמִתְקָפָה

retreat	nesiga	נְסִיגָה (נ)
to retreat (vi)	la'seget	לָסֶגֶת

encirclement	kitur	כִּיתּוּר (ז)
to encircle (vt)	lexater	לְכַתֵּר

bombing (by aircraft)	haftsatsa	הַפְצָצָה (נ)
to drop a bomb	lehatil ptsatsa	לְהָטִיל פְּצָצָה
to bomb (vt)	lehaftsits	לְהַפְצִיץ
explosion	pitsuts	פִּיצוּץ (ז)

shot	yeriya	יְרִיָּה (נ)
to fire (~ a shot)	lirot	לִירוֹת
firing (burst of ~)	'yeri	יְרִי (ז)

to aim (to point a weapon)	lexaven 'neʃek	לְכַוֵּון נֶשֶׁק
to point (a gun)	lexaven	לְכַוֵּון

to hit (the target)	lik'lo'a	לִקְלוֹעַ
to sink (~ a ship)	lehat'bi'a	לְהַטְבִּיעַ
hole (in a ship)	pirtsa	פִּרְצָה (נ)
to founder, to sink (vi)	lit'bo'a	לִטְבּוֹעַ

front (war ~)	χazit	חֲזִית (נ)
evacuation	pinui	פִּינוּי (ז)
to evacuate (vt)	lefanot	לְפַנּוֹת

trench	te'ala	תְּעָלָה (נ)
barbed wire	'tayil dokrani	תַּיִל דּוֹקְרָנִי (ז)
barrier (anti tank ~)	maχsom	מַחְסוֹם (ז)
watchtower	migdal ʃmira	מִגְדַּל שְׁמִירָה (ז)

military hospital	beit χolim tsva'i	בֵּית חוֹלִים צְבָאִי (ז)
to wound (vt)	lif'tso'a	לִפְצוֹעַ
wound	'petsa	פֶּצַע (ז)
wounded (n)	pa'tsu'a	פָּצוּעַ (ז)
to be wounded	lehipatsa	לְהִיפָּצַע
serious (wound)	kaʃe	קָשֶׁה

156. Weapons

weapons	'neʃek	נֶשֶׁק (ז)
firearms	'neʃek χam	נֶשֶׁק חַם (ז)
cold weapons (knives, etc.)	'neʃek kar	נֶשֶׁק קַר (ז)

chemical weapons	'neʃek 'χimi	נֶשֶׁק כִּימִי (ז)
nuclear (adj)	gar'ini	גַּרְעִינִי
nuclear weapons	'neʃek gar'ini	נֶשֶׁק גַּרְעִינִי (ז)

| bomb | ptsatsa | פְּצָצָה (נ) |
| atomic bomb | ptsatsa a'tomit | פְּצָצָה אֲטוֹמִית (נ) |

pistol (gun)	ekdaχ	אֶקְדָּח (ז)
rifle	rove	רוֹבֶה (ז)
submachine gun	tat mak'le'a	תַּת־מַקְלֵעַ (ז)
machine gun	mak'le'a	מַקְלֵעַ (ז)

muzzle	kane	קָנֶה (ז)
barrel	kane	קָנֶה (ז)
calibre	ka'liber	קָלִיבֶּר (ז)

trigger	'hedek	הֶדֶק (ז)
sight (aiming device)	ka'venet	כַּוֶּנֶת (נ)
magazine	maχsanit	מַחְסָנִית (נ)
butt (shoulder stock)	kat	קַת (נ)

| hand grenade | rimon | רִימוֹן (ז) |
| explosive | 'χomer 'nefets | חוֹמֶר נֶפֶץ (ז) |

bullet	ka'li'a	קְלִיעַ (ז)
cartridge	kadur	כַּדּוּר (ז)
charge	te'ina	טְעִינָה (נ)

ammunition	taχ'moʃet	תַּחְמֹשֶׁת (נ)
bomber (aircraft)	maftsits	מַפְצִיץ (ז)
fighter	metos krav	מְטוֹס קְרָב (ז)
helicopter	masok	מָסוֹק (ז)

anti-aircraft gun	totaχ 'neged metosim	תּוֹתָח נֶגֶד מְטוֹסִים (ז)
tank	tank	טַנְק (ז)
tank gun	totaχ	תּוֹתָח (ז)

artillery	arti'lerya	אַרְטִילֶרְיָה (נ)
gun (cannon, howitzer)	totaχ	תּוֹתָח (ז)
to lay (a gun)	leχaven	לְכַוֵּון

shell (projectile)	pagaz	פָּגָז (ז)
mortar bomb	ptsatsat margema	פְּצָצַת מַרְגֵּמָה (נ)
mortar	margema	מַרְגֵּמָה (נ)
splinter (shell fragment)	resis	רְסִיס (ז)

submarine	tso'lelet	צוֹלֶלֶת (נ)
torpedo	tor'pedo	טוֹרְפֶּדוֹ (ז)
missile	til	טִיל (ז)

to load (gun)	lit'on	לִטְעוֹן
to shoot (vi)	lirot	לִירוֹת
to point at (the cannon)	leχaven	לְכַוֵּון
bayonet	kidon	כִּידוֹן (ז)

rapier	'χerev	חֶרֶב (נ)
sabre (e.g. cavalry ~)	'χerev paraʃim	חֶרֶב פָּרָשִׁים (ז)
spear (weapon)	χanit	חֲנִית (נ)
bow	'keʃet	קֶשֶׁת (נ)
arrow	χets	חֵץ (ז)
musket	musket	מוּסְקֵט (ז)
crossbow	'keʃet metsu'levet	קֶשֶׁת מְצוֹלֶבֶת (נ)

157. Ancient people

primitive (prehistoric)	kadmon	קַדְמוֹן
prehistoric (adj)	prehis'tori	פְּרֶהִיסְטוֹרִי
ancient (~ civilization)	atik	עַתִּיק

Stone Age	idan ha''even	עִידָן הָאֶבֶן (ז)
Bronze Age	idan ha'arad	עִידָן הָאָרָד (ז)
Ice Age	idan ha'keraχ	עִידָן הַקֶּרַח (ז)

tribe	'ʃevet	שֵׁבֶט (ז)
cannibal	oχel adam	אוֹכֵל אָדָם (ז)
hunter	tsayad	צַיָּיד (ז)
to hunt (vi, vt)	latsud	לָצוּד
mammoth	ma'muta	מָמוּטָה (נ)

cave	me'ara	מְעָרָה (נ)
fire	eʃ	אֵשׁ (נ)
campfire	medura	מְדוּרָה (נ)

cave painting	pet'roglif	פֶּטְרוֹגְלִיף (ז)
tool (e.g. stone axe)	kli	כְּלִי (ז)
spear	χanit	חֲנִית (נ)
stone axe	garzen ha'even	גַּרְזֶן הָאֶבֶן (ז)
to be at war	lehilaχem	לְהִילָחֵם
to domesticate (vt)	levayet	לְבַיֵּית
idol	'pesel	פֶּסֶל (ז)
to worship (vt)	la'avod et	לַעֲבוֹד אֶת
superstition	emuna tfela	אֱמוּנָה תְּפֵלָה (נ)
rite	'tekes	טֶקֶס (ז)
evolution	evo'luṭsya	אֵבוֹלוּצְיָה (נ)
development	hitpatχut	הִתְפַּתְּחוּת (נ)
disappearance (extinction)	he'almut	הֵיעָלְמוּת (נ)
to adapt oneself	lehistagel	לְהִסְתַּגֵּל
archaeology	arχeʾo'logya	אַרְכֵיאוֹלוֹגְיָה (נ)
archaeologist	arχeʾolog	אַרְכֵיאוֹלוֹג (ז)
archaeological (adj)	arχeʾo'logi	אַרְכֵיאוֹלוֹגִי
excavation site	atar χafirot	אֲתַר חֲפִירוֹת (ז)
excavations	χafirot	חֲפִירוֹת (נ"ר)
find (object)	mimṭsa	מִמְצָא (ז)
fragment	resis	רְסִיס (ז)

158. Middle Ages

people (ethnic group)	am	עַם (ז)
peoples	amim	עַמִּים (ז"ר)
tribe	'ʃevet	שֵׁבֶט (ז)
tribes	ʃvatim	שְׁבָטִים (ז"ר)
barbarians	bar'barim	בַּרְבָּרִים (ז"ר)
Gauls	'galim	גָּאלִים (ז"ר)
Goths	'gotim	גוֹתִים (ז"ר)
Slavs	'slavim	סְלָאבִים (ז"ר)
Vikings	'vikingim	וִיקִינְגִים (ז"ר)
Romans	roma'im	רוֹמָאִים (ז"ר)
Roman (adj)	'romi	רוֹמִי
Byzantines	bi'zantim	בִּיזַנְטִים (ז"ר)
Byzantium	bizantion, bizanṭs	בִּיזַנְטִיוֹן, בִּיזַנְץ (נ)
Byzantine (adj)	bi'zanti	בִּיזַנְטִי
emperor	keisar	קֵיסָר (ז)
leader, chief (tribal ~)	manhig	מַנְהִיג (ז)
powerful (~ king)	rav 'koaχ	רַב־כּוֹחַ
king	'meleχ	מֶלֶךְ (ז)
ruler (sovereign)	ʃalit	שַׁלִּיט (ז)
knight	abir	אַבִּיר (ז)
feudal lord	fe'odal	פֵיאוֹדָל (ז)

| feudal (adj) | fe'o'dali | פֵּיאוֹדָלִי |
| vassal | vasal | וָסָל (ז) |

duke	dukas	דּוּכָּס (ז)
earl	rozen	רוֹזֵן (ז)
baron	baron	בָּרוֹן (ז)
bishop	'biʃof	בִּישׁוֹף (ז)

armour	ʃiryon	שִׁרְיוֹן (ז)
shield	magen	מָגֵן (ז)
sword	'χerev	חֶרֶב (נ)
visor	magen panim	מָגֵן פָּנִים (ז)
chainmail	ʃiryon kaskasim	שִׁרְיוֹן קַשְׂקַשִּׂים (ז)

| Crusade | masa tslav | מַסַּע צְלָב (ז) |
| crusader | tsalban | צַלְבָּן (ז) |

territory	'ʃetaχ	שֶׁטַח (ז)
to attack (invade)	litkof	לִתְקוֹף
to conquer (vt)	liχboʃ	לִכְבּוֹשׁ
to occupy (invade)	lehiʃtalet	לְהִשְׁתַּלֵּט

siege (to be under ~)	matsor	מָצוֹר (ז)
besieged (adj)	natsur	נָצוּר
to besiege (vt)	latsur	לָצוּר

inquisition	inkvi'zitsya	אִינְקְוִוִיזִיצְיָה (נ)
inquisitor	inkvi'zitor	אִינְקְוִוִיזִיטוֹר (ז)
torture	inui	עִינּוּי (ז)
cruel (adj)	aχzari	אַכְזָרִי
heretic	kofer	כּוֹפֵר (ז)
heresy	kfira	כְּפִירָה (נ)

seafaring	haflaga bayam	הַפְלָגָה בַּיָּם (נ)
pirate	ʃoded yam	שׁוֹדֵד יָם (ז)
piracy	pi'ratiyut	פִּירָטִיּוּת (נ)
boarding (attack)	la'alot al	לַעֲלוֹת עַל
loot, booty	ʃalal	שָׁלָל (ז)
treasure	otsarot	אוֹצָרוֹת (ז"ר)

discovery	taglit	תַּגְלִית (נ)
to discover (new land, etc.)	legalot	לְגַלּוֹת
expedition	miʃ'laχat	מִשְׁלַחַת (נ)

musketeer	musketer	מוּסְקֶטֵר (ז)
cardinal	χaʃman	חַשְׁמָן (ז)
heraldry	he'raldika	הֶרַלְדִּיקָה (נ)
heraldic (adj)	he'raldi	הֶרַלְדִּי

159. Leader. Chief. Authorities

king	'meleχ	מֶלֶךְ (ז)
queen	malka	מַלְכָּה (נ)
royal (adj)	malχuti	מַלְכוּתִי

kingdom	mamlaχa	מַמְלָכָה (נ)
prince	nasiχ	נָסִיך (ז)
princess	nesiχa	נְסִיכָה (נ)

president	nasi	נָשִׂיא (ז)
vice-president	sgan nasi	סְגַן נָשִׂיא (ז)
senator	se'nator	סֶנָאטוֹר (ז)

monarch	'meleχ	מֶלֶך (ז)
ruler (sovereign)	ʃalit	שַׁלִיט (ז)
dictator	rodan	רוֹדָן (ז)
tyrant	aruʦ	עָרוּץ (ז)
magnate	eil hon	אֵיל הוֹן (ז)

director	menahel	מְנַהֵל (ז)
chief	menahel, roʃ	מְנַהֵל (ז), רֹאש (ז)
manager (director)	menahel	מְנַהֵל (ז)
boss	bos	בּוֹס (ז)
owner	'baʿal	בַּעַל (ז)

leader	manhig	מַנְהִיג (ז)
head (~ of delegation)	roʃ	רֹאש (ז)
authorities	ʃiltonot	שִׁלְטוֹנוֹת (ז"ר)
superiors	memunim	מְמוּנִים (ז"ר)

governor	moʃel	מוֹשֵׁל (ז)
consul	'konsul	קוֹנְסוּל (ז)
diplomat	diplomat	דִיפְלוֹמָט (ז)
mayor	roʃ ha'ir	רֹאש הָעִיר (ז)
sheriff	ʃerif	שֶׁרִיף (ז)

emperor	keisar	קֵיסָר (ז)
tsar, czar	ʦar	צָאר (ז)
pharaoh	par'o	פַּרְעֹה (ז)
khan	χan	חָאן (ז)

160. Breaking the law. Criminals. Part 1

bandit	ʃoded	שׁוֹדֵד (ז)
crime	'peʃa	פֶּשַׁע (ז)
criminal (person)	po'ʃeʿa	פּוֹשֵׁעַ (ז)

thief	ganav	גַּנָּב (ז)
to steal (vi, vt)	lignov	לִגְנוֹב
stealing (larceny)	gneva	גְּנֵיבָה (נ)
theft	gneva	גְּנֵיבָה (נ)

to kidnap (vt)	laχatof	לַחֲטוֹף
kidnapping	χatifa	חֲטִיפָה (נ)
kidnapper	χotef	חוֹטֵף (ז)

ransom	'kofer	כּוֹפֶר (ז)
to demand ransom	lidroʃ 'kofer	לִדְרוֹש כּוֹפֶר
to rob (vt)	liʃdod	לִשְׁדוֹד

robbery	ʃod	שׁוֹד (ז)
robber	ʃoded	שׁוֹדֵד (ז)
to extort (vt)	lisχot	לִסְחוֹט
extortionist	saχtan	סַחְטָן (ז)
extortion	saχtanut	סַחְטָנוּת (נ)
to murder, to kill	lir'tsoaχ	לִרְצוֹחַ
murder	'retsaχ	רֶצַח (ז)
murderer	ro'tseaχ	רוֹצֵחַ (ז)
gunshot	yeriya	יְרִיָה (נ)
to fire (~ a shot)	lirot	לִירוֹת
to shoot to death	lirot la'mavet	לִירוֹת לַמָוֶת
to shoot (vi)	lirot	לִירוֹת
shooting	'yeri	יְרִי (ז)
incident (fight, etc.)	takrit	תַקְרִית (נ)
fight, brawl	ktata	קְטָטָה (נ)
Help!	ha'tsilu!	הַצִילוּ!
victim	nifga	נִפְגָע (ז)
to damage (vt)	lekalkel	לְקַלְקֵל
damage	'nezek	נֶזֶק (ז)
dead body, corpse	gufa	גוּפָה (נ)
grave (~ crime)	χamur	חָמוּר
to attack (vt)	litkof	לִתְקוֹף
to beat (to hit)	lehakot	לְהַכּוֹת
to beat up	lehakot	לְהַכּוֹת
to take (rob of sth)	la'kaχat be'koaχ	לָקַחַת בְּכוֹחַ
to stab to death	lidkor le'mavet	לִדְקוֹר לְמָוֶת
to maim (vt)	lehatil mum	לְהָטִיל מוּם
to wound (vt)	lif'tso'a	לִפְצוֹעַ
blackmail	saχtanut	סַחְטָנוּת (נ)
to blackmail (vt)	lisχot	לִסְחוֹט
blackmailer	saχtan	סַחְטָן (ז)
protection racket	dmei χasut	דְמֵי חָסוּת (ז"ר)
racketeer	gove χasut	גוֹבֶה חָסוּת (ז)
gangster	'gangster	גַנְגְסְטֶר (ז)
mafia	'mafya	מָאפְיָה (נ)
pickpocket	kayas	כַּיָס (ז)
burglar	porets	פּוֹרֵץ (ז)
smuggling	havraχa	הַבְרָחָה (נ)
smuggler	mav'riaχ	מַבְרִים (ז)
forgery	ziyuf	זִיוּף (ז)
to forge (counterfeit)	lezayef	לְזַיֵיף
fake (forged)	mezuyaf	מְזוּיָף

161. Breaking the law. Criminals. Part 2

rape	'ones	אוֹנֶס (ז)
to rape (vt)	le'enos	לֶאֱנוֹס
rapist	anas	אַנָס (ז)
maniac	'manyak	מַנְיָאק (ז)
prostitute (fem.)	zona	זוֹנָה (נ)
prostitution	znut	זְנוּת (נ)
pimp	sarsur	סַרְסוּר (ז)
drug addict	narkoman	נַרְקוֹמָן (ז)
drug dealer	soχer samim	סוֹחֵר סַמִים (ז)
to blow up (bomb)	lefotsets	לְפוֹצֵץ
explosion	pitsuts	פִּיצוּץ (ז)
to set fire	lehatsit	לְהַצִית
arsonist	matsit	מַצִית (ז)
terrorism	terorizm	טֶרוֹרִיזְם (ז)
terrorist	meχabel	מְחַבֵּל (ז)
hostage	ben aruba	בֶּן עֲרוּבָּה (ז)
to swindle (deceive)	lehonot	לְהוֹנוֹת
swindle, deception	hona'a	הוֹנָאָה (נ)
swindler	ramai	רַמַאי (ז)
to bribe (vt)	leʃaχed	לְשַחֵד
bribery	ʃoχad	שוֹחַד (ז)
bribe	ʃoχad	שוֹחַד (ז)
poison	'ra'al	רַעַל (ז)
to poison (vt)	lehar'il	לְהַרְעִיל
to poison oneself	lehar'il et atsmo	לְהַרְעִיל אֶת עַצְמוֹ
suicide (act)	hit'abdut	הִתְאַבְּדוּת (נ)
suicide (person)	mit'abed	מִתְאַבֵּד (ז)
to threaten (vt)	le'ayem	לְאַיֵים
threat	iyum	אִיוּם (ז)
to make an attempt	lehitnakeʃ	לְהִתְנַקֵש
attempt (attack)	nisayon hitnakʃut	נִיסָיוֹן הִתְנַקְשוּת (ז)
to steal (a car)	lignov	לִגְנוֹב
to hijack (a plane)	laχatof matos	לַחְטוֹף מָטוֹס
revenge	nekama	נְקָמָה (נ)
to avenge (get revenge)	linkom	לִנְקוֹם
to torture (vt)	la'anot	לְעַנוֹת
torture	inui	עִינוּי (ז)
to torment (vt)	leyaser	לְיַיסֵר
pirate	ʃoded yam	שוֹדֵד יָם (ז)
hooligan	χuligan	חוּלִיגָאן (ז)

armed (adj)	mezuyan	מְזוּיָן
violence	alimut	אַלִּימוּת (נ)
illegal (unlawful)	'bilti le'gali	בִּלְתִּי לֶגָלִי

| spying (espionage) | rigul | רִיגוּל (ז) |
| to spy (vi) | leragel | לְרַגֵּל |

162. Police. Law. Part 1

| justice | 'tsedek | צֶדֶק (ז) |
| court (see you in ~) | beit miʃpat | בֵּית מִשׁפָּט (ז) |

judge	ʃofet	שׁוֹפֵט (ז)
jurors	muʃba'im	מוּשׁבָּעִים (ז"ר)
jury trial	χaver muʃba'im	חֶבֶר מוּשׁבָּעִים (ז)
to judge, to try (vt)	liʃpot	לִשׁפּוֹט

lawyer, barrister	oreχ din	עוֹרֵך דִּין (ז)
defendant	omed lemiʃpat	עוֹמֵד לְמִשׁפָּט (ז)
dock	safsal ne'eʃamim	סַפסַל נֶאֱשָׁמִים (ז)

| charge | ha'aʃama | הָאֲשָׁמָה (נ) |
| accused | ne'eʃam | נֶאֱשָׁם (ז) |

| sentence | gzar din | גזַר דִּין (ז) |
| to sentence (vt) | lifsok | לִפסוֹק |

guilty (culprit)	aʃem	אָשֵׁם (ז)
to punish (vt)	leha'aniʃ	לְהַעֲנִישׁ
punishment	'oneʃ	עוֹנֶשׁ (ז)

fine (penalty)	knas	קנָס (ז)
life imprisonment	ma'asar olam	מַאֲסַר עוֹלָם (ז)
death penalty	'oneʃ 'mavet	עוֹנֶשׁ מָוֶת (ז)
electric chair	kise χaʃmali	כִּיסֵא חַשׁמַלִי (ז)
gallows	gardom	גַרדוֹם (ז)

| to execute (vt) | lehotsi la'horeg | לְהוֹצִיא לַהוֹרֵג |
| execution | hatsa'a le'horeg | הוֹצָאָה לַהוֹרֵג (נ) |

| prison | beit 'sohar | בֵּית סוֹהַר (ז) |
| cell | ta | תָא (ז) |

escort (convoy)	miʃmar livui	מִשׁמַר לִיווּי (ז)
prison officer	soher	סוֹהֵר (ז)
prisoner	asir	אָסִיר (ז)

| handcuffs | azikim | אֲזִיקִים (ז"ר) |
| to handcuff (vt) | liχbol be'azikim | לִכבּוֹל בַּאֲזִיקִים |

prison break	briχa	בּרִיחָה (נ)
to break out (vi)	liv'roaχ	לִברוֹחַ
to disappear (vi)	lehe'alem	לְהֵיעָלֵם
to release (from prison)	leʃaχrer	לְשַׁחרֵר

amnesty	χanina	חֲנִינָה (נ)
police	miʃtara	מִשְׁטָרָה (נ)
police officer	ʃoter	שׁוֹטֵר (ז)
police station	taχanat miʃtara	תַּחֲנַת מִשְׁטָרָה (נ)
truncheon	ala	אַלָה (נ)
megaphone (loudhailer)	megafon	מֶגָפוֹן (ז)
patrol car	na'yedet	נַיֶּדֶת (נ)
siren	tsofar	צוֹפָר (ז)
to turn on the siren	lehaf'il tsofar	לְהַפְעִיל צוֹפָר
siren call	tsfira	צְפִירָה (נ)
crime scene	zirat 'peʃa	זִירַת פֶּשַׁע (נ)
witness	ed	עֵד (ז)
freedom	'χofeʃ	חוֹפֶשׁ (ז)
accomplice	ʃutaf	שׁוּתָף (ז)
to flee (vi)	lehiχave	לְהֵיחָבֵא
trace (to leave a ~)	akev	עָקֵב (ז)

163. Police. Law. Part 2

search (investigation)	χipus	חִיפּוּשׂ (ז)
to look for ...	leχapes	לְחַפֵּשׂ
suspicion	χaʃad	חָשָׁד (ז)
suspicious (e.g., ~ vehicle)	χaʃud	חָשׁוּד
to stop (cause to halt)	la'atsor	לַעֲצוֹר
to detain (keep in custody)	la'atsor	לַעֲצוֹר
case (lawsuit)	tik	תִּיק (ז)
investigation	χakira	חֲקִירָה (נ)
detective	balaʃ	בַּלָשׁ (ז)
investigator	χoker	חוֹקֵר (ז)
hypothesis	haʃara	הַשְׁעָרָה (נ)
motive	me'ni'a	מֵנִיעַ (ז)
interrogation	χakira	חֲקִירָה (נ)
to interrogate (vt)	laχkor	לַחְקוֹר
to question (~ neighbors, etc.)	letaʃel	לְתַשְׁאֵל
check (identity ~)	bdika	בְּדִיקָה (נ)
round-up (raid)	matsod	מָצוֹד (ז)
search (~ warrant)	χipus	חִיפּוּשׂ (ז)
chase (pursuit)	mirdaf	מִרְדָף (ז)
to pursue, to chase	lirdof aχarei	לִרְדוֹף אַחֲרֵי
to track (a criminal)	la'akov aχarei	לַעֲקוֹב אַחֲרֵי
arrest	ma'asar	מַאֲסָר (ז)
to arrest (sb)	le'esor	לֶאֱסוֹר
to catch (thief, etc.)	lilkod	לִלְכּוֹד
capture	leχida	לְכִידָה (נ)
document	mismaχ	מִסְמָךְ (ז)
proof (evidence)	hoχaχa	הוֹכָחָה (נ)

to prove (vt)	leho'xiax	לְהוֹכִיחַ
footprint	akev	עָקֵב (ז)
fingerprints	tvi'ot etsba'ot	טְבִיעוֹת אֶצְבָּעוֹת (נ"ר)
piece of evidence	re'aya	רְאָיָה (נ)
alibi	'alibi	אָלִיבִּי (ז)
innocent (not guilty)	xaf mi'pefa	חַף מִפֶּשַׁע
injustice	i 'tsedek	אִי צֶדֶק (ז)
unjust, unfair (adj)	lo tsodek	לֹא צוֹדֵק
criminal (adj)	plili	פְּלִילִי
to confiscate (vt)	lehaxrim	לְהַחְרִים
drug (illegal substance)	sam	סַם (ז)
weapon, gun	'nefek	נֶשֶׁק (ז)
to disarm (vt)	lifrok mi'nefek	לִפְרוֹק מִנֶּשֶׁק
to order (command)	lifkod	לִפְקוֹד
to disappear (vi)	lehe'alem	לְהֵיעָלֵם
law	xok	חוֹק (ז)
legal, lawful (adj)	xuki	חוּקִי
illegal, illicit (adj)	'bilti xuki	בִּלְתִּי חוּקִי
responsibility (blame)	axrayut	אַחְרָיוּת (נ)
responsible (adj)	axrai	אַחְרַאִי

NATURE

The Earth. Part 1

164. Outer space

space	χalal	חָלָל (ז)
space (as adj)	ʃel χalal	שֶׁל חָלָל
outer space	χalal χitson	חָלָל חִיצוֹן (ז)
world	olam	עוֹלָם (ז)
universe	yekum	יְקוּם (ז)
galaxy	ga'laksya	גָּלַקְסְיָה (נ)
star	koχav	כּוֹכָב (ז)
constellation	tsvir koχavim	צְבִיר כּוֹכָבִים (ז)
planet	koχav 'leχet	כּוֹכָב לֶכֶת (ז)
satellite	lavyan	לַוְיָן (ז)
meteorite	mete'orit	מֶטֶאוֹרִיט (ז)
comet	koχav ʃavit	כּוֹכָב שָׁבִיט (ז)
asteroid	aste'ro'id	אַסְטֶרוֹאִיד (ז)
orbit	maslul	מַסְלוּל (ז)
to revolve (~ around the Earth)	lesovev	לְסוֹבֵב
atmosphere	atmos'fera	אַטְמוֹסְפֶּרָה (נ)
the Sun	'ʃemeʃ	שֶׁמֶשׁ (נ)
solar system	ma'a'reχet ha'ʃemeʃ	מַעֲרֶכֶת הַשֶּׁמֶשׁ (נ)
solar eclipse	likui χama	לִיקּוּי חַמָּה (ז)
the Earth	kadur ha''arets	כַּדּוּר הָאָרֶץ (ז)
the Moon	ya'reaχ	יָרֵחַ (ז)
Mars	ma'adim	מַאֲדִים (ז)
Venus	'noga	נוֹגַהּ (ז)
Jupiter	'tsedek	צֶדֶק (ז)
Saturn	ʃabtai	שַׁבְּתַאי (ז)
Mercury	koχav χama	כּוֹכָב חַמָּה (ז)
Uranus	u'ranus	אוּרָנוּס (ז)
Neptune	neptun	נֶפְּטוּן (ז)
Pluto	'pluto	פְּלוּטוֹ (ז)
Milky Way	ʃvil haχalav	שְׁבִיל הֶחָלָב (ז)
Great Bear (Ursa Major)	duba gdola	דּוּבָּה גְּדוֹלָה (נ)
North Star	koχav hatsafon	כּוֹכָב הַצָּפוֹן (ז)
Martian	toʃav ma'adim	תּוֹשַׁב מַאֲדִים (ז)
extraterrestrial (n)	χutsan	חוּצָן (ז)

alien	χaizar	חַייזָר (ז)
flying saucer	tsa'laχat me'o'fefet	צַלַחַת מְעוֹפֶפֶת (נ)
spaceship	χalalit	חֲלָלִית (נ)
space station	taχanat χalal	תַחֲנַת חָלָל (נ)
blast-off	hamra'a	הַמרָאָה (נ)
engine	ma'no'a	מָנוֹעַ (ז)
nozzle	neχir	נְחִיר (ז)
fuel	'delek	דֶלֶק (ז)
cockpit, flight deck	'kokpit	קוֹקפִּיט (ז)
aerial	an'tena	אַנטֶנָה (נ)
porthole	eʃnav	אֶשׁנָב (ז)
solar panel	'luaχ so'lari	לוּחַ סוֹלָרִי (ז)
spacesuit	χalifat χalal	חֲלִיפַת חָלָל (נ)
weightlessness	'χoser miʃkal	חוֹסֶר מִשׁקָל (ז)
oxygen	χamtsan	חַמצָן (ז)
docking (in space)	agina	עֲגִינָה (נ)
to dock (vi, vt)	la'agon	לַעֲגוֹן
observatory	mitspe koχavim	מִצפֶּה כּוֹכָבִים (ז)
telescope	teleskop	טֶלֶסקוֹפּ (ז)
to observe (vt)	litspot, lehaʃkif	לִצפּוֹת, לְהַשׁקִיף
to explore (vt)	laχkor	לַחקוֹר

165. The Earth

the Earth	kadur ha''arets	כַּדוּר הָאָרֶץ (ז)
the globe (the Earth)	kadur ha''arets	כַּדוּר הָאָרֶץ (ז)
planet	koχav 'leχet	כּוֹכָב לֶכֶת (ז)
atmosphere	atmos'fera	אַטמוֹספֶּרָה (נ)
geography	ge'o'grafya	גֵיאוֹגרַפיָה (נ)
nature	'teva	טֶבַע (ז)
globe (table ~)	'globus	גלוֹבּוּס (ז)
map	mapa	מַפָּה (נ)
atlas	'atlas	אַטלָס (ז)
Europe	ei'ropa	אֵירוֹפָּה (נ)
Asia	'asya	אַסיָה (נ)
Africa	'afrika	אַפרִיקָה (נ)
Australia	ost'ralya	אוֹסטרַליָה (נ)
America	a'merika	אָמֶרִיקָה (נ)
North America	a'merika hatsfonit	אָמֶרִיקָה הַצפוֹנִית (נ)
South America	a'merika hadromit	אָמֶרִיקָה הַדרוֹמִית (נ)
Antarctica	ya'beʃet an'tarktika	יַבֶּשֶׁת אַנטָארקטִיקָה (נ)
the Arctic	'arktika	אַרקטִיקָה (נ)

166. Cardinal directions

north	tsafon	צָפוֹן (ז)
to the north	tsa'fona	צָפוֹנָה
in the north	batsafon	בַּצָּפוֹן
northern (adj)	tsfoni	צְפוֹנִי

south	darom	דָרוֹם (ז)
to the south	da'roma	דָרוֹמָה
in the south	badarom	בַּדָרוֹם
southern (adj)	dromi	דרוֹמִי

west	maʿarav	מַעֲרָב (ז)
to the west	maʿa'rava	מַעֲרָבָה
in the west	bamaʿarav	בַּמַעֲרָב
western (adj)	maʿaravi	מַעֲרָבִי

east	mizraχ	מִזרָח (ז)
to the east	miz'raχa	מִזרָחָה
in the east	bamizraχ	בַּמִזרָח
eastern (adj)	mizraχi	מִזרָחִי

167. Sea. Ocean

sea	yam	יָם (ז)
ocean	ok'yanos	אוֹקיָאנוֹס (ז)
gulf (bay)	mifrats	מִפרָץ (ז)
straits	meitsar	מֵיצַר (ז)

land (solid ground)	yabaʃa	יַבָּשָׁה (נ)
continent (mainland)	ya'beʃet	יַבֶּשֶׁת (נ)
island	i	אִי (ז)
peninsula	χatsi i	חֲצִי אִי (ז)
archipelago	arχipelag	אַרכִיפֶּלָג (ז)

bay, cove	mifrats	מִפרָץ (ז)
harbour	namal	נָמָל (ז)
lagoon	la'guna	לָגוּנָה (נ)
cape	kef	כֵּף (ז)

atoll	atol	אָטוֹל (ז)
reef	ʃunit	שׁוּנִית (נ)
coral	almog	אַלמוֹג (ז)
coral reef	ʃunit almogim	שׁוּנִית אַלמוֹגִים (נ)

deep (adj)	amok	עָמוֹק
depth (deep water)	'omek	עוֹמֶק (ז)
abyss	tehom	תְהוֹם (נ)
trench (e.g. Mariana ~)	maχteʃ	מַכתֵש (ז)

current (Ocean ~)	'zerem	זֶרֶם (ז)
to surround (bathe)	lehakif	לְהַקִיף
shore	χof	חוֹף (ז)

coast	χof yam	חוֹף יָם (ז)
flow (flood tide)	ge'ut	גֵּאוּת (נ)
ebb (ebb tide)	'ʃefel	שֵׁפֶל (ז)
shoal	sirton	שִׂרְטוֹן (ז)
bottom (~ of the sea)	karka'it	קַרְקָעִית (נ)

wave	gal	גַּל (ז)
crest (~ of a wave)	pisgat hagal	פִּסְגַּת הַגַּל (נ)
spume (sea foam)	'ketsef	קֶצֶף (ז)

storm (sea storm)	sufa	סוּפָה (נ)
hurricane	hurikan	הוֹרִיקָן (ז)
tsunami	tsu'nami	צוּנָאמִי (ז)
calm (dead ~)	'roga	רוֹגַע (ז)
quiet, calm (adj)	ʃalev	שָׁלֵו

| pole | 'kotev | קוֹטֶב (ז) |
| polar (adj) | kotbi | קוֹטְבִּי |

latitude	kav 'roχav	קַו רוֹחַב (ז)
longitude	kav 'oreχ	קַו אוֹרֶךְ (ז)
parallel	kav 'roχav	קַו רוֹחַב (ז)
equator	kav hamaʃve	קַו הַמַּשְׁוֶה (ז)

sky	ʃa'mayim	שָׁמַיִם (ז"ר)
horizon	'ofek	אוֹפֶק (ז)
air	avir	אֲוִיר (ז)

lighthouse	migdalor	מִגְדַּלּוֹר (ז)
to dive (vi)	litslol	לִצְלוֹל
to sink (ab. boat)	lit'bo'a	לִטְבּוֹעַ
treasure	otsarot	אוֹצָרוֹת (ז"ר)

168. Mountains

mountain	har	הַר (ז)
mountain range	'reχes harim	רֶכֶס הָרִים (ז)
mountain ridge	'reχes har	רֶכֶס הַר (ז)

summit, top	pisga	פִּסְגָּה (נ)
peak	pisga	פִּסְגָּה (נ)
foot (~ of the mountain)	margelot	מַרְגְּלוֹת (נ"ר)
slope (mountainside)	midron	מִדְרוֹן (ז)

volcano	har 'ga'aʃ	הַר גַּעַשׁ (ז)
active volcano	har 'ga'aʃ pa'il	הַר גַּעַשׁ פָּעִיל (ז)
dormant volcano	har 'ga'aʃ radum	הַר גַּעַשׁ רָדוּם (ז)

eruption	hitpartsut	הִתְפָּרְצוּת (נ)
crater	lo'a	לוֹעַ (ז)
magma	megama	מַגְמָה (נ)
lava	'lava	לָאבָה (נ)
molten (~ lava)	lohet	לוֹהֵט
canyon	kanyon	קַנְיוֹן (ז)

gorge	gai	גַּיְא (ז)
crevice	'beka	בֶּקַע (ז)
abyss (chasm)	tehom	תְּהוֹם (נ)
pass, col	ma'avar harim	מַעֲבַר הָרִים (ז)
plateau	rama	רָמָה (נ)
cliff	tsuk	צוּק (ז)
hill	giv'a	גִּבְעָה (נ)
glacier	karχon	קַרְחוֹן (ז)
waterfall	mapal 'mayim	מַפַּל מַיִם (ז)
geyser	'geizer	גֵּייזֶר (ז)
lake	agam	אֲגַם (ז)
plain	miʃor	מִישׁוֹר (ז)
landscape	nof	נוֹף (ז)
echo	hed	הֵד (ז)
alpinist	metapes harim	מְטַפֵּס הָרִים (ז)
rock climber	metapes sla'im	מְטַפֵּס סְלָעִים (ז)
to conquer (in climbing)	liχboʃ	לִכְבּוֹשׁ
climb (an easy ~)	tipus	טִיפּוּס (ז)

169. Rivers

river	nahar	נָהָר (ז)
spring (natural source)	ma'ayan	מַעְיָן (ז)
riverbed (river channel)	afik	אָפִיק (ז)
basin (river valley)	agan nahar	אֲגַן נָהָר (ז)
to flow into …	lehiʃapeχ	לְהִישָׁפֵךְ
tributary	yuval	יוּבַל (ז)
bank (river ~)	χof	חוֹף (ז)
current (stream)	'zerem	זֶרֶם (ז)
downstream (adv)	bemorad hanahar	בְּמוֹרַד הַנָּהָר
upstream (adv)	bema'ale hanahar	בְּמַעֲלֵה הַנָּהָר
inundation	hatsafa	הֲצָפָה (נ)
flooding	ʃitafon	שִׁיטָפוֹן (ז)
to overflow (vi)	la'alot al gdotav	לַעֲלוֹת עַל גְּדוֹתָיו
to flood (vt)	lehatsif	לְהָצִיף
shallow (shoal)	sirton	שִׂרְטוֹן (ז)
rapids	'eʃed	אֶשֶׁד (ז)
dam	'seχer	סֶכֶר (ז)
canal	te'ala	תְּעָלָה (נ)
reservoir (artificial lake)	ma'agar 'mayim	מַאֲגַר מַיִם (ז)
sluice, lock	ta 'ʃayit	תָּא שַׁיִט (ז)
water body (pond, etc.)	ma'agar 'mayim	מַאֲגַר מַיִם (ז)
swamp (marshland)	bitsa	בִּיצָה (נ)
bog, marsh	bitsa	בִּיצָה (נ)

whirlpool	me'ar'bolet	מְעַרְבּוֹלֶת (נ)
stream (brook)	'naxal	נַחַל (ז)
drinking (ab. water)	ʃel ʃtiya	שֶׁל שתִיָה
fresh (~ water)	metukim	מְתוּקִים
ice	'kerax	קֶרַח (ז)
to freeze over (ab. river, etc.)	likpo	לִקפּוֹא

170. Forest

forest, wood	'ya'ar	יַעַר (ז)
forest (as adj)	ʃel 'ya'ar	שֶׁל יַעַר
thick forest	avi ha'ya'ar	עֲבִי הַיַעַר (ז)
grove	xurʃa	חוּרשָׁה (נ)
forest clearing	ka'raxat 'ya'ar	קָרַחַת יַעַר (נ)
thicket	svax	סבַך (ז)
scrubland	'siax	שִׂיחַ (ז)
footpath (troddenpath)	ʃvil	שבִיל (ז)
gully	'emek tsar	עֶמֶק צַר (ז)
tree	ets	עֵץ (ז)
leaf	ale	עָלֶה (ז)
leaves (foliage)	alva	עָלוָה (נ)
fall of leaves	ʃa'lexet	שַׁלֶכֶת (נ)
to fall (ab. leaves)	linʃor	לִנשׁוֹר
top (of the tree)	tsa'meret	צַמֶרֶת (נ)
branch	anaf	עָנָף (ז)
bough	anaf ave	עָנָף עָבֶה (ז)
bud (on shrub, tree)	nitsan	נִיצָן (ז)
needle (of the pine tree)	'maxat	מַחַט (נ)
fir cone	itstrubal	אָצטרוּבָּל (ז)
tree hollow	xor ba'ets	חוֹר בָּעֵץ (ז)
nest	ken	קֵן (ז)
burrow (animal hole)	mexila	מְחִילָה (נ)
trunk	'geza	גֶזַע (ז)
root	'foreʃ	שׁוֹרֶשׁ (ז)
bark	klipa	קלִיפָּה (נ)
moss	taxav	טַחַב (ז)
to uproot (remove trees or tree stumps)	la'akor	לַעֲקוֹר
to chop down	lixrot	לִכרוֹת
to deforest (vt)	levare	לְבָרֵא
tree stump	'gedem	גֶדֶם (ז)
campfire	medura	מְדוּרָה (נ)
forest fire	srefa	שׂרֵיפָה (נ)

to extinguish (vt)	leχabot	לְכַבּוֹת
forest ranger	ʃomer 'yaʿar	שׁוֹמֵר יַעַר (ז)
protection	ʃmira	שְׁמִירָה (נ)
to protect (~ nature)	liʃmor	לִשְׁמוֹר
poacher	tsayad lelo reʃut	צַיָּד לְלֹא רְשׁוּת (ז)
steel trap	mal'kodet	מַלְכּוֹדֶת (נ)
to gather, to pick (vt)	lelaket	לְלַקֵּט
to lose one's way	lit'ot	לִתְעוֹת

171. Natural resources

natural resources	otsarot 'teva	אוֹצְרוֹת טֶבַע (ז"ר)
minerals	mine'ralim	מִינֶרָלִים (ז"ר)
deposits	mirbats	מִרְבָּץ (ז)
field (e.g. oilfield)	mirbats	מִרְבָּץ (ז)
to mine (extract)	liχrot	לִכְרוֹת
mining (extraction)	kriya	כְּרִיָּה (נ)
ore	afra	עַפְרָה (נ)
mine (e.g. for coal)	miχre	מִכְרֶה (ז)
shaft (mine ~)	pir	פִּיר (ז)
miner	kore	כּוֹרֶה (ז)
gas (natural ~)	gaz	גָּז (ז)
gas pipeline	tsinor gaz	צִינוֹר גָּז (ז)
oil (petroleum)	neft	נֵפְט (ז)
oil pipeline	tsinor neft	צִינוֹר נֵפְט (ז)
oil well	be'er neft	בְּאֵר נֵפְט (נ)
derrick (tower)	migdal ki'duaχ	מִגְדַּל קִידּוּחַ (ז)
tanker	meχalit	מֵיכָלִית (נ)
sand	χol	חוֹל (ז)
limestone	'even gir	אֶבֶן גִּיר (נ)
gravel	χatsats	חָצָץ (ז)
peat	kavul	כָּבוּל (ז)
clay	tit	טִיט (ז)
coal	peχam	פֶּחָם (ז)
iron (ore)	barzel	בַּרְזֶל (ז)
gold	zahav	זָהָב (ז)
silver	'kesef	כֶּסֶף (ז)
nickel	'nikel	נִיקֵל (ז)
copper	ne'χoʃet	נְחוֹשֶׁת (נ)
zinc	avats	אָבָץ (ז)
manganese	mangan	מַנְגָּן (ז)
mercury	kaspit	כַּסְפִּית (נ)
lead	o'feret	עוֹפֶרֶת (נ)
mineral	mineral	מִינֶרָל (ז)
crystal	gaviʃ	גָּבִישׁ (ז)
marble	'ʃayiʃ	שַׁיִשׁ (ז)
uranium	u'ranyum	אוּרָנְיוּם (ז)

The Earth. Part 2

172. Weather

weather	'mezeg avir	מֶזֶג אֲוֵויר (ז)
weather forecast	taχazit 'mezeg ha'avir	תַּחֲזִית מֶזֶג הָאֲוֵויר (נ)
temperature	tempera'tura	טֶמְפֶּרָטוּרָה (נ)
thermometer	madχom	מַדחוֹם (ז)
barometer	ba'rometer	בָּרוֹמֶטֶר (ז)
humid (adj)	laχ	לַח
humidity	laχut	לַחוּת (נ)
heat (extreme ~)	χom	חוֹם (ז)
hot (torrid)	χam	חַם
it's hot	χam	חַם
it's warm	χamim	חָמִים
warm (moderately hot)	χamim	חָמִים
it's cold	kar	קַר
cold (adj)	kar	קַר
sun	'ʃemeʃ	שֶׁמֶשׁ (נ)
to shine (vi)	lizhor	לִזְהוֹר
sunny (day)	ʃimʃi	שִׁמְשִׁי
to come up (vi)	liz'roaχ	לִזְרוֹחַ
to set (vi)	liʃ'ko'a	לִשְׁקוֹעַ
cloud	anan	עָנָן (ז)
cloudy (adj)	me'unan	מְעוּנָן
rain cloud	av	עָב (ז)
somber (gloomy)	sagriri	סַגְרִירִי
rain	'geʃem	גֶּשֶׁם (ז)
it's raining	yored 'geʃem	יוֹרֵד גֶּשֶׁם
rainy (~ day, weather)	gaʃum	גָּשׁוּם
to drizzle (vi)	letaftef	לְטַפְטֵף
pouring rain	matar	מָטָר (ז)
downpour	mabul	מַבּוּל (ז)
heavy (e.g. ~ rain)	χazak	חָזָק
puddle	ʃlulit	שְׁלוּלִית (נ)
to get wet (in rain)	lehitratev	לְהִתְרַטֵּב
fog (mist)	arapel	עֲרָפֶל (ז)
foggy	me'urpal	מְעוּרְפָּל
snow	'ʃeleg	שֶׁלֶג (ז)
it's snowing	yored 'ʃeleg	יוֹרֵד שֶׁלֶג

173. Severe weather. Natural disasters

thunderstorm	sufat reʿamim	סוּפַת רְעָמִים (נ)
lightning (~ strike)	barak	בָּרָק (ז)
to flash (vi)	livhok	לִבהוֹק
thunder	ʹraʿam	רַעַם (ז)
to thunder (vi)	lirʹom	לִרעוֹם
it's thundering	lirʹom	לִרעוֹם
hail	barad	בָּרָד (ז)
it's hailing	yored barad	יוֹרֵד בָּרָד
to flood (vt)	lehatsif	לְהָצִיף
flood, inundation	ʃitafon	שִׁיטָפוֹן (ז)
earthquake	reʿidat adama	רְעִידַת אֲדָמָה (נ)
tremor, shoke	reʿida	רְעִידָה (נ)
epicentre	moked	מוֹקֵד (ז)
eruption	hitpartsut	הִתפָּרצוּת (נ)
lava	ʹlava	לָאבָה (נ)
twister	hurikan	הוּרִיקָן (ז)
tornado	torʹnado	טוֹרנָדוֹ (ז)
typhoon	taifun	טַייפוּן (ז)
hurricane	hurikan	הוּרִיקָן (ז)
storm	sufa	סוּפָה (נ)
tsunami	tsuʹnami	צוּנָאמִי (ז)
cyclone	tsiklon	צִיקלוֹן (ז)
bad weather	sagrir	סַגרִיר (ז)
fire (accident)	srefa	שׂרֵיפָה (נ)
disaster	ason	אָסוֹן (ז)
meteorite	meteʹorit	מֶטֶאוֹרִיט (ז)
avalanche	maʹpolet ʃlagim	מַפּוֹלֶת שׁלָגִים (נ)
snowslide	maʹpolet ʃlagim	מַפּוֹלֶת שׁלָגִים (נ)
blizzard	sufat ʃlagim	סוּפַת שׁלָגִים (נ)
snowstorm	sufat ʃlagim	סוּפַת שׁלָגִים (נ)

Fauna

174. Mammals. Predators

predator	χayat 'teref	חַיַּת טֶרֶף (נ)
tiger	'tigris	טִיגְרִיס (ז)
lion	arye	אַרְיֵה (ז)
wolf	ze'ev	זְאֵב (ז)
fox	ʃu'al	שׁוּעָל (ז)
jaguar	yagu'ar	יָגוּאָר (ז)
leopard	namer	נָמֵר (ז)
cheetah	bardelas	בַּרְדְּלָס (ז)
black panther	panter	פַּנְתֵר (ז)
puma	'puma	פּוּמָה (נ)
snow leopard	namer 'ʃeleg	נָמֵר שֶׁלֶג (ז)
lynx	ʃunar	שׁוּנָר (ז)
coyote	ze'ev ha'aravot	זְאֵב הָעֲרָבוֹת (ז)
jackal	tan	תַּן (ז)
hyena	tsa'vo'a	צָבוֹעַ (ז)

175. Wild animals

animal	'ba'al χayim	בַּעַל חַיִּים (ז)
beast (animal)	χaya	חַיָּה (נ)
squirrel	sna'i	סְנָאִי (ז)
hedgehog	kipod	קִיפּוֹד (ז)
hare	arnav	אַרְנָב (ז)
rabbit	ʃafan	שָׁפָן (ז)
badger	girit	גִּירִית (נ)
raccoon	dvivon	דְּבִיבוֹן (ז)
hamster	oger	אוֹגֵר (ז)
marmot	mar'mita	מַרְמִיטָה (נ)
mole	χafar'peret	חֲפַרְפֶּרֶת (נ)
mouse	aχbar	עַכְבָּר (ז)
rat	χulda	חוּלְדָּה (נ)
bat	atalef	עֲטַלֵּף (ז)
ermine	hermin	הֶרְמִין (ז)
sable	tsobel	צוֹבֶּל (ז)
marten	dalak	דָּלָק (ז)
weasel	χamus	חָמוֹס (ז)
mink	χorfan	חוֹרְפָן (ז)

beaver	bone	בּוֹנֶה (ז)
otter	lutra	לוֹטְרָה (נ)
horse	sus	סוּס (ז)
moose	ayal hakore	אַיָּל הַקּוֹרֵא (ז)
deer	ayal	אַיָּל (ז)
camel	gamal	גָּמָל (ז)
bison	bizon	בִּיזוֹן (ז)
wisent	bizon ei'ropi	בִּיזוֹן אֵירוֹפִי (ז)
buffalo	te'o	תְּאוֹ (ז)
zebra	'zebra	זֶבְּרָה (נ)
antelope	anti'lopa	אַנְטִילוֹפָּה (ז)
roe deer	ayal hakarmel	אַיָּל הַכַּרְמֶל (ז)
fallow deer	yaχmur	יַחְמוּר (ז)
chamois	ya'el	יָעֵל (ז)
wild boar	χazir bar	חֲזִיר בָּר (ז)
whale	livyatan	לִוְיָתָן (ז)
seal	'kelev yam	כֶּלֶב יָם (ז)
walrus	sus yam	סוּס יָם (ז)
fur seal	dov yam	דֹּב יָם (ז)
dolphin	dolfin	דּוֹלְפִין (ז)
bear	dov	דֹּב (ז)
polar bear	dov 'kotev	דֹּב קוֹטֶב (ז)
panda	'panda	פַּנְדָּה (נ)
monkey	kof	קוֹף (ז)
chimpanzee	ʃimpanze	שִׁימְפַּנְזֶה (נ)
orangutan	orang utan	אוֹרַנְג-אוּטָן (ז)
gorilla	go'rila	גּוֹרִילָה (נ)
macaque	makak	מָקָק (ז)
gibbon	gibon	גִּיבּוֹן (ז)
elephant	pil	פִּיל (ז)
rhinoceros	karnaf	קַרְנַף (ז)
giraffe	dʒi'rafa	גִ'ירָפָה (נ)
hippopotamus	hipopotam	הִיפּוֹפּוֹטָם (ז)
kangaroo	'kenguru	קֶנְגּוּרוּ (ז)
koala (bear)	ko''ala	קוֹאָלָה (ז)
mongoose	nemiya	נְמִיָּה (נ)
chinchilla	tʃin'tʃila	צִ'ינְצִ'ילָה (נ)
skunk	bo'eʃ	בּוֹאֵשׁ (ז)
porcupine	darban	דַּרְבָּן (ז)

176. Domestic animals

cat	χatula	חֲתוּלָה (נ)
tomcat	χatul	חָתוּל (ז)
dog	'kelev	כֶּלֶב (ז)

horse	sus	סוּס (ז)
stallion (male horse)	sus harba‘a	סוּס הַרְבָּעָה (ז)
mare	susa	סוּסָה (נ)
cow	para	פָּרָה (נ)
bull	ʃor	שׁוֹר (ז)
ox	ʃor	שׁוֹר (ז)
sheep (ewe)	kivsa	כִּבְשָׂה (נ)
ram	'ayil	אַיִל (ז)
goat	ez	עֵז (נ)
billy goat, he-goat	'tayiʃ	תַּיִשׁ (ז)
donkey	χamor	חֲמוֹר (ז)
mule	'pered	פֶּרֶד (ז)
pig	χazir	חֲזִיר (ז)
piglet	χazarzir	חֲזַרְזִיר (ז)
rabbit	arnav	אַרְנָב (ז)
hen (chicken)	tarne'golet	תַּרְנְגֹלֶת (נ)
cock	tarnegol	תַּרְנְגוֹל (ז)
duck	barvaz	בַּרְוָז (ז)
drake	barvaz	בַּרְוָז (ז)
goose	avaz	אַוָּז (ז)
tom turkey, gobbler	tarnegol 'hodu	תַּרְנְגוֹל הוֹדוּ (ז)
turkey (hen)	tarne'golet 'hodu	תַּרְנְגֹלֶת הוֹדוּ (נ)
domestic animals	χayot 'bayit	חַיּוֹת בַּיִת (נ"ר)
tame (e.g. ~ hamster)	mevuyat	מְבוּיָת
to tame (vt)	levayet	לְבַיֵּת
to breed (vt)	lehar'bi‘a	לְהַרְבִּיעַ
farm	χava	חַוָּה (נ)
poultry	ofot 'bayit	עוֹפוֹת בַּיִת (נ"ר)
cattle	bakar	בָּקָר (ז)
herd (cattle)	'eder	עֵדֶר (ז)
stable	urva	אוּרְוָה (נ)
pigsty	dir χazirim	דִּיר חֲזִירִים (ז)
cowshed	'refet	רֶפֶת (נ)
rabbit hutch	arnaviya	אַרְנָבִיָּה (נ)
hen house	lul	לוּל (ז)

177. Dogs. Dog breeds

dog	'kelev	כֶּלֶב (ז)
sheepdog	'kelev ro‘e	כֶּלֶב רוֹעֶה (ז)
German shepherd	ro‘e germani	רוֹעֶה גֶּרְמָנִי (ז)
poodle	'pudel	פּוּדֶל (ז)
dachshund	'taχaʃ	תַּחַשׁ (ז)
bulldog	buldog	בּוּלְדּוֹג (ז)

boxer	'bokser	בּוֹקְסֶר (ז)
mastiff	mastif	מַסְטִיף (ז)
Rottweiler	rot'vailer	רוֹטְווַיילֶר (ז)
Doberman	'doberman	דּוֹבֶּרְמָן (ז)

basset	'baset 'ha'und	בָּאסֶט־הָאוּנְד (ז)
bobtail	bobteil	בּוֹבְּטֵייל (ז)
Dalmatian	dal'mati	דַּלְמָטִי (ז)
cocker spaniel	'koker 'spani'el	קוֹקֶר סְפָּנְיֶאל (ז)

| Newfoundland | nyu'fa'undlend | נְיוּפָאוּנְדְלֶנְד (ז) |
| Saint Bernard | sen bernard | סֶן בֶּרְנָרְד (ז) |

husky	'haski	הָאסְקִי (ז)
Chow Chow	'tʃa'u 'tʃa'u	צָ'אוּ צָ'אוּ (ז)
spitz	ʃpits	שְׁפִּיץ (ז)
pug	pag	פָּאג (ז)

178. Sounds made by animals

barking (n)	nevixa	נְבִיחָה (נ)
to bark (vi)	lin'boax	לִנְבּוֹחַ
to miaow (vi)	leyalel	לְיַלֵּל
to purr (vi)	legarger	לְגַרְגֵּר

to moo (vi)	lig'ot	לִגְעוֹת
to bellow (bull)	lig'ot	לִגְעוֹת
to growl (vi)	linhom	לִנְהוֹם

howl (n)	yelala	יְלָלָה (נ)
to howl (vi)	leyalel	לְיַלֵּל
to whine (vi)	leyabev	לְיַיבֵּב

to bleat (sheep)	lif'ot	לִפְעוֹת
to oink, to grunt (pig)	lexarxer	לְחַרְחֵר
to squeal (vi)	lits'voax	לִצְווֹחַ

to croak (vi)	lekarker	לְקַרְקֵר
to buzz (insect)	lezamzem	לְזַמְזֵם
to chirp (crickets, grasshopper)	letsartser	לְצַרְצֵר

179. Birds

bird	tsipor	צִיפּוֹר (נ)
pigeon	yona	יוֹנָה (נ)
sparrow	dror	דְּרוֹר (ז)
tit (great tit)	yargazi	יַרְגָּזִי (ז)
magpie	orev nexalim	עוֹרֵב נְחָלִים (ז)

| raven | orev ʃaxor | עוֹרֵב שָׁחוֹר (ז) |
| crow | orev afor | עוֹרֵב אָפוֹר (ז) |

| jackdaw | ka'ak | קָאָק (ז) |
| rook | orev hamizra | עוֹרֵב הַמִּזְרָע (ז) |

duck	barvaz	בַּרְוָז (ז)
goose	avaz	אֲוָז (ז)
pheasant	pasyon	פַּסְיוֹן (ז)

eagle	'ayit	עַיִט (ז)
hawk	nets	נֵץ (ז)
falcon	baz	בַּז (ז)
vulture	ozniya	עוֹזְנִיָּה (ז)
condor (Andean ~)	kondor	קוֹנְדּוֹר (ז)

swan	barbur	בַּרְבּוּר (ז)
crane	agur	עָגוּר (ז)
stork	χasida	חֲסִידָה (נ)

parrot	'tuki	תּוּכִּי (ז)
hummingbird	ko'libri	קוֹלִיבְּרִי (ז)
peacock	tavas	טַווָס (ז)

ostrich	bat ya'ana	בַּת יַעֲנָה (נ)
heron	anafa	אֲנָפָה (נ)
flamingo	fla'mingo	פְלָמִינְגוֹ (ז)
pelican	saknai	שַׂקְנַאי (ז)

| nightingale | zamir | זָמִיר (ז) |
| swallow | snunit | סְנוּנִית (נ) |

thrush	kiχli	קִיכְלִי (ז)
song thrush	kiχli mezamer	קִיכְלִי מְזַמֵּר (ז)
blackbird	kiχli ʃaχor	קִיכְלִי שָׁחוֹר (ז)

swift	sis	סִיס (ז)
lark	efroni	עֶפְרוֹנִי (ז)
quail	slav	שְׁלָיו (ז)

woodpecker	'neker	נַקָּר (ז)
cuckoo	kukiya	קוּקִיָּיה (נ)
owl	yanʃuf	יַנְשׁוּף (ז)
eagle owl	'oaχ	אוֹחַ (ז)
wood grouse	seχvi 'ya'ar	שְׂכְווִי יַעַר (ז)

| black grouse | seχvi | שְׂכְווִי (ז) |
| partridge | χogla | חוֹגְלָה (נ) |

starling	zarzir	זַרְזִיר (ז)
canary	ka'narit	קָנָרִית (נ)
hazel grouse	seχvi haya'arot	שְׂכְווִי הַיְעָרוֹת (ז)

| chaffinch | paroʃ | פָּרוּשׁ (ז) |
| bullfinch | admonit | אַדְמוֹנִית (נ) |

seagull	'ʃaχaf	שַׁחַף (ז)
albatross	albatros	אַלְבַּטְרוֹס (ז)
penguin	pingvin	פִּינְגְווִין (ז)

180. Birds. Singing and sounds

to sing (vi)	laʃir	לָשִׁיר
to call (animal, bird)	lits'ok	לִצְעוֹק
to crow (cock)	lekarker	לְקַרְקֵר
cock-a-doodle-doo	kuku'riku	קוּקוּרִיקוּ
to cluck (hen)	lekarker	לְקַרְקֵר
to caw (crow call)	lits'roaχ	לִצְרוֹחַ
to quack (duck call)	legaʾaʾgeʾa	לְגַגֵּעַ
to cheep (vi)	letsayets	לְצַיֵּץ
to chirp, to twitter	letsaftsef, letsayets	לְצַפְצֵף, לְצַיֵּץ

181. Fish. Marine animals

bream	avroma	אַבְרוֹמָה (נ)
carp	karpiyon	קַרְפִּיוֹן (ז)
perch	'okunus	אוֹקוּנוּס (ז)
catfish	sfamnun	שְׂפַמְנוּן (ז)
pike	zeʾev 'mayim	זְאֵב מַיִם (ז)
salmon	'salmon	סַלְמוֹן (ז)
sturgeon	χidkan	חִדְקָן (ז)
herring	ma'liaχ	מָלִיחַ (ז)
Atlantic salmon	iltit	אִילְתִּית (נ)
mackerel	makarel	מָקָרֵל (ז)
flatfish	dag moʃe ra'benu	דַג מֹשֶׁה רַבֵּנוּ (ז)
zander, pike perch	amnun	אַמְנוּן (ז)
cod	ʃibut	שִׁיבּוּט (ז)
tuna	'tuna	טוּנָה (נ)
trout	forel	פוֹרֵל (ז)
eel	tslofaχ	צְלוֹפַח (ז)
electric ray	trisanit	תְּרִיסָנִית (נ)
moray eel	mo'rena	מוֹרֶנָה (נ)
piranha	pi'ranya	פִּירָנְיָה (נ)
shark	kariʃ	כָּרִישׁ (ז)
dolphin	dolfin	דוֹלְפִין (ז)
whale	livyatan	לִוְיָתָן (ז)
crab	sartan	סַרְטָן (ז)
jellyfish	me'duza	מֶדוּזָה (נ)
octopus	tamnun	תַּמְנוּן (ז)
starfish	koχav yam	כּוֹכָב יָם (ז)
sea urchin	kipod yam	קִיפּוֹד יָם (ז)
seahorse	suson yam	סוּסוֹן יָם (ז)
oyster	tsidpa	צִדְפָּה (נ)
prawn	χasilon	חָסִילוֹן (ז)

| lobster | 'lobster | (ז) לוֹבְּסְטֶר |
| spiny lobster | 'lobster koʦani | (ז) לוֹבְּסְטֶר קוֹצָנִי |

182. Amphibians. Reptiles

| snake | naχaʃ | (ז) נָחָשׁ |
| venomous (snake) | arsi | אַרְסִי |

viper	'ʦefa	(ז) צֶפַע
cobra	'peten	(ז) פֶּתֶן
python	piton	(ז) פִּיתוֹן
boa	χanak	(ז) חֶנֶק

grass snake	naχaʃ 'mayim	(ז) נָחָשׁ מַיִם
rattle snake	ʃfifon	(ז) שְׁפִיפוֹן
anaconda	ana'konda	(נ) אֲנָקוֹנְדָה

lizard	leta'a	(נ) לְטָאָה
iguana	igu''ana	(נ) אִיגוּאָנָה
monitor lizard	'koaχ	(ז) כּוֹחַ
salamander	sala'mandra	(נ) סָלָמַנְדְרָה
chameleon	zikit	(נ) זִיקִית
scorpion	akrav	(ז) עַקְרָב

turtle	ʦav	(ז) צָב
frog	ʦfar'de'a	(נ) צְפַרְדֵּעַ
toad	karpada	(נ) קַרְפָּדָה
crocodile	tanin	(ז) תַּנִּין

183. Insects

insect	χarak	(ז) חָרָק
butterfly	parpar	(ז) פַּרְפַּר
ant	nemala	(נ) נְמָלָה
fly	zvuv	(ז) זְבוּב
mosquito	yatuʃ	(ז) יַתּוּשׁ
beetle	χipuʃit	(נ) חִיפּוּשִׁית

wasp	ʦir'a	(נ) צִרְעָה
bee	dvora	(נ) דְּבוֹרָה
bumblebee	dabur	(ז) דַּבּוּר
gadfly (botfly)	zvuv hasus	(ז) זְבוּב הַסּוּס

| spider | akaviʃ | (ז) עַכָּבִישׁ |
| spider's web | kurei akaviʃ | (ז"ר) קוּרֵי עַכָּבִישׁ |

dragonfly	ʃapirit	(נ) שְׁפִּירִית
grasshopper	χagav	(ז) חָגָב
moth (night butterfly)	aʃ	(ז) עָשׁ

| cockroach | makak | (ז) מַקָּק |
| tick | karʦiya | (נ) קַרְצִיָּה |

flea	parʻoʃ	פַּרְעוֹשׁ (ז)
midge	yavχuʃ	יַבְחוּשׁ (ז)
locust	arbe	אַרְבֶּה (ז)
snail	χilazon	חִילָזוֹן (ז)
cricket	tsartsar	צְרָצַר (ז)
firefly	gaχlilit	גַחְלִילִית (נ)
ladybird	parat moʃe ra'benu	פָּרַת מֹשֶׁה רַבֵּנוּ (נ)
cockchafer	χipuʃit aviv	חִיפּוּשִׁית אָבִיב (נ)
leech	aluka	עֲלוּקָה (נ)
caterpillar	zaχal	זַחַל (ז)
earthworm	to'laʻat	תוֹלַעַת (נ)
larva	'deren	דֶרֶן (ז)

184. Animals. Body parts

beak	makor	מָקוֹר (ז)
wings	kna'fayim	כְּנָפַיִם (נ"ר)
foot (of the bird)	'regel	רֶגֶל (נ)
feathers (plumage)	pluma	פְּלוּמָה (נ)
feather	notsa	נוֹצָה (נ)
crest	tsitsa	צִיצָה (נ)
gills	zimim	זִימִים (ז"ר)
spawn	beitsei dagim	בֵּיצֵי דָגִים (נ"ר)
larva	'deren	דֶרֶן (ז)
fin	snapir	סְנַפִּיר (ז)
scales (of fish, reptile)	kaskasim	קַשְׂקַשִׂים (ז"ר)
fang (canine)	niv	נִיב (ז)
paw (e.g. cat's ~)	'regel	רֶגֶל (נ)
muzzle (snout)	partsuf	פַּרְצוּף (ז)
mouth (cat's ~)	loʻa	לוֹעַ (ז)
tail	zanav	זָנָב (ז)
whiskers	safam	שָׂפָם (ז)
hoof	parsa	פַּרְסָה (נ)
horn	'keren	קֶרֶן (נ)
carapace	ʃiryon	שִׁרְיוֹן (ז)
shell (mollusk ~)	konχiya	קוֹנְכִייָה (נ)
eggshell	klipa	קְלִיפָּה (נ)
animal's hair (pelage)	parva	פַּרְוָה (נ)
pelt (hide)	or	עוֹר (ז)

185. Animals. Habitats

habitat	beit gidul	בֵּית גִידוּל (ז)
migration	hagira	הֲגִירָה (נ)
mountain	har	הַר (ז)

| reef | ʃunit | שׁוּנִית (נ) |
| cliff | 'sela | סֶלַע (ז) |

forest	'ya'ar	יַעַר (ז)
jungle	'dʒungel	ג׳וּנְגֶל (ז)
savanna	sa'vana	סָוַנָּה (נ)
tundra	'tundra	טוּנְדְּרָה (נ)

steppe	arava	עֲרָבָה (נ)
desert	midbar	מִדְבָּר (ז)
oasis	neve midbar	נְוֵה מִדְבָּר (ז)

sea	yam	יָם (ז)
lake	agam	אֲגַם (ז)
ocean	ok'yanos	אוֹקְיָאנוֹס (ז)

swamp (marshland)	bitsa	בִּיצָה (נ)
freshwater (adj)	ʃel 'mayim metukim	שֶׁל מַיִם מְתוּקִים
pond	breχa	בְּרֵיכָה (נ)
river	nahar	נָהָר (ז)

den (bear's ~)	me'ura	מְאוּרָה (נ)
nest	ken	קֵן (ז)
tree hollow	χor ba'ets	חוֹר בָּעֵץ (ז)
burrow (animal hole)	meχila	מְחִילָה (נ)
anthill	kan nemalim	קַן נְמָלִים (ז)

Flora

tree	ets	עֵץ (ז)
deciduous (adj)	naʃir	נָשִׁיר
coniferous (adj)	maχtani	מַחְטָנִי
evergreen (adj)	yarok ad	יָרוֹק עַד
apple tree	ta'puaχ	תַּפּוּחַ (ז)
pear tree	agas	אַגָּס (ז)
sweet cherry tree	gudgedan	גּוּדְגְּדָן (ז)
sour cherry tree	duvdevan	דּוּבְדְּבָן (ז)
plum tree	ʃezif	שְׁזִיף (ז)
birch	ʃadar	שָׁדָר (ז)
oak	alon	אַלּוֹן (ז)
linden tree	'tilya	טִילְיָה (נ)
aspen	aspa	אַסְפָּה (נ)
maple	'eder	אֶדֶר (ז)
spruce	a'ʃuaχ	אַשּׁוּחַ (ז)
pine	'oren	אוֹרֶן (ז)
larch	arzit	אַרְזִית (נ)
fir tree	a'ʃuaχ	אַשּׁוּחַ (ז)
cedar	'erez	אֶרֶז (ז)
poplar	tsaftsefa	צַפְצָפָה (נ)
rowan	ben χuzrar	בֶּן־חֻזְרָר (ז)
willow	arava	עֲרָבָה (נ)
alder	alnus	אַלְנוּס (ז)
beech	aʃur	אָשׁוּר (ז)
elm	bu'kitsa	בּוּקִיצָה (נ)
ash (tree)	mela	מֵילָה (נ)
chestnut	armon	עַרְמוֹן (ז)
magnolia	mag'nolya	מַגְנוֹלְיָה (נ)
palm tree	'dekel	דֶּקֶל (ז)
cypress	broʃ	בְּרוֹשׁ (ז)
mangrove	mangrov	מַנְגְרוֹב (ז)
baobab	ba'obab	בָּאוֹבָּב (ז)
eucalyptus	eika'liptus	אֵיקָלִיפְּטוּס (ז)
sequoia	sek'voya	סָקְווֹיָה (נ)

bush	'siaχ	שִׂיחַ (ז)
shrub	'siaχ	שִׂיחַ (ז)

| grapevine | 'gefen | גֶּפֶן (ז) |
| vineyard | 'kerem | כֶּרֶם (ז) |

raspberry bush	'petel	פֶּטֶל (ז)
blackcurrant bush	'siaχ dumdemaniyot ʃχorot	שִׂיחַ דּוּמְדְּמָנִיּוֹת שְׁחוֹרוֹת (ז)
redcurrant bush	'siaχ dumdemaniyot adumot	שִׂיחַ דּוּמְדְּמָנִיּוֹת אֲדוּמּוֹת (ז)
gooseberry bush	χazarzar	חֲזַרְזַר (ז)

acacia	ʃita	שִׁיטָה (נ)
barberry	berberis	בֶּרְבֶּרִיס (ז)
jasmine	yasmin	יַסְמִין (ז)

juniper	ar'ar	עַרְעָר (ז)
rosebush	'siaχ vradim	שִׂיחַ וְרָדִים (ז)
dog rose	'vered bar	וֶרֶד בָּר (ז)

188. Mushrooms

mushroom	pitriya	פִּטְרִיָּה (נ)
edible mushroom	pitriya ra'uya lema'aχal	פִּטְרִיָּה רְאוּיָה לְמַאֲכָל
poisonous mushroom	pitriya ra'ila	פִּטְרִיָּה רְעִילָה (נ)
cap	kipat pitriya	כִּיפַּת פִּטְרִיָּה (נ)
stipe	'regel	רֶגֶל (נ)

cep, penny bun	por'tʃini	פּוֹרְצִ'ינִי (ז)
orange-cap boletus	pitriyat 'kova aduma	פִּטְרִיַּת כּוֹבַע אֲדוּמָּה (נ)
birch bolete	pitriyat 'ya'ar	פִּטְרִיַּת יַעַר (נ)
chanterelle	gvi'onit ne'e'χelet	גְּבִיעוֹנִית נֶאֱכֶלֶת (נ)
russula	χarifit	חֲרִיפִית (נ)

morel	gamtsuts	גַּמְצוּץ (ז)
fly agaric	zvuvanit	זְבוּבָנִית (נ)
death cap	pitriya ra'ila	פִּטְרִיָּה רְעִילָה (נ)

189. Fruits. Berries

fruit	pri	פְּרִי (ז)
fruits	perot	פֵּירוֹת (ז״ר)
apple	ta'puaχ	תַּפּוּחַ (ז)
pear	agas	אַגָּס (ז)
plum	ʃezif	שְׁזִיף (ז)

strawberry (garden ~)	tut sade	תּוּת שָׂדֶה (ז)
sour cherry	duvdevan	דֻּבְדְּבָן (ז)
sweet cherry	gudgedan	גּוּדְגְּדָן (ז)
grape	anavim	עֲנָבִים (ז״ר)

raspberry	'petel	פֶּטֶל (ז)
blackcurrant	dumdemanit ʃχora	דּוּמְדְּמָנִית שְׁחוֹרָה (נ)
redcurrant	dumdemanit aduma	דּוּמְדְּמָנִית אֲדוּמָּה (נ)
gooseberry	χazarzar	חֲזַרְזַר (ז)
cranberry	χamutsit	חֲמוּצִית (נ)

orange	tapuz	תַּפּוּז (ז)
tangerine	klemen'tina	קְלֶמֶנְטִינָה (נ)
pineapple	'ananas	אֲנָנָס (ז)
banana	ba'nana	בַּנָנָה (נ)
date	tamar	תָּמָר (ז)

lemon	limon	לִימוֹן (ז)
apricot	'miʃmeʃ	מִשְׁמֵשׁ (ז)
peach	afarsek	אֲפַרְסֵק (ז)
kiwi	'kivi	קִיוִוי (ז)
grapefruit	eʃkolit	אֶשְׁכּוֹלִית (נ)

berry	garger	גַּרְגֵּר (ז)
berries	gargerim	גַּרְגֵּרִים (ז"ר)
cowberry	uχmanit aduma	אוּכְמָנִית אֲדוּמָה (נ)
wild strawberry	tut 'ya'ar	תּוּת יַעַר (ז)
bilberry	uχmanit	אוּכְמָנִית (נ)

190. Flowers. Plants

| flower | 'peraχ | פֶּרַח (ז) |
| bouquet (of flowers) | zer | זֵר (ז) |

rose (flower)	'vered	וֶרֶד (ז)
tulip	tsiv'oni	צִבְעוֹנִי (ז)
carnation	tsi'poren	צִיפּוֹרֶן (ז)
gladiolus	glad'yola	גְּלַדִיוֹלָה (נ)

cornflower	dganit	דְּגָנִית (נ)
harebell	pa'amonit	פַּעֲמוֹנִית (נ)
dandelion	ʃinan	שִׁינָן (ז)
camomile	kamomil	קָמוֹמִיל (ז)

aloe	alvai	אַלְוַוי (ז)
cactus	'kaktus	קַקְטוּס (ז)
rubber plant, ficus	'fikus	פִיקוּס (ז)

lily	ʃoʃana	שׁוֹשַׁנָּה (נ)
geranium	ge'ranyum	גֵּרַנְיוּם (ז)
hyacinth	yakinton	יָקִינְטוֹן (ז)

mimosa	mi'moza	מִימוֹזָה (נ)
narcissus	narkis	נַרְקִיס (ז)
nasturtium	'kova hanazir	כּוֹבַע הַנָּזִיר (ז)

orchid	saχlav	סַחְלָב (ז)
peony	admonit	אַדְמוֹנִית (נ)
violet	sigalit	סִיגָלִית (נ)

pansy	amnon vetamar	אַמְנוֹן וְתָמָר (ז)
forget-me-not	ziχ'rini	זִכְרִינִי (ז)
daisy	marganit	מַרְגָּנִית (נ)
poppy	'pereg	פֶּרֶג (ז)
hemp	ka'nabis	קָנָאבִּיס (ז)

mint	'menta	מִנְתָּה (נ)
lily of the valley	zivanit	זִיוֹנִית (נ)
snowdrop	ga'lantus	גָּלַנְטוּס (ז)

nettle	sirpad	סִרְפָּד (ז)
sorrel	χumʻa	חוּמְעָה (נ)
water lily	nufar	נוּפָר (ז)
fern	ʃaraχ	שֶׁכָךְ (ז)
lichen	χazazit	חֲזָזִית (נ)

conservatory (greenhouse)	χamama	חֲמָמָה (נ)
lawn	midʃaʼa	מִדְשָׁאָה (נ)
flowerbed	arugat praχim	עֲרוּגַת פְּרָחִים (נ)

plant	'tsemaχ	צֶמַח (ז)
grass	'deʃe	דֶּשֶׁא (ז)
blade of grass	givʻol 'esev	גִּבְעוֹל עֵשֶׂב (ז)

leaf	ale	עָלֶה (ז)
petal	ale ko'teret	עָלֶה כּוֹתֶרֶת (ז)
stem	givʻol	גִּבְעוֹל (ז)
tuber	'pkaʻat	פְּקַעַת (נ)

| young plant (shoot) | 'nevet | נֶבֶט (ז) |
| thorn | kots | קוֹץ (ז) |

to blossom (vi)	lif'roaχ	לִפְרוֹחַ
to fade, to wither	linbol	לִנְבּוֹל
smell (odour)	'reaχ	רֵיחַ (ז)
to cut (flowers)	ligzom	לִגְזוֹם
to pick (a flower)	liktof	לִקְטוֹף

191. Cereals, grains

grain	tvuʼa	תְּבוּאָה (נ)
cereal crops	dganim	דְּגָנִים (ז"ר)
ear (of barley, etc.)	ʃi'bolet	שִׁיבּוֹלֶת (נ)

wheat	χita	חִיטָה (נ)
rye	ʃifon	שִׁיפוֹן (ז)
oats	ʃi'bolet ʃuʻal	שִׁיבּוֹלֶת שׁוּעָל (נ)

| millet | 'doχan | דּוֹחַן (ז) |
| barley | seʻora | שְׂעוֹרָה (נ) |

maize	'tiras	תִּירָס (ז)
rice	'orez	אוֹרֶז (ז)
buckwheat	ku'semet	כּוּסֶמֶת (נ)

pea plant	afuna	אֲפוּנָה (נ)
kidney bean	ʃuʻit	שְׁעוּעִית (נ)
soya	'soya	סוֹיָה (נ)
lentil	adaʃim	עֲדָשִׁים (נ"ר)
beans (pulse crops)	pol	פּוֹל (ז)

REGIONAL GEOGRAPHY

192. Politics. Government. Part 1

politics	po'litika	פּוֹלִיטִיקָה (נ)
political (adj)	po'liti	פּוֹלִיטִי
politician	politikai	פּוֹלִיטִיקַאי (ז)
state (country)	medina	מְדִינָה (נ)
citizen	ezraχ	אֶזְרָח (ז)
citizenship	ezraχut	אֶזְרָחוּת (נ)
national emblem	'semel leʾumi	סֶמֶל לְאוּמִי (ז)
national anthem	himnon leʾumi	הִמְנוֹן לְאוּמִי (ז)
government	memʃala	מֶמְשָׁלָה (נ)
head of state	roʃ medina	רֹאש מְדִינָה (ז)
parliament	parlament	פַּרְלָמֶנְט (ז)
party	miflaga	מִפְלָגָה (נ)
capitalism	kapitalizm	קַפִּיטָלִיזְם (ז)
capitalist (adj)	kapita'listi	קַפִּיטָלִיסְטִי
socialism	sotsyalizm	סוֹצְיָאלִיזְם (ז)
socialist (adj)	sotsya'listi	סוֹצְיָאלִיסְטִי
communism	komunizm	קוֹמוּנִיזְם (ז)
communist (adj)	komu'nisti	קוֹמוּנִיסְטִי
communist (n)	komunist	קוֹמוּנִיסְט (ז)
democracy	demo'kratya	דֶמוֹקְרַטְיָה (נ)
democrat	demokrat	דֶמוֹקְרָט (ז)
democratic (adj)	demo'krati	דֶמוֹקְרָטִי
Democratic party	miflaga demo'kratit	מִפְלָגָה דֶמוֹקְרָטִית (נ)
liberal (n)	libe'rali	לִיבֶּרָלִי (ז)
Liberal (adj)	libe'rali	לִיבֶּרָלִי
conservative (n)	ʃamran	שַׁמְרָן (ז)
conservative (adj)	ʃamrani	שַׁמְרָנִי
republic (n)	re'publika	רֶפּוּבְּלִיקָה (נ)
republican (n)	republi'kani	רֶפּוּבְּלִיקָנִי (ז)
Republican party	miflaga republi'kanit	מִפְלָגָה רֶפּוּבְּלִיקָנִית (נ)
elections	bχirot	בְּחִירוֹת (נ"ר)
to elect (vt)	livχor	לִבְחוֹר
elector, voter	mats'biʿa	מַצְבִּיעַ (ז)
election campaign	masa bχirot	מַסָע בְּחִירוֹת (ז)
voting (n)	hatsba'a	הַצְבָּעָה (נ)
to vote (vi)	lehats'biʿa	לְהַצְבִּיעַ

175

suffrage, right to vote	zχut hatsba'a	זְכוּת הַצְבָּעָה (נ)
candidate	mu'amad	מוּעֲמָד (ז)
to run for (~ President)	lehatsig mu'amadut	לְהַצִּיג מוּעֲמָדוּת
campaign	masa	מַסָע (ז)

| opposition (as adj) | opozitsyoni | אוֹפּוֹזִיצְיוֹנִי |
| opposition (n) | opo'zitsya | אוֹפּוֹזִיצְיָה (נ) |

visit	bikur	בִּיקוּר (ז)
official visit	bikur riʃmi	בִּיקוּר רִשְׁמִי (ז)
international (adj)	benle'umi	בֵּינְלְאוּמִי

| negotiations | masa umatan | מַשָׂא וּמַתָּן (ז) |
| to negotiate (vi) | laset velatet | לָשֵׂאת וְלָתֵת |

193. Politics. Government. Part 2

society	χevra	חֶבְרָה (נ)
constitution	χuka	חוּקָה (נ)
power (political control)	ʃilton	שִׁלְטוֹן (ז)
corruption	ʃχitut	שְׁחִיתוּת (נ)

| law (justice) | χok | חוֹק (ז) |
| legal (legitimate) | χuki | חוּקִי |

| justice (fairness) | 'tsedek | צֶדֶק (ז) |
| just (fair) | tsodek | צוֹדֵק |

committee	'va'ad	וַעַד (ז)
bill (draft law)	hatsa'at χok	הַצָעַת חוֹק (נ)
budget	taktsiv	תַקְצִיב (ז)
policy	mediniyut	מְדִינִיוּת (נ)
reform	re'forma	רֵפוֹרְמָה (נ)
radical (adj)	radi'kali	רָדִיקָלִי

power (strength, force)	otsma	עוֹצְמָה (נ)
powerful (adj)	rav 'koaχ	רַב־כּוֹחַ
supporter	tomeχ	תוֹמֵךְ (ז)
influence	haʃpa'a	הַשְׁפָּעָה (נ)

regime (e.g. military ~)	miʃtar	מִשְׁטָר (ז)
conflict	siχsuχ	סִכְסוּךְ (ז)
conspiracy (plot)	'keʃer	קֶשֶׁר (ז)
provocation	provo'katsya, hitgarut	פְּרוֹבוֹקַצְיָה, הִתְגָרוּת (נ)

to overthrow (regime, etc.)	leha'diaχ	לְהַדִיחַ
overthrow (of a government)	hadaχa mikes malχut	הֲדָחָה מִכֵּס מַלְכוּת (נ)
revolution	mahapeχa	מַהְפֵּכָה (נ)

| coup d'état | hafiχa | הֲפִיכָה (נ) |
| military coup | mahapaχ tsva'i | מַהֲפָךְ צְבָאִי (ז) |

| crisis | maʃber | מַשְׁבֵּר (ז) |
| economic recession | mitun kalkali | מִיתוּן כַּלְכָּלִי (ז) |

demonstrator (protester)	mafgin	מַפְגִּין (ז)
demonstration	hafgana	הַפְגָּנָה (נ)
martial law	miʃtar tsva'i	מִשְׁטָר צְבָאִי (ז)
military base	basis tsva'i	בָּסִיס צְבָאִי (ז)
stability	yatsivut	יַצִּיבוּת (נ)
stable (adj)	yatsiv	יַצִּיב
exploitation	nitsul	נִיצוּל (ז)
to exploit (workers)	lenatsel	לְנַצֵּל
racism	giz'anut	גִּזְעָנוּת (נ)
racist	giz'ani	גִּזְעָנִי (ז)
fascism	faʃizm	פָשִׁיזְם (ז)
fascist	faʃist	פָשִׁיסְט (ז)

194. Countries. Miscellaneous

foreigner	zar	זָר (ז)
foreign (adj)	zar	זָר
abroad (in a foreign country)	beχul	בְּחוּ"ל
emigrant	mehager	מְהַגֵּר (ז)
emigration	hagira	הֲגִירָה (נ)
to emigrate (vi)	lehager	לְהַגֵּר
the West	ma'arav	מַעֲרָב (ז)
the East	mizraχ	מִזְרָח (ז)
the Far East	hamizraχ haraχok	הַמִּזְרָח הָרָחוֹק (ז)
civilization	tsivili'zatsya	צִיבִילִיזַצְיָה (נ)
humanity (mankind)	enoʃut	אֱנוֹשׁוּת (נ)
the world (earth)	olam	עוֹלָם (ז)
peace	ʃalom	שָׁלוֹם (ז)
worldwide (adj)	olami	עוֹלָמִי
homeland	mo'ledet	מוֹלֶדֶת (נ)
people (population)	am	עַם (ז)
population	oχlusiya	אוֹכְלוּסִיָּה (נ)
people (a lot of ~)	anaʃim	אֲנָשִׁים (ז"ר)
nation (people)	uma	אֻמָּה (נ)
generation	dor	דּוֹר (ז)
territory (area)	ʃetaχ	שֶׁטַח (ז)
region	ezor	אֵזוֹר (ז)
state (part of a country)	medina	מְדִינָה (נ)
tradition	ma'soret	מָסוֹרֶת (נ)
custom (tradition)	minhag	מִנְהָג (ז)
ecology	eko'logya	אֵקוֹלוֹגְיָה (נ)
Indian (Native American)	ind'yani	אִינְדִיאָנִי (ז)
Gypsy (masc.)	tso'ani	צוֹעֲנִי (ז)
Gypsy (fem.)	tso'aniya	צוֹעֲנִיָּה (נ)

Gypsy (adj)	tso'ani	צוֹעֲנִי
empire	im'perya	אִימְפֶּרְיָה (נ)
colony	ko'lonya	קוֹלוֹנְיָה (נ)
slavery	avdut	עַבְדוּת (נ)
invasion	pliʃa	פְּלִישָׁה (נ)
famine	'ra'av	רָעָב (ז)

195. Major religious groups. Confessions

| religion | dat | דָת (נ) |
| religious (adj) | dati | דָתִי |

faith, belief	emuna	אֱמוּנָה (נ)
to believe (in God)	leha'amin	לְהַאֲמִין
believer	ma'amin	מַאֲמִין

| atheism | ate'izm | אָתֵאִיזם (ז) |
| atheist | ate'ist | אָתֵאִיסט (ז) |

Christianity	natsrut	נַצְרוּת (נ)
Christian (n)	notsri	נוֹצְרִי (ז)
Christian (adj)	notsri	נוֹצְרִי

Catholicism	ka'toliyut	קָתוֹלִיוּת (נ)
Catholic (n)	ka'toli	קָתוֹלִי (ז)
Catholic (adj)	ka'toli	קָתוֹלִי

Protestantism	protes'tantiyut	פְּרוֹטֶסְטַנְטִיוּת (נ)
Protestant Church	knesiya protes'tantit	כְּנֵסִיָה פְּרוֹטֶסְטַנְטִית (נ)
Protestant (n)	protestant	פְּרוֹטֶסְטַנְט (ז)

Orthodoxy	natsrut orto'doksit	נַצְרוּת אוֹרְתוֹדוֹקְסִית (נ)
Orthodox Church	knesiya orto'doksit	כְּנֵסִיָה אוֹרְתוֹדוֹקְסִית (נ)
Orthodox (n)	orto'doksi	אוֹרְתוֹדוֹקְסִי

Presbyterianism	presbiteryanizm	פְּרֶסְבִּיטֶרְיָאנִיזם (ז)
Presbyterian Church	knesiya presviteri''anit	כְּנֵסִיָה פְּרֶסְבִּיטֶרְיָאנִית (נ)
Presbyterian (n)	presbiter'yani	פְּרֶסְבִּיטֶרְיָאנִי (ז)

| Lutheranism | knesiya lute'ranit | כְּנֵסִיָה לוּתֶרָנִית (נ) |
| Lutheran (n) | lute'rani | לוּתֶרָנִי (ז) |

| Baptist Church | knesiya bap'tistit | כְּנֵסִיָה בַּפְּטִיסְטִית (נ) |
| Baptist (n) | baptist | בַּפְּטִיסְט (ז) |

Anglican Church	knesiya angli'kanit	כְּנֵסִיָה אַנְגְלִיקָנִית (נ)
Anglican (n)	angli'kani	אַנְגְלִיקָנִי (ז)
Mormonism	mor'monim	מוֹרְמוֹנִים (ז)
Mormon (n)	mormon	מוֹרְמוֹן (ז)

Judaism	yahadut	יַהֲדוּת (נ)
Jew (n)	yehudi, yehudiya	יְהוּדִי (ז), יְהוּדִיָה (נ)
Buddhism	budhizm	בּוּדְהִיזם (ז)
Buddhist (n)	budhist	בּוּדְהִיסְט (ז)

Hinduism	hindu'izm	הִינְדוּאִיזְם (ז)
Hindu (n)	'hindi	הִינְדִי (ז)
Islam	islam	אִיסְלָאם (ז)
Muslim (n)	'muslemi	מוּסְלְמִי (ז)
Muslim (adj)	'muslemi	מוּסְלְמִי
Shiah Islam	islam 'ʃi'i	אָסְלָאם שִׁיעִי (ז)
Shiite (n)	'ʃi'i	שִׁיעִי (ז)
Sunni Islam	islam 'suni	אָסְלָאם סוּנִי (ז)
Sunnite (n)	'suni	סוּנִי (ז)

196. Religions. Priests

priest	'komer	כּוֹמֶר (ז)
the Pope	apifyor	אַפִּיפְיוֹר (ז)
monk, friar	nazir	נָזִיר (ז)
nun	nazira	נְזִירָה (נ)
pastor	'komer	כּוֹמֶר (ז)
abbot	roʃ minzar	רֹאש מִנְזָר (ז)
vicar (parish priest)	'komer hakehila	כּוֹמֶר הַקְּהִילָה (ז)
bishop	'biʃof	בִּישׁוֹף (ז)
cardinal	χaʃman	חַשְׁמָן (ז)
preacher	matif	מַטִּיף (ז)
preaching	hatafa, draʃa	הַטָּפָה, דְּרָשָׁה (נ)
parishioners	χaver kehila	חָבֵר קְהִילָה (ז)
believer	ma'amin	מַאֲמִין (ז)
atheist	ate'ist	אָתָאִיסְט (ז)

197. Faith. Christianity. Islam

Adam	adam	אָדָם
Eve	χava	חַוָּה
God	elohim	אֱלוֹהִים
the Lord	adonai	אֲדוֹנָי
the Almighty	kol yaχol	כָּל יָכוֹל
sin	χet	חֵטְא (ז)
to sin (vi)	laχato	לַחֲטוֹא
sinner (masc.)	χote	חוֹטֵא (ז)
sinner (fem.)	χo'ta'at	חוֹטֵאת (נ)
hell	gehinom	גֵּיהִינוֹם (ז)
paradise	gan 'eden	גַּן עֵדֶן (ז)
Jesus	'yeʃu	יֵשׁוּ
Jesus Christ	'yeʃu hanotsri	יֵשׁוּ הַנּוֹצְרִי

the Holy Spirit	'ruax ha'kodeʃ	רוּחַ הַקּוֹדֶשׁ (ז)
the Saviour	mo'ʃiˤa	מוֹשִׁיעַ (ז)
the Virgin Mary	'miryam hakdoʃa	מִרְיָם הַקְּדוֹשָׁה
the Devil	satan	שָׂטָן (ז)
devil's (adj)	stani	שְׂטָנִי
Satan	satan	שָׂטָן (ז)
satanic (adj)	stani	שְׂטָנִי
angel	malʾax	מַלְאָךְ (ז)
guardian angel	malʾax ʃomer	מַלְאָךְ שׁוֹמֵר (ז)
angelic (adj)	malʾaxi	מַלְאָכִי
apostle	ʃa'liax	שָׁלִיחַ (ז)
archangel	arximalax	אַרְכִימַלְאָךְ (ז)
the Antichrist	an'tikrist	אַנְטִיכְרִיסְט (ז)
Church	knesiya	כְּנֵסִיָּה (נ)
Bible	tanax	תַּנַ"ךְ (ז)
biblical (adj)	tanaxi	תַּנַ"כִי
Old Testament	habrit hayeʃana	הַבְּרִית הַיָשָׁנָה (נ)
New Testament	habrit haxadaʃa	הַבְּרִית הַחֲדָשָׁה (נ)
Gospel	evangelyon	אֶוַונְגֶּלְיוֹן (ז)
Holy Scripture	kitvei ha'kodeʃ	כִּתְבֵי הַקּוֹדֶשׁ (ז"ר)
Heaven	malxut ʃa'mayim, gan 'eden	מַלְכוּת שָׁמַיִם (נ), גַּן עֵדֶן (ז)
Commandment	mitsva	מִצְוָה (נ)
prophet	navi	נָבִיא (ז)
prophecy	nevu'a	נְבוּאָה (נ)
Allah	'alla	אַלְלָה
Mohammed	mu'xamad	מוּחַמָד
the Koran	kurʾan	קוֹרְאָן (ז)
mosque	misgad	מִסְגָּד (ז)
mullah	'mula	מוּלָא (ז)
prayer	tfila	תְּפִילָה (נ)
to pray (vi, vt)	lehitpalel	לְהִתְפַּלֵל
pilgrimage	aliya le'regel	עֲלִיָה לְרֶגֶל (נ)
pilgrim	tsalyan	צַלְיָין (ז)
Mecca	'meka	מֶכָּה (נ)
church	knesiya	כְּנֵסִיָּה (נ)
temple	mikdaʃ	מִקְדָּשׁ (ז)
cathedral	kated'rala	קָתֶדְרָלָה (נ)
Gothic (adj)	'goti	גוֹתִי
synagogue	beit 'kneset	בֵּית כְּנֶסֶת (ז)
mosque	misgad	מִסְגָּד (ז)
chapel	beit tfila	בֵּית תְּפִילָה (ז)
abbey	minzar	מִנְזָר (ז)
convent	minzar	מִנְזָר (ז)
monastery	minzar	מִנְזָר (ז)
bell (church ~s)	pa'amon	פַּעֲמוֹן (ז)

bell tower	migdal pa'amonim	מִגְדַּל פַּעֲמוֹנִים (ז)
to ring (ab. bells)	letsaltsel	לְצַלְצֵל
cross	tslav	צְלָב (ז)
cupola (roof)	kipa	כִּיפָּה (נ)
icon	ikonin	אִיקוֹנִין (ז)
soul	neʃama	נְשָׁמָה (נ)
fate (destiny)	goral	גּוֹרָל (ז)
evil (n)	'ro'a	רוֹעַ (ז)
good (n)	tuv	טוּב (ז)
vampire	arpad	עַרְפָּד (ז)
witch (evil ~)	maxʃefa	מַכְשֵׁפָה (נ)
demon	ʃed	שֵׁד (ז)
spirit	'ruax	רוּחַ (נ)
redemption (giving us ~)	kapara	כַּפָּרָה (נ)
to redeem (vt)	lexaper al	לְכַפֵּר עַל
church service	'misa	מִיסָה (נ)
to say mass	la'arox 'misa	לַעֲרוֹךְ מִיסָה
confession	vidui	וִידוּי (ז)
to confess (vi)	lehitvadot	לְהִתְוַדּוֹת
saint (n)	kadoʃ	קָדוֹשׁ (ז)
sacred (holy)	mekudaʃ	מְקוּדָשׁ
holy water	'mayim kdoʃim	מַיִם קְדוֹשִׁים (ז"ר)
ritual (n)	'tekes	טֶקֶס (ז)
ritual (adj)	ʃel 'tekes	שֶׁל טֶקֶס
sacrifice	korban	קוֹרְבָּן (ז)
superstition	emuna tfela	אֱמוּנָה תְפֵלָה (נ)
superstitious (adj)	ma'amin emunot tfelot	מַאֲמִין אֱמוּנוֹת תְפֵלוֹת
afterlife	ha'olam haba	הָעוֹלָם הַבָּא (ז)
eternal life	xayei olam, xayei 'netsax	חַיֵּי עוֹלָם (ז"ר), חַיֵּי נֶצַח (ז"ר)

MISCELLANEOUS

198. Various useful words

background (green ~)	'reka	רֶקַע (ז)
balance (of the situation)	izun	אִיזּוּן (ז)
barrier (obstacle)	mixʃol	מִכְשׁוֹל (ז)
base (basis)	basis	בָּסִיס (ז)
beginning	hatxala	הַתְחָלָה (נ)
category	kate'gorya	קָטֵגוֹרְיָה (נ)
cause (reason)	siba	סִיבָּה (נ)
choice	bxina	בְּחִינָה (נ)
coincidence	hat'ama	הַתְאָמָה (נ)
comfortable (~ chair)	'noax	נוֹחַ
comparison	haʃva'a	הַשְׁוָואָה (נ)
compensation	pitsui	פִּיצוּי (ז)
degree (extent, amount)	darga	דַרְגָה (נ)
development	hitpatxut	הִתְפַּתְחוּת (נ)
difference	'ʃoni	שׁוֹנִי (ז)
effect (e.g. of drugs)	efekt	אֶפֶקְט (ז)
effort (exertion)	ma'amats	מַאֲמָץ (ז)
element	element	אֶלֶמֶנְט (ז)
end (finish)	sof	סוֹף (ז)
example (illustration)	dugma	דוּגְמָה (נ)
fact	uvda	עוּבְדָה (נ)
frequent (adj)	tadir	תָדִיר
growth (development)	gidul	גִידוּל (ז)
help	ezra	עֶזְרָה (נ)
ideal	ide'al	אִידֵיאָל (ז)
kind (sort, type)	sug	סוּג (ז)
labyrinth	mavox	מָבוֹךְ (ז)
mistake, error	ta'ut	טָעוּת (נ)
moment	'rega	רֶגַע (ז)
object (thing)	'etsem	עֶצֶם (ז)
obstacle	maxsom	מַחְסוֹם (ז)
original (original copy)	makor	מָקוֹר (ז)
part (~ of sth)	'xelek	חֵלֶק (ז)
particle, small part	xelkik	חֶלְקִיק (ז)
pause (break)	hafuga	הֲפוּגָה (נ)
position	emda	עֶמְדָה (נ)
principle	ikaron	עִיקָרוֹן (ז)
problem	be'aya	בְּעָיָה (נ)
process	tahalix	תַהֲלִיךְ (ז)

progress	kidma	קִדְמָה (נ)
property (quality)	txuna, sgula	תְּכוּנָה, סְגוּלָה (נ)
reaction	tguva	תְּגוּבָה (נ)
risk	sikun	סִיכּוּן (ז)
secret	sod	סוֹד (ז)
series	sidra	סִדְרָה (נ)
shape (outer form)	tsura	צוּרָה (נ)
situation	matsav	מַצָב (ז)
solution	pitaron	פִּיתָרוֹן (ז)
standard (adj)	tikni	תִּקְנִי
standard (level of quality)	'teken	תֶּקֶן (ז)
stop (pause)	hafsaka	הַפְסָקָה (נ)
style	signon	סְגְנוֹן (ז)
system	ʃita	שִׁיטָה (נ)
table (chart)	tavla	טַבְלָה (נ)
tempo, rate	'ketsev	קֶצֶב (ז)
term (word, expression)	musag	מוּשָׂג (ז)
thing (object, item)	'xefets	חֵפֶץ (ז)
truth (e.g. moment of ~)	emet	אֱמֶת (נ)
turn (please wait your ~)	tor	תּוֹר (ז)
type (sort, kind)	min	מִין (ז)
urgent (adj)	daxuf	דָחוּף
urgently	bidxifut	בִּדְחִיפוּת
utility (usefulness)	to''elet	תּוֹעֶלֶת (נ)
variant (alternative)	girsa	גִירְסָה (נ)
way (means, method)	'ofen	אוֹפֶן (ז)
zone	ezor	אֵזוֹר (ז)